Philippe Vonnard, Nicola Sbetti, Grégory Quin (Eds.)
Beyond Boycotts

Rethinking the Cold War

Edited by
Kirsten Bönker and Jane Curry

Volume 1

Beyond Boycotts

Sport during the Cold War in Europe

Edited by
Philippe Vonnard, Nicola Sbetti and Grégory Quin

Afterword by
Martin Polley

ISBN 978-3-11-068429-2
e-ISBN (PDF) 978-3-11-052909-8
e-ISBN (EPUB) 978-3-11-052673-8

Library of Congress Cataloging-in-Publication Data
A CIP catalog record for this book has been applied for at the Library of Congress.

Bibliographic information published by the Deutsche Nationalbibliothek
The Deutsche Nationalbibliothek lists this publication in the Deutsche Nationalbibliografie;
detailed bibliographic data are available on the Internet at http://dnb.dnb.de.

© 2019 Walter de Gruyter GmbH, Berlin/Boston
This volume is text- and page-identical with the hardback published in 2018.
Cover: 1974 FIFA World cup, the two captains of West and East Germany shook their hand
just before the game, © FIFA photography archives collections
Printing and binding: CPI books GmbH, Leck
♾ Printed on acid-free paper
Printed in Germany

www.degruyter.com

Preface and Acknowledgments

The idea of this book saw the light during discussions we held at a panel organized as part of the Fifth Meeting of Young Researchers in Contemporary History, in Barcelona, July 2015. In regard to the call for paper and our respective research interests – the shared edition of a book on European football, paired with writing a report on the arrival of rhythmic gymnastics at the Olympic Games for one of us and concluding a thesis on UEFA for the other – the Cold War theme was clearly at the centre of our concerns and discussions. Therefore, we thought it would be very interesting to organize a panel on this topic. Even though the organizers accepted our proposal, we were still wondering whether we would get any replies. But to our great surprise, over a dozen researchers answered our call favourably!

There was, however, a small issue: give the quality of the contributions, the two hours allowed per panel were largely insufficient a space for discussions. Moreover, the cosmopolitan aspect of the interested individuals (nearly a dozen different nationalities were represented) would make for extended exchanges. So we faced this situation and set up a two-days symposium preceding the event. The panellists soon agreed upon this solution, which delighted us and motivated us to pursue the process. This is where we need to cordially thank the staff of Barcelona's Olympic Museum for providing us with a room and technical resources, ensuring the symposium ran smoothly. The intensity and quality of the exchanges, coupled with a general good disposition and socially enriching moments, made this symposium a special event that will remain, we are sure, in most attendees' memories.

The exchanges worked so well that a second symposium was organized in July 2016, on the theme of sports leaders, and a third one in July 2017, this time around female leaders, always at the same place. Another one is already taking shape for 2018. These Barcelonian exchanges have even materialized in the form of a network: the Réseau d'Etudes des Relations Internationales Sportives (RERIS), which has now a website: www.reris.net

This book embodies, to our greatest pleasure, this network's first publication. As such, we need to thank Nicola Sbetti who kindly took upon himself the heavy burden of editing this volume with us. In addition to his extensive knowledge of international sports relations and his undeniably critical mind, Nicola's presence was absolutely appropriate, seeing as we met him during a CESH (European Committee for Sports History) symposium organized in November 2013 in Barcelona, already on Catalan ground.

Because of the large number of contributors, we were unable to publish all the papers in this book. Therefore, it will be paired with a special issue published in the journal *Sport in History* in the second semester of 2017. We thus want to take advantage of this occasion to cordially thank everyone who took part in the symposium of 2015 as well as the contributors to this volume.

Besides, we give our regards to the publishing house De Gruyter for trusting a group of young researchers and giving them the opportunity to publish their research in a quality collection. We wish to thank Elise Wintz and Kristen Bönker in particular for their supervising and availability. Finally, we want to wholeheartedly thank Shani D'Cruze for the quality of her proofreading, as well as Julie Cocaigne for translating our introduction. We are also forever grateful to the University of Lausanne for handling most of the various financing needs.

We hope that this volume will open new questions on Sport in the Cold War and will spark off new debates to be discussed in Barcelona … or anywhere else of course!

Lausanne, Summer 2017
Philippe Vonnard
Grégory Quin

Table of Contents

Philippe Vonnard, Nicola Sbetti, and Grégory Quin
Introduction —— 1

First Part. Creating relations between European states. Sport as tool of diplomacy

Nicola Sbetti
Playing at the border of the Cold War
 The case of the city of Trieste (1945–1948) —— 17

by Daniel Svensson and Anna Åberg
An Even Colder War?
 Specialization and Scientization in the Training methods for Cross-Country Skiing from the 1940s in Sweden and the Soviet Union —— 33

Juan Antonio Simón
Athletes of Diplomacy:
 Francoism, Sport and the Cold War during the 1960s —— 55

Second part. A European space of exchanges. Crossing the Iron Curtain with sport

Sylvain Dufraisse
The emergence of Europe-wide collaboration and competition:
 Soviet sports interactions in Europe. 1945–mid-1960s. —— 71

Philippe Vonnard and Kevin Marston
Building bridges between separated Europeans:
 The role of UEFA's competitions in East-West exchanges (1955–1964) —— 85

Stefan Scholl
Cooperation and conflict:
 The case of the European Sports Conference in the 1970s and 1980s —— 109

Third Part. Globalizing sport. Europe as a site of international sporting diplomacy

François Doppler-Speranza
"Shooting Hoops with Foreign Teams":
  Basketball Ambassadors on US Military Bases in France (1916–1961) —— 135

Claire Nicolas
The Ghana Young Pioneers
  Intertwining global connections to build a Pan-Africanist youth —— 157

Souvik Naha
"The Russian deadpan expert" vs "America's white hope":
  The personal, the national, and the global in the "Cold War" of chess —— 179

Quentin Tonnerre and Grégory Quin
A forgotten "ping-pong diplomacy"?
  About the Chinese ping-pong players' tour of Switzerland (1972) —— 195

Martin Polley
Afterword —— 213

Bibliography —— 219

Contributors (by alphabetical order)
  Biographies —— 229

Index —— 233

Philippe Vonnard, Nicola Sbetti, and Grégory Quin
Introduction

"Divided but not disconnected"[1]: studying a new "paradigm" for the history of sport during the Cold War

"When Tito rhymes with Franco".[2] This sentence is the title of an article published on 27 December 1955 in the journal *France Football*, after the match held between Real Madrid and JSD Partizan of Belgrade the evening before as part of the first European Champions Clubs' Cup.[3] The fixture made quite an impression as it opposed two countries who did not then maintain diplomatic relations because of their strongly divergent political opinions on the international stage: one was Francoist, a champion of anticommunism, the other Titoist, which, although it was part of the "non-aligned" countries that were more open to relations with the West than other European communist countries, was nonetheless anti-Francoist. On top of these difficulties, there was also a symbolic element, namely El Caudillo Franco and Marshal Tito themselves, who supported each respective club. All the diplomacy of the UEFA leaders was required, as well as the help of journalists from the newspaper *L'Equipe*, as the two countries did not have proper legations, their respective embassies in Paris had to deliver the visas. Both teams faced a journey of over 20 hours of travel for their players to go and play in the opposition country, the fixture being a two-legged match, first in Madrid in December, and then in Belgrade in January. Eventually, football beat all obstacles, and both fixtures went smoothly. If the context of the mid-1950s – at the beginning of what historians then called "the Thaw" – favoured these rapprochements, the football authorities still managed quite the "*coup de force*".

This example highlights the ability of the game, and of sport more generally, to defy the international political context, and also shows the complexity of in-

---

1 Hochscherf, Tobias, Laucht, Christopher and Andrew Plowman (eds.). *Divided, but not Disconnected: German Experiences of the Cold War*. New York: Berghahn Books, 2011.
2 "Quand Tito rime avec Franco". *France football*, 27 December 1955.
3 About this competition, see: Vonnard, Philippe. A Competition that Shook European Football: the Origins of the European Champion Clubs' Cup, 1954–1955. *Sport in History* 34 (2014): 595–619.

ternational sports exchanges, as they involve many agents, whether they officiate in the state sphere or not. These analyses are not new and have already been revealed by authors who work on international sports relations.[4] However, as Yohan Ariffin recently indicated,[5] studies still remain largely permeated by a realist paradigm,[6] meaning that they mainly focus on the role of the states and how they use sport in order to increase their power on the international stage.

The particular nature of the Cold War can explain this tendency that states had to consider sport as a means for political confrontation and political conflict between the two great powers, the United States and the Soviet Union, nevertheless they managed to avoid armed confrontation in Europe – even though, as Béatrice Heuser justly reminded us, in some so-called "peripheral" African, South American and Asian regions, it had been the cause of particularly atrocious mass physical actions all along.[7] This peculiar configuration implied the total involvement of governments in every social field, with the underlying aim to show the superiority of one bloc over the other. In a text published in 2001, Tony Shaw clearly highlighted this aspect when he said:

> Virtually everything, from sport to ballet to comic books and space travel, assumed political significance and hence potentially could be deployed as a weapon both to shape opinion at home and to subvert societies abroad.[8]

---

[4] For an overview on sport studies in international relations, see: Keys, Barbara. International Relations. In *Routledge Companion to Sports History*, Steven Pope and John Nauright (eds.), 248–267. London and New York: Routlege, 2010; Dichter, Heather. Sport History and Diplomatic History. *H-Diplo* 122 (2014), http://h-diplo.org/essays/PDF/E122.pdf; Sbetti, Nicola and Umberto Tulli, La fine di una reciproca negazione: riflessioni sullo sport nella storia delle relazioni internazionali, *Ricerche di storia politica* 2 (2016): 193–202. For a theoretical reflection, see: Beacom, Aaron. Sport in International Relations: A Case for Cross-disciplinary Investigation. *Sport in History* 20 (2000): 1–23; Murray, Stuart. The Two Halves of Sports-Diplomacy. *Diplomacy & Statecraft* 23 (2012): 575–592.
[5] Ariffin, Yohan. Sport and Global Politics: Still an Unchartered Territory? In *Playing to Build Europe. Turning Points in the Europeanization of Football (1914–1989)*, Philippe Vonnard, Grégory Quin and Nicolas Bancel (eds.), 223–229. Oxford: Peter Lang, 2016.
[6] Numerous books exist on the subject of theories in international relations, see in particular: Burchill, Scott et al. (eds.), *Theories of International Relations*. Basingstoke: Palgrave Macmillan, 2013; De Senarclens, Pierre and Yohan Ariffin. *La politique internationale. Théories et enjeux contemporains*. Paris: Armand Colin, 2015.
[7] Heuser, Béatrice. Looking Back: a Quarter of a Century After the Cold War. *Cold War History* 14 (2014): 455–459.
[8] Shaw, Tony. The Politics of Cold War Culture. *Journal of Cold War Studies* 3 (2001): 59–76. Many other texts addressed these various subjects. For a good synthesis of literature on the Cold War, see: Romero, Federico. Cold War Historiography at the Crossroads. *Cold War History*

On this topic, sport was also a very attractive means for the two superpowers to show off their supremacy, even more so since totalitarian regimes,[9] but also several democracies,[10] had already demonstrated the efficiency of sport as part of political propaganda during the interwar period. Moreover, this situation was also amplified by the increasing importance of the sporting field on an international level, which can be explained by the combined efforts of the expansion of practice on every continent, decolonization – as demonstrated by numerous authors, sport was one of the best means for recently independent countries to get recognized on the international stage – as well as external factors, such as the development of air transport.[11]

Therefore, the main competitions (first and foremost the Olympic Games, but also world championships organized in various disciplines, several of which were inaugurated during this period) have become occasions to bring together more and more audiences, whether on site or behind small screens, as sports events saw an increase in media coverage from the 1960s onward. For instance, the Olympic Games of Helsinki (1952), in which the Soviet Union participated in for the first time,[12] gathered 4,099 athletes (3,714 men and 385 women) from 69 countries. One year before the fall of the Berlin Wall, 8,465 athletes (6,279 men

---

14 (2014): 685–703; and the introduction of: Buton, Philippe, Olivier Büttner and Michael Hastings (eds.). *La Guerre froide vue d'en bas*. Paris: CNRS Editions, 2016.
9 For a synthesis of the use of sport by totalitarian regimes, see in particular: Teichler, Hans-Joachim. *Internationale Sportpolitik im Dritten Reich*. Schorndorf: K. Hofmann, 1991; Arnaud, Pierre and James Riordan (eds.). *Sport et relations internationales (1900–1941): les démocraties face au fascisme et au nazisme*. Paris: L'Harmattan, 1998; Aja Gonzalez, Teresa (ed.). *Sport y autoritarismos. La utilización del deporte por el comunismo y el fascismo*. Madrid: Alianza Editorial, 2002; Bolz, Daphné. *Les arènes totalitaires: fascisme, nazisme et propagande sportive. Hitler, Mussolini et les jeux du stade*. Paris: CNRS Ed, 2009; Bensoussan, Georges, Dietschy, Paul, François, Caroline and Hubert Strouk (eds.). *Sport, corps et sociétés de masse. Le projet d'un homme nouveau*. Paris: Armand Colin, 2011.
10 For a good example, see: Beck, Peter. *Scoring for Britain: International Football and International Politics, 1900–1939*. London: F. Cass, 1999.
11 For more details on this internationalization of sports, see the introductions to the following: Malz, Arié, Rohdewald, Stefan and Stefan Wiederkehr (eds.). *Sport zwischen Ost und Est. Beiträge zur Sportgeschichte Osteuropas im 19. Und 20. Jahrhundert*. Osnabruck: Fibre, 2007; Singaravélou, Pierre and Julien Sorez (eds.). *L'Empire des sports. Une histoire de la mondialisation culturelle*. Paris: Belin, 2010; Dichter, Heather and Andrew Johns (eds.). *Diplomatic Games. Sport Statecraft and International Relations Since 1945*. Lexington Kentucky: University Press of Kentucky, 2014.
12 About these games, see: Niggli, Nicholas. Diplomatie sportive et Relations internationales: Helsinki 1952, les 'Jeux olympique de la Guerre froide'. *Relations internationales* 112 (2002): 467–485; Dufraisse, Sylvain. The Emergence of Europe-wide Collaboration and Competition: Soviet Sports Interactions in Europe, 1945– mid-1960s, in this volume.

and 2,186 women) from 159 countries went to Seoul (1988).¹³ The same effect applied to the number of participating countries in the Football World Cup. While 16 teams played the final phase in 1954, 30 years later there were 24. Moreover, in 1954 only about 40 teams applied for the qualifying rounds, but in 1986, there were nearly 130. On top of this increase in participation, we can add the increase in broadcasting, as ever since the Winter Games of Cortina d'Ampezzo in 1956, television insinuated itself into the game¹⁴ via the Eurovision network created in 1954.¹⁵ In view of this situation, Maurice Roche suggested that big sporting fixtures were now to be considered, much like World Fairs, as "mega-events". ¹⁶ Even though this statement was issued about more recent fixtures, it undeniably stemmed from the Cold War.

The increasing importance of sport on the international stage consequently awarded the sporting field a particular place in state politics during this "fifty-years war". ¹⁷

Studying "Sport in the Cold War" in Europe

Our reflection was inspired by the words of Andrew Johns who, in the introduction to *Diplomatic Games* published in 2014 – a book which offers various case studies on sport at an international level after 1945 – highlights the complexity of sport in international relations. Johns indeed observes: "in short, sport is at once parochial and universal, unifying and dividing, and has the potential to fundamentally affect the relations between individuals and nations".¹⁸ In light of these words, it seems therefore necessary to expand the focus to the case of sport during the Cold War.¹⁹

---

13 Official number given by the Olympic Studies Centre.
14 Anonymous, Installations techniques pour la radiophonie et la télévision lors des Jeux Olympiques d'Hiver à Cortina d'Ampezzo, 1956. *Bulletin de l'U.E.R* 8 (1956): 345–358.
15 Heinrich-Franke, Christian. Jean d'Arcy et la naissance de l'Eurovision. In *Jean d'Arcy. Penser la communication au XXe siècle*, by Marie-Françoise Lévy (eds.), 147–156. Paris: Publications de la Sorbonne, 2013.
16 Roche, Maurice. *Mega-events and Modernity: Olympics and Expos in the Growth of Global Culture*. London and New York: Routledge, 2000.
17 Soutou, George-Henri. *La guerre de cinquante ans. Le conflit Est-Ouest, 1943–1990*. Paris: Fayard, 2001.
18 Johns, Andrew. Introduction. Competing in the Global Arena: Sport and Foreign Relations since 1945. In, *Diplomatic Games*, Dichter and Johns (eds.), 1–18, here 3.
19 For a reflection that also emphasizes this complexity, see: Jackson, Steven and Stephen Haigh. Between and Beyond Politics: Sport and Foreign Policy in a Globalizing World. *Sport*

Thus, our ambition is to remain mainly focused on the European continent, while pursuing two main goals. First, we propose studies pertaining to new *places* throughout Europe regarding the idea of "Sport in the Cold War". Therefore, we agreed on the premise that no contribution would focus on the Olympic Games. The idea is, to put it a little provocatively, to go "beyond boycotts" and show that "Sport in the Cold War" took various forms and happened in many different places. Moreover, the purpose is to maintain our focus away from the two great powers and to show that the European territory as a whole was a particularly important place for sport during the Cold War. Second, this publication aims to go beyond a descriptive view of "Sport in the Cold War" and thus offers a more complex *theoretical* opinion. Although the idea is not to call into question the use of sport by the United States as a political confrontation tool – several authors in this book offer new case studies that take this approach – we wish however to widen the perspective and speak about the ability of the sporting field to give enemy blocs a few moments of collaboration, or even to create the conditions for an anticipation of politics, as was demonstrated by the now renowned case of the "ping-pong diplomacy" between China and the United States in 1971.[20] From this point of view, we were inspired by recent studies published on the Cold War that highlight the fact that the two blocs might have been divided, but they were never completely disconnected.[21] Thus, the two great powers definitely maintained more exchanges than they would officially admit, and circulations,[22] transfers of technology[23] or even expertise networks

---

in *Society* 11 (2008): 349–358; Frank, Robert. Internationalisation du sport et diplomatie sportive. In *Pour l'histoire des relations internationales*, Robert Frank (ed.), 387–405, Paris: Presses Universitaires de France, 2012.

20 Many studies have been published on this topic. For a stat of art see : Tonnerre, Quentin et Grégory Quin. A forgotten "ping-pong diplomacy"? About the Chinese ping-pong players' tour of Switzerland (1972), in this volume.

21 Hochscherf, Laucht and Plowman. *Divided, but not Disconnected*; Mitter, Rana and Patrick Major (eds.). *Across the Blocs: Cold War Cultural and Social History*, London: Frank Cass, 2004; Fleury, Antoine and Lubor Jilek (eds.). *Une Europe malgré tout, 1945–1990*. Bruxelles: P.I.E. Peter Lang, 2008; Autio-Sarasmo, Sari and Katalin Miklossy (eds.). *Reassessing Cold War Europe*. London: Routledge, 2011; Romijn, Peter, Scott-Smith, Giles and Joes Segal (eds.). *Divided Dreamworlds? The Cultural Cold War in East and West*. Amsterdam: Amsterdam University Press, 2012; Bönker, Kirsten, Obertreis, Julia and Sven Gramp (eds.). *Television Beyond and Across the Iron Curtain*. Cambridge: Cambridge Scholars, 2016; Mikkonen, Simo and Pekka Suutari (eds.). *Music, Art and Diplomacy. East-West Cultural Interactions and the Cold War*. London: Routledge, 2016.

22 Dufraisse, Sylvain, Sophie Momzikoff and Rafael Pedemonte. Les soviétiques hors d'URSS: quels voyages pour quelles expériences? *Les Cahiers Sirice* 16 (2016): 35–46.

– some created in the interwar period[24] – existed between them. Moreover, as has been shown by numerous studies pertaining to the case of new tools or agents of diplomacy,[25] or even diplomacy in a global perspective,[26] states are not the only actors on the international stage. In the sporting field, ever since the 1930s, multiple agents have participated in the development of what Barbara Keys has called the "international sport community", [27] whose actors tend to stay away from international politics. Such is particularly the case with international sports organizations, as they gradually turn from being mere diplomatic spaces to acting in international relations, a position they reinforce during the Cold War.[28] Indeed, they can force states to unify (as shown in the case of the unified German team during the Olympic Games of 1964 and 1968) or, to a lesser extent, they help maintain constant bonds between divided countries and thus participate in the rapprochement between conflicting states on the international stage.[29]

This book thus covers an ambitious programme, especially since we chose not to sequence the period, although being aware of the risks as this "War" was global and long, affected by moments of unrest and others of quiet.[30] The

---

23 This type of thinking is particularly popular with researchers working in the technical field (mainly infrastructures and telecommunication), especially as part of the Tension of Europe network –www.tensionofeurope.eu.
24 Kott, Sandrine. Par-delà la Guerre froide. Les organisations internationales et les circulations Est-Ouest (1947–1973). *Vingtième Siècle. Revue d'histoire* 109 (2011): 143–154.
25 About these renewals, see the special issue: Fleury, Antoine and Georges-Henri Soutou (eds.). Les nouveaux outils de la diplomatie au XXe siècle. *Relation internationale* 212 (2006); Genin, Vincent, Osmont, Mathieu and Thomas Raineau. *Reshaping Diplomacy. Network, Practices and Dynamics of Socialization in European Diplomacy since 1919*. Bruxelles: P.I.E. Peter Lang, 2016.
26 Badel, Laurence and Stanislas Jeannesson. Introduction. Une histoire globale de la diplomatie? *Monde(s)* 5 (2014): 6–26; Holmes, Alison and Simon Rofe. *Global Diplomacy. Theories, Types and Models*. Boulder, CO: Westview Press, 2016.
27 Keys, Barbara. *Globalizing Sport. National Rivalry and International Community in the 1930s*. London: Harvard University Press, 2006.
28 Bernasconi, Gabriel. De l'Universalisme au transnational: le Comité international olympique, acteur atypique des relations internationales. *Bulletin de l'Institut Pierre Renouvin* 31 (2010): 151–159; Beacom, Aaron, *International Diplomacy and the Olympic Movement: The New Mediators*, Basingstoke: Palgrave Macmillan, 2012.
29 For an example, see: Mittag, Jürgen. Negotiating the Cold War? Perspectives in Memory Research on the UEFA, the Early European Football Competitions and the European Nations Cups. In *European Football and Collective Memory*, Wolfram Pyta, Nils Havemann (eds.), 40–63. Palgrave Macmillan: Basingstoke, 2015.
30 An abundant literature now addresses the Cold War from a global angle. For instance, see: Muehlenbeck, Philip E. *Religion and the Cold War: A Global Perspective*. Nashville: Vanderbilt

main aim of this contribution is to highlight further the complexity of sport in international relations. In order to do so, the authors have submitted new case studies based on often hitherto unpublished documents from new archival sources. These texts also take stock of the current state of knowledge on the topic – a general bibliography proposing a summary of the field can be found at the end of the book – so as to open reflection for future research.

The ten contributions thus provide support for a discussion on the place of sport during the Cold War and lead to debating the hypothesis that, because of its particular position on the international stage, but also the capitalist values notably conveyed within the main international sports organizations since the second part of the 1970s,[31] the sporting field has played a part in the crumbling and the collapse of the communist bloc at the end of the 1980s.

Sport and the Cold War: a brief overview of the existing literature

Without being exhaustive, and if we set aside specific collective works on the topic,[32] the studies carried out on this subject can be assembled into four major categories.

First, some authors focused on the commitment of the American[33] and Soviet[34] states in the sporting field. The playing ground being a place where one

---

University Press, 2012; Oreskes, Naomi and John Krige (eds.). *Science and Technology in the Global Cold War*. Cambridge: MIT Press, 2014; Bott, Sandra, Hanhimäki, Jussi M., Schaufelbuehl, Janick and Marco Wyss (eds.). *Neutrality and Neutralism in the Global Cold War: Between or Within the Blocs?* London: Routledge, 2015.

31 Young, Christopher, Tomlinson, Alan and Richard Holt (eds.). *Sport and the Transformation of Modern Europe: States, Media and Markets, 1950–2010*. London: Routledge, 2011.

32 See in particular: Wagg, Steven and David L. Andrews (eds.). *East Plays West: Sport and Cold War*. London & New York: Routledge, 2007; Bertling, Christoph and Evelyne Mertin (eds.). *Freunde oder Feinde? Sportberichterstattung in Ost und West während des Kalten Kriegs*. Gütersloh: Medienfabrik, 2013; and the two special issues: Terret, Thierry (ed.). Sport in Eastern Europe during the Cold War. *The International Journal of the History of Sport* 26 (2009); Graf, Maximilian, Meisinger, Agnes and Wolfgang Weber (eds.). Sport im Kalten Krieg, *Zeitgeschichte* 4 (2015).

33 For a synthesis, see: Gygax, Jérôme. *Olympisme et guerre froide culturelle: le prix de la victoire américaine*. Paris: l'Harmattan, 2012.

34 Riordan, James. *Sport, Politics and Communism*. Manchester: Manchester University Press, 1991; Peppard, Victor and James Riordan. *Playing Politics: Soviet Sport Diplomacy to 1992*. Greenwich: JAI Press Inc., 1992; Tomilina, Natalia (ed.). *Belye igry pod grifom 'sekretno', sovetskij soûz i*

could measure the success of one system (or ideology) over another, the athletes' preparation (infrastructures, training, medicalization, etc.) would require heavy state investments. Other cases, such as East Germany, have also been studied with the same focus.[35]

Other work emphasizes confrontations during international competitions. Here, we think in particular of memorable events such as the 1972 ice hockey "Summit Series",[36] the basketball contest finals between the USA and the USSR during the Munich Olympic Games the same year,[37] or else Francoist Spain's refusal to go to the Soviet Union to play the 1960 UEFA European Nations' Cup.[38] With this in mind however, the events that actually held the academic attention were the boycott of the 1980 Olympic Games by several countries from the capitalist bloc and in response, the boycott of the 1984 Games by the countries of the communist bloc.[39] Besides, a focus has been put on the stakes surrounding applications such as the city of Berlin's at the end of the 1960s.[40]

---

zimnie olimpiady, 1956–1988 [The white games under the clutches of secrecy, the Soviet Union and the winter games, 1956–1988]. Moscow: MFD, 2013.

35 In the wake of Joachim Teichler's pioneer works, the organization of sport in Germany has been studied especially. However, these studies contain elements on international impact. For recent studies, see in particular: Balbier, Uta. A Game, a Competition, an Instrument? High Performance, Cultural Diplomacy and German Sport from 1950 to 1972. The International Journal of the History of Sport 26 (2009): 539–555. Dennis, Michael and Jonathan Grix. *Sport Under Communism: Behind the East German 'Miracle'*. Basingstoke: Palgrave Macmillan, 2012; Wiese, René. *Kaderschmieden des 'Sportwunderlandes' die Kinder- und Jugendsportschulen der DDR*. Hildesheim: Arete-Verl., 2012; McDougal, Alan. *The people's game. Football, state and society in East Germany*. Cambridge : Cambridge University Press, 2014.

36 See for instance: Wilson, J. J. 27 Remarkable Days: The 1972 Summit Series of Ice Hockey Between Canada and the Soviet Union. *Totalitarian Movements and Political Religions* 5 (2004): 271–280; Soares, Joan. Our Way of Life against Theirs. In *Diplomatic Games*, 251–296.

37 Archambault, Fabien. Trois secondes de Guerre froide. La finale olympique de Munich en 1972. In *Le Continent basket. L'Europe et le basket-ball au XXe siècle*, Fabien Archambault, Loïc Artiaga and Gérard Bosc (eds.), 159–190, Peter Lang: Bruxelles, 2015. And for a longer viewpoint of these basketball confrontations between the USA and the USSR, see: Witherspoon, Kevin. 'Fuzz Kids' and 'Musclemen'. In *Diplomatic Games*, 297–326.

38 Ramos, Ramón. *¡Que vienen los rusos!: España renuncia a la Eurocopa de 1960 por decisión de Franco*. Granada: Comares, 2012.

39 Many texts have been published about these two boycotts. For a general view of these two events, see: Mertin, Evelyne. The Soviet Union and the Olympic Games of 1980 and 1984. In *East Plays West*, 235–252. For recent works on the boycott of the Olympic Games of 1980, see in particular: Sarantakes, Nicholas Evans. *Dropping the Torch: Jimmy Carter, the Olympic Boycott, and the Cold War*. Cambridge: Cambridge University Press, 2010 and Tulli, Umberto. Boicottate le Olimpiadi del Gulag! I diritti umani e la campagna contro le Olimpiadi di Mosca, *Ricerche di Storia Politica* 1 (2013): 3–24. For 1984, see: Gygax, Jérôme. Le retrait soviétique des Jeux de Los

Another element that proved to be interesting for researchers was the athletes, as they were studied as vectors for their bloc's ideology. For instance, we can list the cases of the gymnast Nadia Comăneci,[41] the football player László Kubala,[42] or the athlete Emile Zátopek.[43] Likewise, the case of athletes who fled from the communist bloc has also been studied.[44]

Finally, the last category pertains to how the great powers used some international organizations for their own profit. The main case studied here is that of the International Olympic Committee (IOC) since for other organizations, though a few studies do exist, the Cold War is not at the heart of the subject but is only included in a larger institutional history.[45] As a matter of fact, the recent publication of a special issue on how the international organizations negotiated the Cold War should, in addition to several contributions in this book, galvanize further studies on this topic.[46] About the IOC, researchers have mainly tried to understand the USSR's arrival in and influence on the IOC,[47] as well as the Amer-

---

Angeles: Enjeux idéologiques et diplomatie publique américaine (1983–1984). In *Le Pouvoir des anneaux: les Jeux olympiques à la lumière de la politique 1896–2004*, Pierre Milza, Philippe Tétart and François Jequier (eds.), 299–325, Paris: Vuibert, 2004; Edelman, Robert, The Russians are Not Coming! The Soviet Withdrawal from the Games of the XXIII Olympiad. *The International Journal of the History of Sport* 32 (2015): 9–36. Also, for a theoretical reflection about the boycotts of sporting events, see: Monin, Eric and Christophe Maillard. Pour une typologie du boycottage aux Jeux olympiques. *Relations internationales* 162 (2015): 173–198; Giuntini, Sergio. *L'Olimpiade dimezzata. Storia e politica del boicottaggio nello sport*. Sedizioni, Milano, 2009.

40 Cary, Noel. Olympics in Divided Berlin? Popular Culture and Political Imagination at the Cold War Frontier, *Cold War History* 11 (2011): 291–316.

41 Even though the book is closer to a novel than a scientific study, see: Lafon, Lola. *La Petite Communiste qui ne souriait jamais*. Arles: Actes Sud, 2014.

42 Simon, Juan Antonio. Fútbol y cine en el franquismo: la utilización política del héroe deportivo en la España de Franco. *Historia y comunicación social* 17 (2012): 69–84.

43 Fortune, Yohann. Emil Zatopek dans la guerre froide: de la soumission à la rébellion (1948–1968). *Sciences Sociales et Sport* 5 (2012): 53–86.

44 See for instance: Rider, Toby. Eastern Europe's Unwanted: Exiled Athletes and the Olympic Games, 1948–1964. *Journal of Sport History* 40 (2013): 435–453.

45 Roger, Anne and Thierry Terret. *European Athletics. Une histoire continentale de l'athlétisme*, Stuttgart: Neuer Sportverlag, 2012; Ottogali-Mazzacavallo, Cécile, Thierry Terret and Gérard Six. *L'histoire de l'escrime: 1913–2013, un siècle de Fédération internationale d'escrime*, Biarritz: Atlantica, 2013. Also, a few other contributions in: Archambault, Artiaga and Bosc (eds.), *Le continent basket*.

46 About this topic, see the special issue: Negotiating the Cold War. The Case of International Sport Bodies during the First Period of the Cold War (1946–1971). *Sport in History* 37 (2017) coordinated by Grégory Quin and Philippe Vonnard.

47 Charitas, Pascal. La Commission d'Aide Internationale Olympique (CAIO): Un instrument de propagande soviétique? (1951–1962). *Sport History Review* 40 (2008): 143–166; Mertin, Evelyne.

ican commitment to this organization.⁴⁸ They have also analysed how the case of the two Germanys was treated.⁴⁹ Besides, other authors have questioned the impact of the Cold War on the governance of the organization.⁵⁰

In the meantime, we also need to underline that our study is part of the recent increase in interest in research about the place of sport in international relations,⁵¹ but also of new interrogation of "Sport in the Cold War" more generally. As a matter of fact, in parallel to our process, three established researchers, namely Robert Edelman, Christian Ostermann and Christopher Young, have been carrying out an ambitious project, called "The Global History of Sport in the Cold War". This project gathers no less than 77 researchers, who work to bring a new vision of the topic, especially by proposing studies that pertain to all five continents.⁵²

This brief overview of existing literature shows that several topics pertaining to what could be called "Sport in the Cold War" have been broached. However, it also highlights the prevalence of a vision focused on sport as a power tool for states. Yet, if this aspect is undeniable, it should be noted that sports relations

---

Sowjetisch-deutsche Sportbeziehungen im "Kalten Krieg". Sankt Augustin: Akademia Verlag, 2009; Parks, Jenifer. *Red Sport, Red Tape: the Olympic Games, the Soviet Sports Bureaucracy, and the Cold War, 1952–1980*. PhD, University of North Carolina en 2009.
48 Rider, Toby. *Cold War Games: Propaganda, the Olympics, and US Foreign Policy*. Urbana: University of Illinois Press, 2016.
49 Hughes, Gerald and Rachel Owen. 'The Continuation of Politics by Other Means': Britain, the Two Germanys and the Olympic Games, 1949–1972. *Contemporary European History* 18 (2009): 443–474.
50 Clastres, Patrick. Paix par le sport et guerre froide: le neutralisme pro-occidental du Comité international olympique. In *Culture et Guerre froide*, Jean-François Sirinelli and Georges-Henri Soutou (eds.), 121–137. Paris: PUPS, 2008: Keys, Barbara. The International Olympic Committee and Global Culture during the Cold War. In *Les relations culturelles internationales au XXe siècle. De la diplomatie culturelle à l'acculturation*, Anne Dulphy, Robert Frank, Marie-Anne Matard-Bonucci and Pascal Ory (eds.), 291–298. Bruxelles: P.I.E Peter Lang, 2010.
51 Since 2014, several publications have addressed the link between sport and diplomacy: Pigman, Geoffray Alan. International Sport and Diplomacy's Public Dimension: Governments, Sporting Federations and the Global Audience. *Diplomacy & Statecraft* 25 (2014): 94–114; "Diplomacy and Sport". *Diplomacy & Statecraft*, 27 (2016) special issue coordinated by Simon Rofe and Heather Dichter. Moreover, it is important to put in evidence several thesis defences addressing this topic and more largely the case of sport in international relations: Sbetti, Nicola. *Giochi diplomatici. Sport e politica estera nell'Italia del secondo dopoguerra (1943–53)*. PhD, University of Bologna, 2015; Dufraisse, Sylvain. *Les "Héros du sport". La fabrique de l'élite sportive soviétique (1934–1980)*. PhD, University Paris 1-Panthéon-Sorbonne, 2016; Vonnard, Philippe. *Genèse du football européen. De la FIFA à l'UEFA (1930–1960)*. PhD, University of Lausanne, 2016.
52 For more information on this project, see: https://www.wilsoncenter.org/article/the-global-history-sport-the-cold-war.

do not solely develop in those directions. Moreover, they often take place within a competitive setting, itself the object of preliminary negotiation and eventual agreement by the countries taking part in the contest. Taking all of this into account, this book offers a more "open" approach to the sports phenomenon during the Cold War, based primarily on the case of Europe.

Book outline

The book is divided into three parts, each dealing with a specific geographical scale.

The first part addresses the national level, where the authors mainly focus on the use of sport by states as a tool of power on the international stage. Although it sounds like a classical approach, the three contributions propose new grounds to show that the investments and the aims vary strongly depending on the state. **Nicola Sbetti** studies the sports-politics development of Trieste, a city that became a border between the East and the West even before the Cold War between the two great powers really broke out. **Daniel Svensson** and **Anna Åberg** propose a comparison between the training of Swedish and Soviet skiers, an approach that helps question the commitment of the state in both countries. Finally, **Juan Antonio Simon** re-evaluates the commitment of Francoism in sport and shows that from the end of the 1950s, sport became an important issue for the regime. However, the lack of financial investment did not allow Spain to really shine on the international stage and, in that sense, the relationship between Francoism and sport cannot equate to Hitlerite or Mussolinian predecessors.

The second part deals with the European continental scale and considers more specifically the role of sport in the rapprochement between the two blocs. The authors' intention is to highlight the brilliant ability of sport to create bridges between countries in a period when several of them are politically divided. **Sylvain Dufraisse** agreed with the recent developments of the history of transnational circulations and shows that numerous Soviet athletes actually travelled in the Western bloc. **Philippe Vonnard** and **Kevin Marston** address the opportunity a sports organization, namely UEFA (Union des associations européennes de football) had to create bonds between its member associations, from both sides of the Iron Curtain, through competitions it organized (International Youth Tournament and European Nations' Cup). As for **Stefan Scholl**, he studies a parastatal organization that has not yet been analysed, namely the European Sports Conference. Created during the 1970s, it has the particularity of being an organization made of political and sports leaders from both blocs.

The author thus explores the possibilities, while also showing the difficulties, of creating an East-West dialogue within the organization.

The third part broaches the question of transcontinental exchanges. Researchers try here to think about the possible influences the two superpowers may have had on sports politics or the development of practice within states. Also, they question the impact of the representations in European countries of the conflict between the two giant powers. **François Doppler** studies the influence of the American army in the development of basketball in France after the Second World War. His contribution questions the American government's sports politics within its army stationed in Europe. **Claire Nicolas** takes the opposite stance as she studies the Soviet influence on the implementation of the Ghana Young Pioneer movement. However, in the wake of the development of postcolonial studies, her contribution also shows that over time, a third way was actually developed by Ghana, which corresponded with its position on the international stage. In his contribution, **Souvik Naha** considers the chess summit of 1972 opposing the Soviet, Boris Spassky and the American, Bobby Fischer. By compiling several news titles from different European countries, the author shows that the match was really carried by the Cold War, as some journalists did not hesitate to recall the context or even to use stereotypes to describe both protagonists. But Souvik Naha also underlines that this viewpoint is actually a construction of reality and that it does not correspond exactly to the way the match itself was played, as despite Fischer's mischief, both protagonists were above all chess players fighting for the supreme title in a given field. Finally, through their contribution, **Quentin Tonnerre** and **Grégory Quin** analyse the motives and resonances existing around the Chinese ping-pong tour of Switzerland in 1972. Their main hypothesis is that, regarding its international popular success and the apolitical discourse of its leaders since the end of the Second World War, sport started to be a new "tool of diplomacy", especially used to establish relationships with "new" countries, allowing governments to cross some ideological borders. Thus, as a small and neutral European power, Switzerland implemented various strategies, including sport, to negotiate with the bigger countries during the Cold War.

The book concludes with an afterword by **Martin Polley**, director of the prestigious International Centre for Sports History and Culture at De Montfort University in Leicester, UK. As a specialist in sports questions at an international level,[53] Martin Polley brings an interesting perspective on the contributions and

---

53 As part of his research on British sports diplomacy, he addressed the place of sport in international relations, in particular during the period of the Cold War. His key publications are: Pol-

offers research prospects that could be developed in the years to come on the topic of "Sport in the Cold War", and more largely on studies about sport in international relations.

Philippe Vonnard, Nicola Sbetti, Grégory Quin

---

ley, Martin. *Moving the Goalposts: A History of Sport and Society Since 1945*. London & New York: Routledge, 1998; Polley, Martin. *The British Olympics: Britain's Olympic Heritage 1612–2012*. London: English Heritage, 2011.

First Part. Creating relations between European states. Sport as tool of diplomacy

Nicola Sbetti
Playing at the border of the Cold War
The case of the city of Trieste (1945–1948)

Introduction

On 5 March 1946, in his famous Fulton speech, by affirming: 'From Stettin in the Baltic to Trieste in the Adriatic, an iron curtain has descended across the Continent',[1] Winston Churchill indicated the Julian city as a border of the emerging Cold War. From the end of the Second World War in 1945 until at least 1948, when the Socialist Federal Republic of Yugoslavia (SFRY) was expelled from the Cominform (the organization which coordinated the Communist parties internationally, under Soviet direction), the city of Trieste, which was claimed by Italy and the SFRY and occupied by Anglo-American troops as part of the Free Territory of Trieste (FTT), become a 'symbol of the dispute' between Washington and Moscow and 'the ideal and strategic point of the meeting between two civilizations of the East and of the West'.[2] So, in Trieste the end of the war, which saw the victory of the anti-fascist Alliance over the Axis powers, did not stop tensions and conflicts because the long existing ethnic cleavage (Italian vs. South Slavic) was now intersected by that between Communists and anti-Communists, which ideologically shaped the Cold War.

In this context, sport, as much as other cultural activities, could not stay neutral. Its practice was deeply influenced by the intersection of the ethnic and political conflicts that shaped the life of the city. Even before the Long Telegram of George F. Kennan and the Marshall Plan or the Sovietization of Eastern Europe and the creation of the Cominform, which were decisive for the emergence of the Cold War, Trieste become one of the first places where sport became an arena of confrontation between two different ways of imagining the future, with the further complexity that the Communist vs. anti-Communist cleavage was interconnected with the ethnic one.

By looking at the specific case of the Italian population, the aim of this chapter is to analyse how the ideological conflict, fundamental in the emergence of

---

[1] Churchill, Winston. The Sinews of Peace (The Iron Curtain Speech). Westminster College, Fulton, 5 March 1946.
[2] Quoted in: Cattaruzza, Marina. *L'Italia e il confine orientale*. Bologna: Il Mulino, 2007, here 303.

the Cold War, influenced the development of sporting activities in a contested and occupied city like Trieste, from its liberation from the Third Reich in spring 1945 until the Tito-Stalin split in 1948. Particular attention will be dedicated to the interactions among the political, institutional and sporting actors in order to understand how they influenced sporting practice at local, national, international and transnational level.

This work is based on the documents from the Prime Minister's Cabinet (PCM) in the Italian National Archives (ACS), from the Italian National Olympic Committee (CONI) and from the International Olympic Committee (IOC) archives, articles in the Italian political and sporting press and the existing literature. While the case of Trieste is widely studied from a political and diplomatic point of view, as will be later described, there are only few studies of the history of sport in the free territory of Trieste. The most important work, that of Fabien Archambault, is focused almost exclusively on the case of football.[3]

The political context of the city, then how the different political cultures used sport activities for their goal and finally two case studies, will be analysed. The first of these, the parable of Triestina and Amatori Ponziana football teams, is a significant example on how far political and ethnic divisions could influence sporting practice. The second, the contested passage of the Giro d'Italia in Trieste, shows that not only is sport deeply influenced by the political milieu but that a particular sporting event can have the impact to influence the political life of a city.

The political context

It is impossible to understand the significance of playing sport for the Italian population in Trieste in the years following the end of the Second World War without considering the broader political context.

Historically Trieste, a city and seaport in north-eastern Italy, had been populated by a melting pot of different ethnic and cultural groups, where the Italian majority coexisted with significant South Slavic, German and Jewish minorities.

---

[3] Archambault, Fabien. Le football à Trieste de 1945 à 1954. Un affaire d'État. *Vingtième Siècle* 111 (2011): 49–58. For the literature on the political and diplomatic history of Trieste see footnotes 4–6. For analysis of the attempts of the FTT to gain an international sporting recognition see: Sbetti, Nicola. Neutrally anti-Communists. International Sports Institutions and the Case of Trieste (1945–1954). *Sport in History* (in press). For an Italian perspective on the sport in the FTT see: Sbetti, Nicola. *Giochi diplomatici. Sport e politica estera nell'Italia del second dopoguerra (1943–1953)*. Treviso: Ludica (in press).

The whole region was part of the Austro-Hungarian Empire until the end of the First World War. However, these territories were claimed by both Italian and South Slavic nationalists, causing strains between the two populations. After 1919, when the Treaty of Versailles was signed and Trieste became part of the Kingdom of Italy, those tensions increased.[4] In fact, during the 1930s, the Italian Fascist government increased the discriminatory attitude towards the Slavic minority, which suffered a process of "Italianization". The Slavic languages were forbidden and Slovenian place-names and peoples' surnames were changed.[5]

During the Second World War, the Italian Fascist government supported the 1941 Nazi invasion of Yugoslavia and annexed some Yugoslavian territories, including Ljubljana and Split. In the late summer of 1943, with the fall of Mussolini and the decision of the Badoglio government to switch its alliance, the situation changed. Italy lost all its East Adriatic territories in the Balkans, including Trieste, which was then incorporated into the Third Reich. During the war, the majority of the Italian population remained neutral and just tried to survive. However, a significant part decided to remain loyal to the Nazi regime even after 8 September 1943. In this choice, the fear of Communism and Slavic hegemony played a significant role, which did not exist elsewhere in Italy for those who choose to follow Mussolini in the Salò Republic.[6] Others, with anti-Fascist sympathies, decided to become partisans; the majority entered the local anti-Fascist Italian Resistance Forces (CLN) and collaborated with the Liberation Front of the Slovene Nation (OF), which was part of the National Liberation Army of Yugoslavia (NLAY).[7] The situation changed in the autumn of 1944, after NLAY claimed Trieste. Tito affirmed, as a non-negotiable condition, that the only way for the Italian partisans to fight the Nazi-fascist forces was to be part of the Yugoslavian resistance.[8] This diktat had a shattering impact on the Italian resistance movement of the Trieste region. Obliged to choose between a national and a political loyalty, the Italian Communist partisans choose the second one. So, the Italian Communist brigades, in the name of internationalist solidary, entered the Yugoslavian resistance breaking the anti-Fascist alliance, that in the rest of the pen-

---

4 Cattaruzza. *L'Italia e il confine orientale*, here 15–41.
5 Sluga, Glenda. Identità nazionale italiana e fascismo: alieni, allogeni e assimilazione sul confine nord-orientale italiano. In *Nazionalismi di frontiera. Identità contrapposte sull'Adriatico nord-orientale, 1850–1950*, Marina Cattaruzza (ed.), 171–202. Soveria Mannelli: Rubbettino, 2003.
6 Cattaruzza. *L'Italia e il confine orientale*, here 246–59.
7 Scotti, Giacomo. *"Bono taliano". Gli italiani in Jugoslavia dal 1941 al 1943*. Milano: La Pietra, 1977, here 7.
8 Pupo, Raoul. *Trieste 1945*. Roma: Laterza, 2014, here 58–61.

insula unified Socialists, Communists, Republicans, Catholics and Monarchists. On the contrary, the rest of the Julian CNL tried to represent the feelings of those Italian populations who were anti-Fascist but not pro-Communist and wanted Italy to maintain the sovereignty of the region. However, by trying simultaneously to defend their "anti-Fascism" and their "Italian patriotism" they became marginalized or eliminated with the accusation of treason or even Fascism by the pro-Communist side of the Resistance movement. This dramatic rupture in the Italian anti-Fascist front had important consequences not only during the war but also at the end of the hostilities.[9]

Inevitably the process that led to the liberation of Trieste from the Nazis in the spring of 1945 reflected this complexity. The city was claimed by both Italy and Yugoslavia, and was considered significant by the Allies because of the strategic relevance of its port. In the diplomatic dispute, the power dynamic between Rome and Belgrade was imbalanced. While Socialist Yugoslavia, which thanks to Tito's partisans had liberated itself from the Nazis, was in a strong position from a political and military point of view, Italy was a former enemy country, with no real control of its territory and which had to rely on the Anglo-American armies to protect its interests. On 1 May 1945, immediately after the two cores of the Triestinean resistance had started two concurrent uprisings against the Nazis,[10] the city was occupied by the Yugoslavian Army, which anticipated the arrival of the British VIII Army, led by the New Zealander General Freyberg. Having won the "race for Trieste",[11] Tito refused to give control of the city to the Allies. Therefore, for 40 days, in an atmosphere of uncertainty, marked by riots, violence, vengeance and hasty trials against the "enemies of the people", the city remained under Yugoslavian control.[12]

While the majority of the Slovenian population and a significant part of the Italian working class embraced the Yugoslav troops as true liberators, on the other hand, for the non-Communist Italian population, even the anti-Fascists, the days of Yugoslavian rule were perceived as one of the darkest moments in the history of the city. After all, for the Italian bourgeoisie, the Yugoslavian occu-

---

9 See for example, Valdevit, Giampaolo. *Il dilemma di Trieste. Guerra e dopoguerra in uno scenario europeo.* Gorizia: LEG, 1999, here 98–9 and http://www.kozina.com/premik/porita.pdf.
10 The Italian and Yugoslavian Communist partisans led the first uprising, and the non-Communist Italian partisans with former members of the Italian police the second one.
11 Cox, Geoffrey. *The race for Trieste.* London: Kimber, 1977.
12 Pupo, *Trieste 1945*.

pation represented an "overturning of the ethnic and social balance in place since the years of the Habsburgs".[13]

The Yugoslavian refusal to withdraw their troops provoked strong military-diplomatic tension, but in the end, Tito had to give in to Allied pressure. On 9 June 1945, the Morgan line, which divided the occupation zone of the Allies from that of the Yugoslavians, was drawn and three days later the Yugoslavian Army left Trieste to the Anglo-American occupation force. Despite the fact that this situation should have been provisional, in the end the Morgan line became definitive, especially after the end of the peace treaty negotiations. While the Soviets supported Belgrade's position, to make Trieste a Yugoslavian city, the UK and the USA rejected this option. In the end, French mediation prevailed. With the peace treaty, Italy could retain Gorizia and Monfalcone, but lost the Istrian Peninsula and 81 per cent of the Julian Venetia territory. The peace treaty formally created the FTT, which should have been ruled by a UN-nominated governor. However, because of the opposing vetoes among the winning powers over the nomination of the governor, the FTT remained divided by the Morgan line into an "A Zone", which included Trieste and was occupied by the Anglo-American forces, and a "B Zone", occupied by the Yugoslavs.[14]

For three years Trieste became a barrier against the expansion – perceived as unrestrained – of Communism in Western Europe. The SFRY seemed to be the most loyal and aggressive ally of the USSR, and "Tito's administration more 'Stalinist' than Stalin".[15] However, while Tito aimed to control the city, Stalin was not ready to start a war for Trieste, and this soon become one of the many causes of strain between the two leaders. In the summer of 1948 the split between Belgrade and Moscow and the expulsion of the SFRY from the Cominform changed the scenario. With the Yugoslavian exit from the Soviet bloc, Trieste ceased to be a border of the Cold War.[16] The Western powers saw Tito as an important leader

---

13 Purini, Piero. *Metamorfosi etniche. I cambiamenti di popolazione a Trieste, Gorizia, Fiume e in Istria, 1914–1975.* Udine: Kappa Vu, 2010, here 215.
14 On the diplomatic case of Trieste see for example: De Castro, Diego. *La Questione di Trieste. L'Azione politica e diplomatica italiana dal 1943 al 1954.* Trieste: LINT, 1981; Duroselle, Jean-Baptiste. *Le conflit de Trieste 1943–54.* Institut de sociologie de l'Université libre de Bruxelles, 1966; Pupo, Raoul. *La rifondazione della politica estera italiana: la questione giuliana (1944–1946).* Udine: Del Bianco,1979; Valdevit, Giampaolo. *La questione di Trieste, 1941–1954. Politica internazionale e contesto locale.* Milano: Franco Angeli, 1986.
15 Crockatt, Richard. *Cinquant'anni di Guerra Fredda.* Roma: Salerno, 1997, here 102.
16 On the Tito-Stalin split see among the others: Banac, Ivo. *With Stalin Against Tito: Cominformist Splits in Yugoslav Communism.* Ithaca: Cornell University Press, 1988; Lees, Lorraine M. *Keeping Tito Afloat. The United States, Yugoslavia, and the Cold War.* University Park, Pennsylva-

for their anti-Soviet strategy and, in order to gain his favour, they paid less attention to Italian aspirations. At the same time, the decreased international pressure on Trieste opened the path to a higher degree of economic and administrative integration of the "A Zone" into Italy. In the meantime, the "B Zone" had gradually become substantially included into the SFRY.[17]

In 1954, with the London Memorandum which ratified the status quo, the "Case of Trieste" found a solution. The SFRY regained formal possession of the "B Zone", while, with the withdrawal of the Allied armies, Italy obtained sovereignty over Trieste and the "A Zone". However, only in 1975 with the Osimo Treaty did Italy and the SFRY reach a formal mutual recognition of their borders.

Sport in a contested city

The political destiny of Trieste was chosen by the Paris Peace Conference and the Morgan line became a division between the Soviet and the American spheres of influence; its population lived in a situation of permanent mobilization. Violent groups were often protagonists of aggression, fights, and vandalism toward the political enemy and their headquarters. Although the ethnic cleavage was certainly important in these *amicus-hostis* divisions, it was the Cold War axis which played a major role. In fact, the Julian Communist Party (PCRG), despite some internal disagreement and the embarrassment of the Italian Communist Party, declared itself in favour of the inclusion of Trieste in the SFRY, in the name of socialist internationalism and anti-imperialism.[18]

In this situation sport was more than just a game. It soon became a weapon in the low-intensity conflict fought in order to claim the Julian city. From 1945 until 1948, both sides, with the mediation of the Allied authorities, tried to symbolically "occupy" the city with sporting activities in order to both build and to

---

nia: Penn State University Press, 1997; Perović, Jeronim. The Tito-Stalin Split: A Reassessment in Light of New Evidence. *Journal of Cold War Studies* 9 (2007): 32–63.

17 See Seton-Watson, Christopher. *La politica estera della Repubblica italiana*. In *La politica estera italiana (1860–1985)*, Richard J. B. Bosworth and Sergio Romano (eds.), 331–360, here 346. Bologna: Il Mulino, 1991; Varsori, Antonio. *L'Italia nelle relazioni internazionali dal 1943–1992*. Roma-Bari: Laterza, 1998, here 63.

18 Pons, Silvio. Mosca, il PCI e la questione di Trieste (1943–1948). In *Dagli Archivi di Mosca. L'URSS il Cominform e il PCI (1943–1951)*, Francesca Gori and Silvio Pons (eds.), 85–134. Roma: Carocci, 1998. See also: Terzuolo, Eric R. *Red Adriatic: The Communist Parties of Italy and Yugoslavia*. London: Westview Press, 1985; Capano, Fabio. Fighting for Trieste: Nationalism and Political Violence at the Edge of the Iron Curtain. *Journal of Modern Italian Studies* 21 (2016): 603–626.

demonstrate the consensus of the population. From the sporting point of view, the pro-Italian, anti-Communist side was represented by the local committees of CONI and its federations, meanwhile the Italo-Slovenian pro-Communist side was represented by an organization which was called the Unione dei Circoli di Educazione Fisica per il litorale e Trieste (UCEF).

Until September 1943 Trieste was an Italian city and its teams played in the Italian championships. So, despite the Anglo-American occupation, and the possibility that Trieste would became the main city of a free territory, all the teams which had an Italian and a non-Communist background expressed their desire to continue to participate in the Italian competitions. This request was fully support by CONI and the other Italian sport institutions, which were well aware that the participation of Triestinean teams in the Italian championship was a strong claim to the Italian character of Trieste. It is not exaggerated to say that the support of the Italian sport institutions, far from limiting itself to the symbolic aspects, soon become a true "occupation" of the "A Zone" by them. Not only was it decided that the Triestinean clubs continued to participate in the Italian championships but, despite the fact that the city was ruled by the Allied Military Government (AMG), they kept control of sporting activity as had happened before the war and Trieste was explicitly chosen as the location for congresses and championships of almost all Italian sport federations. Despite its economic problems, in 1946 CONI decided to support its Trieste committee with a monthly subsidy and in the following year, with 3 per cent of the gross of the local revenue of *Totocalcio*, the football betting system which would maintain Italian sport for almost five decades.[19] Furthermore, CONI with the full support of all the sporting newspapers, launched a subscription to support sport activity in the Trieste region.[20] Despite the fact that Trieste had lost Italian sovereignty, CONI also financed the construction of the first covered swimming pool in Italy after the war.[21]

The sporting institutions were not left alone. Through the Office for the Border Areas (UZC), the Italian government subsidized all the organizations that defended the "Italianness" of conflict areas, like Bolzano and Trieste. While the

---

19 Arch. CONI, Giunta 30 September 1946–1 October 1946 and Arch. CONI, Giunta 7 May 1947.
20 La stampa sportiva del CONI lancia una sottoscrizione nazionale per lo sport giuliano e tridentino, *La Gazzetta dello Sport*, 15 September 1945.
21 Arch. CONI, Consiglio Nazionale, 28 September 1953. See also Arch. CONI, Giunta 18–19 January 1950, Giunta 4 April 1951, Giunta 29 September 1952, Giunta 23 December 1952, Giunta 25 March 1953.

government generally showed little interest in supporting Italian sport,[22] when the destiny of a city like Trieste was at stake, it radically changed its attitude and fully supported pro-Italian sporting activities with a secret influx of money.[23] The pro-Italian and non-Communist teams were informally regularly subsidized, however because according to the UZC in football and basketball "one strong team was more useful that three modest" ones, the support was not equal for all the teams and depended on political criteria.[24]

In the eyes of the Italian authorities this political intervention in sport was necessary to fight against the involvement of the Italian-Slovenian pro-Communist side in the city's sport activities. In fact, since August 1945, with the creation of UCEF, which operated from the area between Monfalcone and Pula, sport became a political tool. As was written in the UCEF statute, its goal was to "educate and consolidate the moral and physical forces of the population of Trieste and its coast, and develop the anti-fascist idea and reinforce the Italian-Slovenian solidarity".[25] For Tito the concept of "Italian-Slovenian brotherhood" was not just a slogan but was part of a broader political strategy for winning the hearts and minds of the Italian city's workers, to reinforce Yugoslavian claims to Trieste.[26] In the name of socialist internationalism and anti-imperialism, UCEF, whose officials were close to the PCRG, included athletes from any nationality and focused on the most popular disciplines such as football, cycling, basketball and swimming. In fact, a significant number of the Italian working class of Trieste joined UCEF. Because of the antagonism with CONI, which was defined as "Fascist" in order to delegitimize it,[27] when UCEF sporting activity crossed Trieste's borders it was more likely to head for SFRY and the East rather than Italy and the West. This was also because CONI and the Italian federation boy-

---

[22] Sbetti, Nicola. La "diplomazia sportiva" italiana nel secondo dopoguerra: attori e istituzioni (1943–1955). *Diritto dello Sport* 1 (2016): 27–44.

[23] D'Amelio, Diego. *La difesa di Trieste. Strategie e culture politiche delle forze italiane nella battaglia per il confine orientale (1945–1954)*. In *La difesa dell'Italianità. L'Ufficio per le zone di confine a Bolzano, Trento e Trieste*, Diego D'Amelio, Andrea Di Michele and Giorgio Mezzalira (eds.), 381–414. Bologna: Il Mulino, 2015.

[24] Gheda, Paolo and Federico Robbe. *Andreotti e l'Italia di confine. Lotta politica e nazionalizzazione delle masse (1947–1954)*. Guerini: Milano, 2015, here 96–97.

[25] UCEF Statue in Arch. CIO, D. RM01, Tries/001.

[26] Pirjevec, Jože. Italiani e sloveni: cent'anni di rapporti conflittuali (1848–1954). In *La difesa dell'italianità*. D'Amelio, Di Michele and Mezzalira, 355–379.

[27] UCEF. *Il Progresso*, 14 October 1946.

cotted UCEF activity and imposed sanctions on athletes and teams who participated in UCEF competitions.[28]

UCEF also tried to gain international recognition by claiming to be the representative of the FTT, something which was denied by the IOC and the ISFs. In fact, exploiting their stronger position in international sport institutions and taking advantage of their visceral anti-Communism, Italy managed successfully to delegitimize UCEF, describing it as a purely political organization.[29]

Nonetheless, a "Trieste national team", linked to UCEF played some unofficial international games against some Eastern bloc countries in 1947 and 1948, and participated in the international sporting events organized in the Cominform countries. For example, a Trieste team took part in the sports competitions of the World Festival of Youth and Students (an event which aimed to reinforce solidarity among the youth of the Eastern bloc countries and the Communist youth in Western countries) in the Festivals which were held in Prague in 1947, in Budapest in 1949, in East Berlin in 1951 and Bucharest in 1953.[30]

However, this international activity was drastically reduced after 1948. When the SFRY, their neighbour and supporter, left Cominform the UCEF teams saw their economic support ended. This was a direct consequence of the fact that the PCRG had decided to remain loyal to Moscow instead of Belgrade and this brought an end to all the projects for Italian-Slovenian solidarity, including sport. Significantly also, the economic support from the Italian government to pro-Italian non-Communist sport gradually reduced in the 1950s.[31]

During its short experience, strongly linked with the historical evolution of the FTT, UCEF played a relevant role in involving the working class of the city in sporting activities which were far from apolitical. Its role, however was soon forgotten because the ostracism of the Italian sport institutions and the opposition coming from the SFRY after 1948 contributed to erase the memory of this experience.[32]

---

28 See for example, L'UVI e la "Coppa della Pace", Agenzia Italiana Sportiva, 6 October 1949 and the Memorandum of the Trieste Olympic Committee, Arch. CIO. D. RM01, Tries/001.
29 Sbetti, Neutrally anti-Communists.
30 See Giuntini, Sergio. Lo sport italiano ai Festival mondiali della gioventù. *Il Calendario del Popolo* 673 (2003): 20–24; Impiglia, Marco. Goliardi in gara. I Giochi mondiali universitari prima delle Universiadi. *Lancillotto e Nausica* 1 (1997): 8–39, here 22–25.
31 Pirjevec. Italiani e sloveni: cent'anni di rapporti conflittuali.
32 Sbetti, Nicola and Nicolò Falchi. *Trieste val ben una sassata*. Ivrea: Bradipolibri (in press).

The case of football

Football, whose popularity was challenged only by cycling, was probably the discipline in which the political and ethnic tensions that divided the city emerged more regularly. For three seasons, from 1946 to 1949, Trieste found itself in the peculiar condition of having two football teams in the First Division of two different nations: Triestina in Italian and Amatori Ponziana in Yugoslavian football.

Amatori Ponziana was founded in the summer of 1946 through a split from Ponziana, the team of the popular quarter of San Giacomo. The division was mainly due to political reasons; the team was based in the most pro-Communist area of Trieste. However, there were sporting and economic reasons as well. The Italian Football Federation (FIGC) did not included either Ponziana or Edera Trieste in the first two divisions but only in the third (Serie C), and the Yugoslavians financially supported the new team. These three factors help to explain the choice of the several Italian players who decided to play for the Amatori Ponziana. For those who truly believed in Communism it was mainly a political choice, but for many others the decision to cross the "Morgan line" was a consequence of the opportunity to play in the First Division rather than the Third and have better salaries. For Belgrade, the possibility to have a team from Trieste in the Yugoslavian championship was an extraordinary card to play at the diplomatic table. It was for that reason the team was strongly subsidized. This gave the opportunity to Amatori Ponziana, which was formally an amateur team, to offer "refunds" three times higher than the salary which the players had previously had in Italy.[33]

In consequence, the presence of Triestina in the Italian league assumed an even more heightened political meaning. If the simple participation of Triestina in Serie A validated the idea that Trieste was an Italian city, the celebration that the Triestinean team received each time it played away reinforced this narration. For example, on 22 April 1946, when the *alabardati* went to the capital to play Rome, Prime Minister Alcide De Gasperi, who usually did not intervene in sporting events, was not only present at the game but took part in a patriotic ceremony which celebrated Triestina and the Italian character of Trieste.[34] The month before, when the members of the Inter-Allied Commission, tasked with establishing the ethnic composition of the contested area, attended the game between

---

[33] Sbetti and Falchi. *Trieste val ben una sassata*. See also Sadar, Giuliano. *Una lunga giornata di bora. Trieste e la Triestina, storie di calcio attraverso terre di confine*. Arezzo: Limina, 2003; Archambault, *Le football à Trieste*.

[34] Roma-Triestina 0 – 0. *Corriere dello Sport*, 23 April 1946.

Triestina and Juventus, they assisted in a nationalistic moment which was often staged by the supporters. Despite the loss, at the end of the games the fans recalled the players of both teams and all the stadium applauded them singing the chorus: "Italia, Italia". *La Gazzetta dello Sport* commented "Again, sport, in a simple and spontaneous way, is serving the country".[35]

After having finished the north leg of the 1945–1946 championship in eighth place, during the summer of 1946 the AMG started to query the suitability of Trieste's stadium for security reasons. So, on 27 September, despite the fact that Milan's players had already arrived in Trieste, the AMG forbade playing the championship game there, and those games planned at home in the following weeks.[36] Beyond the sporting advantage of playing in their own stadium, Triestina officials were fully aware of the political significance of playing in the contested city so they publicly expressed their desire to "stay in Trieste" despite the decision.[37] However, faced with Allied inflexibility, they were obliged to ask for the location of the game to be changed or for it to be played in the neutral venue of Udine.[38] Furthermore, the decision did not only affect Triestina but also Amatori Ponziana. This anomaly lasted for around ten games, when Triestina played only two games in Udine, against Rome and Inter Milan. Starting from 15 December, in the game against Sampdoria, the situation become normalized and the supporters were back in their own stadium.[39]

If the diplomatic work to secure the return to the stadium was successful, on the sporting side, with only 18 points, the season ended with the team at the bottom rung of the ladder; a result that for the Italian parliament was unacceptable. In order to reinforce claims of the "Italianness" of Trieste it was necessary that Triestina played in Serie A, so on 26 July two MPs of the Christian Democracy party, Angelo Salizzoni and Benigno Zaccagnini, asked for "an intervention of the Government".[40] In their speech they underlined that the participation of Triestina in the Italian league was "one of the few links between Trieste and the homeland" and considering that "with lavish helps" from Belgrade the Amatori Ponziana participated in the main Yugoslavian championship, a relegation should be avoided, especially because the team had "played away from its sta-

---

35 Grandinate. *La Gazzetta dello Sport*, 13 March 1946.
36 Il comando militare alleato proibisce Triestina Milan. *La Gazzetta dello Sport*, 28 September 1946.
37 La Triestina vuol restare a Trieste. *La Gazzetta dello Sport*, 1 October 1946.
38 La Triestina non si ritira. *La Gazzetta dello Sport*, 11 October 1946.
39 Triestina – Sampdoria 1–1. *La Gazzetta dello Sport*, 16 December 1946.
40 ACS, PCM 1944–1947, fasc. 3-2-5, n° 116278.

dium the first part of the season".[41] The political pressure worked because on 29 July 1947 the FIGC assembly, despite some discussions, decided to admit Triestina as an extra team (meaning that 21 rather than the usual 20 teams played) for the 1947–1948 Serie A. However, from a formal point of view, the decision was autonomously taken by the FIGC and would not have been possible if the other two teams which were relegated (Brescia and Venezia) had not declared themselves in favour of this solution.[42] According to both these teams, the government and the FIGC, the political relevance of having Triestina in the First Division, was more important than observing the sporting rule.

In the following years, in order to make sure that the team could maintain a competitive standard, the Italian government gave important unofficial subsidies to Triestina. Thanks to those and a capable coach such as Nereo Rocco the *alabardati* manage to finish second in the 1947–1948 season and eighth in the following two.[43]

Curiously, in the same season as the "non relegation" of Triestina, Amatori Ponziana should also have been relegated from the Yugoslavian First Division, but, as a political decision, they were allowed to keep their spot for the following year.[44] Amatori Ponziana played three years in the Yugoslavian championship but after the Tito-Stalin split, the rupture between Italian and Yugoslavian Communists, with the subsequent end of all the projects linked to Italo-Slovenian solidarity, Belgrade stopped any kind of economic support for the Triestinean team. At the end of the season Amatori Ponziana players and staff returned to Italy and either reunited with Ponziana in Serie C or joined other clubs, with players obliged to suffer a six-month ban for having played in the SFRY.[45]

---

41 ACS, PCM 1944–1947, fasc. 3–2–5, n° 116278.
42 ACS, PCM 1944–1947, fasc. 3–2–5, n° 116278. See also Il congresso di Perugia leva le tende. *La Gazzetta dello Sport*, 30 July 1947.
43 Di Ragogna, Dante. *Undici ragazzi*. Trieste: Pro Sport Editore, 1985, here 86.
44 Sbetti and Falchi, *Trieste val ben una sassata*.
45 Sbetti and Falchi, *Trieste val ben una sassata*. See also Sadar, *Una lunga giornata di bora*; Archambault, *Le football à Trieste*.

The Giro d'Italia 1946 in Trieste

Sport is not just a reflex of the political situation but, provoking emotions in the people, has the possibility to influence the political situation.[46] The passage of the Giro d'Italia in 1946 represents a clear example.

In the 1940s cycling was one of the most popular sports in Italy and the Giro d'Italia, was the most important event in the Italian sporting calendar. The first Giro after the war was raced in the summer of 1946, one year before Tour de France, from 15 June until 7 July. Since its inception, it assumed a meaning which went far beyond sport. For two years Italy had been split in two by the war and the first Giro began just 13 days after the referendum of 2 June 1946, which transformed Italy into a Republic; it had the symbolic mission to reunite the country.[47]

For the organizers, it was unimaginable to think of a race without including Trieste, while its destiny was at stake. Furthermore, on 16 of August 1945, the SFRY had tried to exploit a cycle race in order to reinforce its claim over Trieste. In fact, the city was the starting point of an amateur stage race called "From the Adriatic to the Black Sea". Although the goal of this race was to strengthen Yugoslav-Bulgarian relationships, the choice of Trieste was a clear political assertion that the city belonged to Yugoslavia.[48] So, despite the fact that the Paris Peace Conference, in which its geopolitical destiny had to be discussed, was scheduled for that July, in April 1946 the organizers of *La Gazzetta dello Sport* announced that Trieste would be included in the course and they managed to obtain – or at least this was what they declared – a first authorization from the Allied authorities, which controlled the area.[49]

The news brought much enthusiasm, as well as a degree of anxiety. The Giro was a widely recognized symbol of Italianness and in a divided city like Trieste this aspect was not necessarily shared. That is why, before authorizing the race, in order to be sure not to irritate the Allied authorities, on 27 May the government asked Consul Giorgio Bombassei de Vettor to investigate whether the Allied authorities had any problem with the passage of the Giro through Trieste.[50] On 4 June the government was informed that the authorization required could not

---

46 Sbetti, Nicola and Umberto Tulli. La fine di una reciproca negazione: riflessioni sullo sport nella storia delle relazioni internazionali. *Ricerche di storia politica* 2 (2016): 193–202.
47 See for example: Marchesini, Daniele. *L'Italia del Giro d'Italia*. Bologna: Il Mulino, 1996.
48 *Lo sport in Jugoslavia*. Novi Sad: FSJ, 1955.
49 Questo è il giro d'Italia. *La Gazzetta dello Sport*, 12 April 1946.
50 ACS, PCM, 1951–1954, Fasc. 14.4 n° 29708.

be granted because "In the existing situation the AMG consider absolutely inappropriate that the race entered the A Zone".[51]

However, the organizers did not give up. Furthermore, the early stages of the Giro strengthened the argument of those forces who wanted the arrival of the race in Trieste. In fact a team called Wilier Triestina, whose symbol recalled those of the contested Adriatic city and which was formed by cyclists from north east Italy, dominated the first stages of the race. Its captain, the Triestinean Giordano Cottur, won the first stage in Turin and dedicated the victory to "our beloved Trieste"[52] instigating a wave of patriotism in the sporting press, which glorified the links between Cottur, Trieste, Italy and the Giro.[53] Another Wilier cyclist, the Venetian Bevilacqua, won the second and the fourth stages, reinforcing this narrative. In the meantime, the diplomatic work of the organizer was successful and on 19 June the AMG changed its mind, authorizing the Rovigo-Trieste stage.[54]

Although the Italian press suggested that in Trieste everyone was enthusiastic for the arrival of the cyclists,[55] the situation was much more conflicted. As well as the Allied troops, there were operating in the town paramilitary units and political groups not only earlier enlisted with the Julian CLN partisans or with the Italian-Slovenian Communist partisans but also Italian nationalist and filo-fascist militia. These had helped heighten the tensions, especially after March when the Interallied Commission arrived with the task of establishing the ethnic composition of the contested area. The Giro proclaimed itself a symbol of "Italianness" and, by doing so, it become a target for those who were opposed to the idea of the "Italianness" of Trieste.

So, on 30 June, as soon as the caravan entered the "A Zone", near the village of Pieris there was an ambush. Blocked by some handcrafted barricades, the cyclists were hit by a hail of stones and only after the security guards had shot some bullets did the aggressors disperse into the countryside. The reports of the facts were divergent. In the Italian newspapers anti-Communists described the ambush as premeditated and added colourful details, whereas pro-Communists spoke about a spontaneous reaction of the population. In any case in Trieste the news arrived around 16.46 with this text:

---

51 ACS, PCM, 1951–1954, Fasc. 14.4 n° 29708.
52 I protagonisti della giornata. *Corriere dello Sport*, 17 June 1946.
53 Commozione profonda. *La Gazzetta dello Sport*, 16 June 1946.
54 ACS, PCM, 1951–1954, Fasc. 14.4 n° 29708. See also Il Giro a Trieste. *Corriere dello Sport*, 20 June 1946.
55 See for example: L'eco della speranza. *La Gazzetta dello Sport*, 30 June 1946.

> Two kilometres east of Peris [...] a big barrel was put in the street in front of the cyclists. Some stones were thrown at [the cyclists] and they stopped. The police who were following the race were able to break up the small crowd at the side of the road. While the agents were doing this, there were some shots and an agent was injured. The police returned fire.[56]

In subsequent reports the shooting was scaled down, but the news caused a series of heated reactions. The cyclists, with some exceptions, suffered only minor physical consequences from the attack, but the majority of them – especially those interested in winning the general rank – wanted to abandon the race. However, a small but fierce group lead the Wilier Triestina riders, wanted to continue at any cost. This stage of the race was cancelled, but the group of those who wanted to continue was escorted by the military in a lorry as far as Barcola, from where the race restarted. Those seven kilometres raced by a small group of 17 athletes assumed a highly political symbolism. It was only thanks to their willingness that the *Gazzetta dello Sport* could affirm that the Giro was stronger than the stones.[57]

Cottur, who passed the finishing line first, and all his colleagues who arrived in Trieste were met by a triumphal celebration from the Italian and non-Communist crowd. However, as already mentioned, the arrival of the race was all but peaceful. After the news of the ambush arrived in Trieste, violence against the Slovene community, who were considered responsible, flared and the headquarters of the Italian-Slovenian solidarity were destroyed. The day after the race two concurrent strikes were declared: one by the Julian CLN, the other by the antifascist Italian-Slovenian Union. The disorders continued, leaving three dead, 138 injured and more than 400 arrests.[58]

Taking place on the eve of the peace treaty, the Giro of 1946 assumed a clear political relevance. The stage in Trieste was wanted more by the organizers than the government, whose priority was to maintain good relations. Most of all, the passage of an Italian symbol such as the Giro in a contested city was a clear way to claim the "Italianness" of Trieste and that is the reason why it was attacked by those who were against the sovereignty of Rome. The Giro returned peacefully to Trieste only in 1949, when after the Tito-Stalin split there was less tension in the city and the AMG authorized the passage in Trieste of the "Pink race", which occurred without any troubles.

---

56 Un comunicato dell'Agenzia Nazioni Unite. *La Gazzetta dello Sport*, 1 June 1946.
57 Trieste maglia rosa. *La Gazzetta dello Sport*, 2 June 1946. See also: Foot, John. *Pedalare! La grande avventura del ciclismo italiano*. Milano: Rizzoli, 2011, here 92–104.
58 Cattaruzza. *L'Italia e il confine orientale*, 299.

Conclusion

Immediately after the Second World War in the months when the war alliance was crumbling but still in place, in the city of Trieste, the political and ideological divisions that caused the Cold War were already underway. The sport activities that in the past had developed themselves mainly along ethnic lines became separated by political divisions as well.

With the destruction caused by the war and the political conflicts, playing sport could seem a priority. Furthermore, for many Triestinean youngsters being successful in a professional sport could mean economic safety. In any case, whether they were professional or amateur, the political background of the athletes become crucial in the choice between CONI and UCEF teams, even though the economic aspects could sometimes overcome the political ones.

Until 1948, teams like Triestina, Wilier Triestina or athletes like Mitri and Cottur become the symbol of the "Italianness" of Trieste, but in Trieste not all the Italians agreed with that vision. A significant part of the working class preferred to identify with the players of Amatori Ponziana and the activities linked to UCEF. The Italian and Yugoslavian governments played an active role in supporting those experiences. With the Tito-Stalin split and the decision taken by the PCRG to remain loyal to Moscow rather than Belgrade, UCEF continued its activities but with both the Italian and the Yugoslavian border closed and without the Yugoslavian economic support it tended to withdraw into itself.

Because of its ability to provoke emotions and its symbolic link with identity, sport activity did not only reflect political divisions, but influenced materially the political life of the city. The fact that the passage in Trieste of a symbolic race such as the Giro d'Italia provoked an ambush against it, and a subsequent reaction against the political instigators which ended with death, wounding, arrests and a day with two concurrent general strikes, sums up the power of sport in a conflictual milieu.

In conclusion, looking at the case of sport in a contested and divided city like Trieste after the Second World War is particularly interesting for several reasons. First, it shows how national governments used sport as a political tool. Second it highlights the differences between the more direct intervention of a Socialist government and the more hidden one – so as to protect the supposed independence of the sporting institutions – of a liberal-democrat government. Third it demonstrates the relative autonomy of the sport intuitions, which were often more nationalist and less pragmatic than the government, as the passage of the 1946 Giro clearly demonstrates. Finally, on a local scale, it anticipates many questions and problems that emerged during throughout the Cold War period.

by Daniel Svensson and Anna Åberg
An Even Colder War?

Specialization and Scientization in the Training methods for Cross-Country Skiing from the 1940s in Sweden and the Soviet Union

Introduction

The Cold War was a period of increasing international competition in sports. With the participation of more countries and the gradual restoration of elite athlete communities in countries which had been damaged by the Second World War, the need for rational preparation and training grew. For cross-country skiing, this was certainly true as the Soviet Union entered the international scene in the 1950s.

Scientization of training methods, in endurance training in general and in cross-country skiing in particular, accelerated in the 1950s.[1] In several European countries physiologists influenced physical practice in many areas of society (such as industry, domestic work, military and education). The labs that produced this new knowledge also had links to the military sector. Athletes were often hesitant about this new development, but in the hardening competition on the international level, sport associations saw new methods as necessary to stay competitive.

In this paper, we study the official (state-funded and published by governing organizations of sport, such as the Swedish Ski Association) training advice given to prospective elite skiers in Sweden and the Soviet Union from the late 1940s onwards. How was training advice affected by the Cold War context? In what ways did Sweden differ from the Soviet Union? What type of organizations took an interest in training and what ideas about the athletic body did they express? The question of how ties between rational training and military purposes influenced individual skiers in Europe can shed new light on how the Cold War affected sports and vice versa.

---

[1] Svensson, Daniel. Scientizing Performance in Endurance Sports: The Emergence of "Rational Training" in Cross-country Skiing, 1930–1980. PhD, Kungliga Tekniska Högskolan, Stockholm, 2016.

The comparative method within historical research has been widely discussed, especially in the light of the emerging fields of *historie croisée* and transnational history.[2] Meanwhile, as Heinz-Gerhard Haupt has pointed out, although comparison has its pitfalls, it has a place in what he calls, an *histoire problème*, guided by theoretical reflections.[3] In this article, using the theory of sportification, we want to compare training methods in two countries on either side of the Iron Curtain, during the postwar period, focusing on skiing, a sport in which these were two of four leading nations during this period.

The scientization of training in Sweden and the Soviet Union will be analysed using the theory of sportification. According to this theory, certain key factors such as rationalization, standardization, specialization and professionalization occur in all sports. In essence, sportification means that sports develop in similar, predictable ways, becoming more rational, systematic, organized and professional.[4] Earlier research in sport history highlights training as one area where sportification is evident, and cross-country skiing is no exception.[5] Today, newer sport-like activities such as competitive gaming (e-sport) undergo similar developments. Recent additions to the theory have argued that certain "technologies of sportification", among them training manuals such as those studied here, have been an important tool for those who have advocated scientization of training.[6] This article can add to this development of sportification theory by comparing two politically and culturally different countries and their respective approaches to scientific training in cross-country skiing. Does the sportification process change under different national and international po-

---

[2] For example, Kocka, Jürgen. Comparison and Beyond. *History and Theory* 42 (2003): 39–44; Friberg, Katarina, Mary Hilson and Natasha Vall. Reflections on Transnational Comparative History from an Anglo-Swedish Perspective. *Historisk Tidsskrift* 127 (2007): 717–737; Levine, Philippa. Is Comparative History Possible? *History and Theory* 53 (2014): 331–347.

[3] Haupt, Heinz-Gerhard. Comparative History – A Contested Method. *Historisk Tidsskrift* 127 (2007): 697–716, here 714.

[4] Goksøyr, Matti. *Sivilisering, modernisering, sportifisering: fruktbare begreper i idrettshistorisk forskning?* Oslo: Oslo Universitet, 1988; Guttmann, Allen. *From Ritual to Record. The Nature of Modern Sports*. New York: Columbia University Press, 1978, 54–55; Yttergren, Leif. *Täflan ä rlifvet: idrottens organisering och sportifiering i Stockholm 1860–1898*. Stockholm: Stockholmia, 1996, 21–22.

[5] For example, Yttergren, Leif. *Träna är livet: träning, utbildning och vetenskap i svensk friidrott, 1888–1995*. Malmö: idrottsforum.org, 2012; Svensson. *Scientizing Performance in Endurance Sports*.

[6] Svensson, Daniel. Technologies of Sportification – Practice, Theory and Co-Production of Training Knowledge in Cross-country Skiing Since the 1950s. *European Studies in Sports History* 9 (2016): 1–29.

litical contexts, such as the Cold War? The sportification process is inherently transnational, as it includes organization (on all levels, not least internationally) and regimentation.

The texts studied here are the training manuals published by leading training scientists and organizations. For Sweden, we use the official training manuals published by the Swedish Ski Association. For the Soviet Union we use books and collections of articles written by researchers working as educators and scientists at the skiing faculties and research laboratories of different state institutes of physical culture in the Soviet Union.[7]

We will begin with a short introduction about the organizations and other actors involved in the respective countries. Then we will move on with a detailed discussion of the development of training in Sweden and the Soviet Union, and end with a comparison and a discussion about the differences and similarities we have found.

The organizations of training and sport science in Sweden and the Soviet Union

For a comparison between how two countries worked with scientization of training, it is important to look closely at the institutions and organizations involved in the process. Below we present a general background.

In Sweden, the leading centre for sport-related physiology was the Royal Central Institute of Gymnastics (GCI), today known as the Swedish School of Sport and Health Sciences. The GCI had been founded in 1813 but their department of physiology was opened in 1941. The physiologists there (among them Per-Olof Åstrand, Bengt Saltin and Björn Ekblom) made important contributions to Swedish and international work physiology, and they saw sports as an important outlet for their research. They were the architects behind the "rational training" model in Sweden, introducing interval training, carbohydrate loading, high-altitude training and acclimatization periods, bicycle ergometer testing and much more.[8]

---

[7] The names as well as the affiliation of these institutes changed slightly over the studied period, but the main structure remained.
[8] See, Schantz, Peter. Along Paths Converging to Bengt Saltin's Early Contributions in Exercise Physiology. *Scandinavian Journal of Medicine and Science in Sports* 25 (2015): 7–15; Svensson, Daniel. How Much Sport is There in Sport Physiology? Practice and Ideas in the Stockholm

The other main actor driving the scientization of skiing was the Swedish Ski Association. It was on their initiative, following an embarrassing Swedish failure in the Olympic Winter Games in Oslo in 1952 that in 1954 scientists from the GCI were engaged in testing and analysing the physical performance of cross-country skiers in the Swedish national team. Soon these scientists had completely changed the theoretical base for training, even if it took much longer for training to change in practice. The Swedish Ski Association was, compared to its counterparts in other leading winter sport nations such as Norway, an early adopter of scientific training. This rather dramatic change in training ideology was motivated by increasing international competition, mainly represented by the Soviet Union who also had ambitious plans for increasing sport performance through science.[9]

In the Soviet Union, sport and physical health was a central issue for the state from the start. Sports were an important means of activating and educating the workers in the rapidly urbanizing and industrializing state. Two means to inspire the populace and engage them were to create an elite of professional athletes as role models and to use competition as a means of encouraging people to both watch and participate. In the early days of the Soviet state, in the context of the civil war and so called war communism, control over all sports clubs and organizations were given to the newly formed Central Board of Universal Military Training. After the war this organization changed and the militarization of sports came under criticism during the 1920s, especially from scientists, many of whom worked at the Moscow State Institute of Physical Culture. This Institute was created in 1918 and, together with the already existing Lesgaft Institute of Physical Culture in St Petersburg, was tasked with the education of physical culture instructors. In the early 1930s, similar institutes were also set up in Kiev, Tbilisi and Stalingrad, and state research institutes for physical culture were created in Tbilisi, Leningrad, Moscow and Kharkov.[10] By that time, the criticism regarding the competitive nature of sports and physical culture had been mostly silenced, and from the mid-1920s onwards, competition became central to Soviet

---

School of Physiology at GCI, 1941–1969. *The International Journal of the History of Sport* 30 (2013): 892–913.

9 Svensson. Technologies of Sportification – Practice.

10 Grant, Susan. *Physical Culture and Sport in Soviet Society: Propaganda, Acculturation, and Transformation in the 1920s and 1930s*. New York: Routledge, 2013, here 30–33, 181; Riordan, James. *Sport in Soviet Society: Development of Sport and Physical Education in Russia and the USSR*. Cambridge: Cambridge University Press, 1977, here 69–70, 77, 146.

sports ideology.[11] Further, a re-militarization took place, with sports again becoming a means of providing pre-military training and overall fitness in order to prepare for the nation's defence, not least through the "Ready for Labour and Defence" programme (GTO, Gotov k Trudu i Oborone), consisting of a badge and ranking system for all Soviet citizens. The two-fold goal of the GTO was to broaden participation in sports as well as to establish a "mass base" from which to draw star athletes and soldiers, and skiing was one of the mandatory categories.[12] In 1934 the official title "distinguished master of sport" was instated, and this year can be seen as a starting point for the formation of a Soviet sports elite through the development of structural frameworks, hierarchies, models of behaviour and internationalization.[13] Earlier, the Soviet Union had stayed out of "bourgeoise" international events (such as the Olympic Games) and international federations and committees, choosing instead to encourage a proletarian sport system through the creation of and participation in the Socialist Workers' Sport International. During the 1930s, however, the attitude towards the Western sports system changed and opened up for later memberships in the international sports federations after the Second World War.[14] Although the country came out of the war bearing many losses and with an exhausted and physically weak population, it also came out with a newborn patriotism and a will to, as O'Mahoney has put it, "claim further victory on the sports field of the world".[15] This meant, among other things, joining international sports federations and starting to compete in the "bourgeoise" international competitions; the Soviet Union joined the International Ski Federation (FIS) in 1946.[16]

---

[11] Gounot, André. De L'hygiène du corps à l'obsession des records. Les mutations politiques et idéologiques de la fizkul'tura en russie, 1921–1937. *Science Sociales et Sport* 6 (2013): 9–34, here 21–31.
[12] Grant. *Physical Culture and Sport in Soviet Society*, 37–41; Riordan. *Sport in Soviet Society*, 129; Kobchenko, Kateryna. Emancipation within the Ruling Ideology: Soviet Women in Fizkul'tura and Sport in the 1920s and 1930s. In *Euphoria and Exhaustion: Modern Sport in Soviet Culture and Society*, Nikolaus Katzer, Sandra Budy, Alexander Kohring and Manfred Zeller (eds.), 250–267. Chicago: Chicago University Press; Frank, William D. *Everyone to Skis!: Skiing in Russia and the Rise of Soviet Biathlon*. DeKalb, Ill.: Northen Illinois University Press, 2015, 81.
[13] Dufraisse, Sylvain. Les "Héros du Sport". La fabrique de l'élite sportive Soviétique (1934–1980). *Bulletin de l'Institut Pierre Renouvin* 44 (2016): 143–151, here 147.
[14] Keys, Barbara. *Globalizing Sport: National Rivalry and International Community in the 1930s*. London: Harvard University Press, 2006, here 161–162, 169–172.
[15] O'Mahony, Mike. *Sport in the USSR: Physical Culture – Visual Culture*. London: Reaktion Books, 2006, here 152
[16] Riordan. *Sport in Soviet Society*, 365.

Training instruction in Sweden: from experiential to scientific training

In Sweden there was a clear shift from "natural", experiential training in the 1940s to a more scientific approach in the 1970s. The changes in training ideology came due to a scientific turn initiated by the Swedish Ski Association, together with the leading institution of physiology research in Sweden, the Royal Central Institute of Gymnastics (GCI). However, the scientific turn was also the result of a changing and growing transnational sport community, with increasing participation and competition.

Before the scientific turn, in 1948, the training manuals were written by the Swedish training ideologist Gösta Olander, who apart from being active as a coach for the national team was also a hotel manager at Vålådalen alpine station in the mountains outside Östersund, a filmmaker, writer and tourist guide. Olander's views on training were based on experience and tradition, rather than science. He advocated a holistic method that built on practical experience, and he saw the movements of the Sami people and of mountain wildlife as a source of inspiration for would-be athletes. He even refers to the classic idea of *mens sana in corpore sano* – a sound mind in a sound body.[17] A few years later, such references would be replaced by scientific test results. This change was inspired by research tracing its roots to the Copenhagen School of Physiology, which intensified when Soviet skiers started to make an impact on the international scene and was widely discussed and negotiated within the international sport organizations (such as the IOC and FIS).[18] The national process of scientizing training in endurance sports was both part of and affected by an international context.

For Olander, the natural variations of the landscape were not a problem but rather a potential advantage, if used correctly. Olander recommended running on the moors and slopes during the summer, while running in deep snow or skiing during the winter.[19] Olander was not alone in appreciating the mountains as an arena for training – some of his international colleagues had already advocated

---

17 Olander, Gösta. *Träningsråd för skidåkare*. Stockholm: Swedish Ski Association, 1948, 1950, 1952, here 4.

18 For example, Svensson. How Much Sport is there in Sport Physiology?; Schantz, Along Paths Converging to Bengt Saltin's Early Contributions in Exercise Physiology; Åstrand, Per-Olof. Physiological Aspects on Cross-country Skiing at the High Altitudes. *FIS Bulletin* 8 (1962):1–41, here 24.

19 Olander. *Träningsråd för skidåkare*, 4–5.

training in mountain landscapes in the 1930s.[20] He did not use any of the scientific language found in later editions of the official training manual, such as lactic acid threshold, periodization or oxygen uptake. Olander was also modest about the universality of his training model, and stated that "what suits one, may not suit the other at all".[21] At the time, Swedish skiing was still a male-dominated endeavour, even though there were also Swedish Championship races arranged for female skiers from 1917. In Olander's manual, there is no sign of female skiers whatsoever. He repeatedly talks about men or boys, and all the pictures show male skiers. The pictures in Olander's book are quite interesting. They show male skiers running in snow, running in mountains, sawing wood, and of course skiing. Only one image shows anything that could be linked to a more scientific training regime, and that is a picture of a male skier training with a bicycle inner tube.[22] Almost to anchor this rather unusual picture in Olander's natural training ideology, the bicycle tube training is done with the tube wrapped around a birch tree.

Following the Swedish failure in the Oslo Olympic Winter Games in 1952, the Swedish Ski Association removed most of Olander's exercises within the Ski Association and replaced his training manuals with new editions, this time written by physiologists and/or officials within the Swedish Ski Association who had a background at the Royal Central Institute of Gymnastics (GCI). When physiologists and educated officials took over the duty of writing these manuals, the advice on training gradually changed.

In the 1958 edition, written by the former GCI student Calle Briandt, Olander's naturalistic training was already being replaced by a more scientific approach.[23] There was much less focus on the role of landscape and mind, and much more on physiology. Oxygen uptake and other concepts from physiology were introduced. In terms of practical training, Briandt argued for more intervals, higher intensity and in general a scientific base. Briandt, himself a supporter of scientific training and organized development of talent, was one of the architects behind the Swedish system for elite sport education at upper-secondary level, the so called Riksidrottsgymnasium which started in 1972.

The scientific turn in Swedish skiing was clearly manifested through changes in training practice illustrated by these manuals. As the official publications of the Swedish Ski Association, the manuals represented the training

---

20 Yttergren. *Träna är livet: träning, utbildning och vetenskap i svensk friidrott, 1888–1995*, 85–87.
21 Olander. *Träningsråd för skidåkare*, 3.
22 Olander. *Träningsråd för skidåkare*, 7.
23 Briandt, Calle. *Träningsråd i längdlöpning*. Stockholm: Swedish Ski Association, 1958, 1962.

theory advocated by the most influential sport leaders and work physiologists in the country. These manuals were published at uneven intervals, from the 1940s onwards. Most were printed in at least two editions, and here we therefore list all the editions where applicable.

After Olander ceased to be seen as the leading training ideologist, Briandt held the position throughout the 1950s and 1960s, informally and with the aid of physiologists from GCI. His manual from 1958 was reprinted in 1962 and 1965, with the same content. It was a clear step away from much of what Gösta Olander had focused on. Briandt mentions "rational ski training" at the beginning of the text and states that those who undergo such training can testify that it is not only efficient but also fun.[24] In contrast to Olander, Briandt also argues that a stopwatch should be used in training sessions as it works to stimulate and enhance the training effect.[25] And unlike his predecessor, Briandt provides a detailed training programme with more focus on interval training and constant increase in intensity. In line with the scientization of training, the use of a training log for evaluation of training is recommended.[26] This is also the first time that something similar to carbohydrate loading before a competition, an idea developed by GCI physiologists, is described in the official training advice.[27]

Briandt was also involved in the new manual from 1967 which he co-authored together with the national team coach and former elite skier Lennart Larsson.[28] Larsson also had a background at GCI and was a supporter of scientific training if paired with experience and individualization.[29] With the entrance of Lennart Larsson, the editorial team for the training manual now included both practical, experiential knowledge (represented by the former elite skier Larsson) and theoretical, scientific knowledge (represented by the former GCI student Briandt). This setup meant that while the base of the manual came from physiology, it also had a practical perspective which made it more useful for skiers.

In 1970, GCI physiologist Sune Wehlin was responsible for the training manual. He started by claiming that the era of forestry workers as the best skiers was coming to an end, and that Sweden now was in need of a more scientific ap-

---

24 Briandt. *Träningsråd i längdlöpning*, 3.
25 Briandt. *Träningsråd i längdlöpning*, 5.
26 Briandt. *Träningsråd i längdlöpning*, 19.
27 Briandt. *Träningsråd i längdlöpning*, 24.
28 Larsson, Lennart and Briandt, Calle. *Träningsråd i längdlöpning*. Stockholm: Swedish Ski Association, 1967.
29 Interview with Lennart Larsson, 7 January 2013.

proach to secure future success in international competitions.[30] This volume is also the most detailed concerning ski wax, with an entire chapter devoted to different types of wax, discussion of weather conditions etcetera.[31] Ski wax is not discussed by Olander in his 1948 manual, but sporadically appears in the other earlier volumes.

By 1974, the scientization process had really made its mark on the training manuals. Already in the first sentence the word "rational" is used to describe a scientifically guided training setup. The new feature in this volume was the emphasis put on the individuality of the skier. Ulf Bergh clearly stated that what science could provide was not an exact training programme that would work for everyone, but rather a scientific base of leading principles which each skier then had to adapt to their own qualifications and preferences.[32] Nevertheless, Bergh and his co-authors did not abstain from making detailed training programmes, with advice regarding periodization, intensity and amount. They also provided detailed numbers on oxygen uptake, pulse, lactic acid concentration and other indicators to explain the effect of certain types of training, such as rollerskiing.[33] Another notable change in the 1974 edition was the return of psychological factors, which had been more or less absent in the previous editions. In Olander's manual from the 1948, psychological factors were very important even though Olander did not talk about psychology but rather about the importance of enjoying training and never becoming a "training machine" as that may lead to losing "the spark".[34] We thus see that the psychological aspects of training were absent during the first decades of scientization, but returned during the 1970s in a scientific form, as sport psychology and mental training.

In summary, the official training advice given by the Swedish Ski Association shifted quite dramatically from the natural, experiential training of Gösta Olander in the 1940s and early 1950s, to a scientific approach designed by physiologists in the 1970s. It is interesting to see this change in relation to the Cold War context, as the removal of Olander from the leading position was sparked by Swedish failure in the 1952 Winter Olympics in Oslo, and a fear that Soviet skiers were going to be more and more successful (which they were, starting in Falun two years later). The increasing competition of the early Cold War was an important factor in the Swedish change of training ideology, and like in so many other

---

30 Swedish Ski Association. Åk skidor. Täby: Larson, 1970, here 7.
31 Swedish Ski Association, Åk skidor, 87–106.
32 Bergh, Ulf (ed.). Längdlöpning på skidor: träningsråd. Bjästa: CeWe-förlaget, 1974, here 5.
33 Bergh. Längdlöpning på skidor: träningsråd, 32.
34 Olander. Träningsråd för skidåkare, 4.

areas of Swedish society, science was the solution.[35] Even if the Swedish Ski Association took an interest in other nations and their approach to training, there was a firm belief that close cooperation with science would result in more Swedish medals. This may seem like an obvious development, given sportification theory and its emphasis on continuous specialization and rationalization. However, Norway did not make a similar scientific turn until much later, in the 1970s.[36] An important explanation of the early Swedish attempts to make training more scientific was that it was part of a larger rationalization movement, which affected not only sports but industry, the military, schools, household work and much more.[37] Without this connection, it is hard to see how such ambitious research on athletes could have been financed. Swedish sport-related research was therefore implicitly political, closely linked to military research and ambitions which were clearly connected to the Cold War arms race. This was an era when "success in the sports realm reflected [a] superior managerial, geopolitical, and fiduciary ideology".[38]

Training instructions in the Soviet Union: periodization for the pride of the nation

In 1948, the Central Committee of the USSR named skiing one of the prioritized sports to be developed within the Soviet Union, as an activity having both a use in everyday life, as well as being indispensable for the army. Skiing had long been a sport closely connected with the armed forces, and although skiing developed as a mass phenomenon before the war, the military constituted an exceptionally large proportion of practitioners. Not least during the Finnish-Soviet war, skiing was proved to be of central strategic value, when Finnish troops opposed the Soviet army mainly through guerrilla warfare on skis. Finnish tactics and skills were then adopted by the Soviet troops in the following war efforts.[39] After the war, images of the Soviet skiing troops would become iconic, and ski-

---

35 Svensson. How Much Sport is There in Sport Physiology?
36 Sandbakk, Øyvind and Espen Tønnesen (eds.). *Den norske langrennsboka*. Oslo: Aschehoug, 2012.
37 Svensson. How Much Sport is There in Sport Physiology?
38 Wagg, Stephen and David L. Andrews (eds.). *East Plays West: Sport and the Cold War*. Routledge, London, 2007, here 45.
39 Frank. *Everyone to Skis!: Skiing in Russia and the Rise of Soviet Biathlon*, 88–89; Harlamov, N. I., Krivcov, M. M. Обучение и тренировка лыжника [The Education and Training of the Skier]. Moscow: Voennoe Izdatel'stvo, 1949, here 9; Riordan, *Sport in Soviet Society*, 140.

ing acquired an important symbolic value through its connection to the Great Patriotic War; in the words of William Frank it became an "all-encompassing Soviet metaphor".[40] This symbolic value, in combination with a view of skiing as embodying ideals of endurance, moral and physical health, courage and the possibility for mass participation, while also speaking to a nationalist narrative about skiing as originating in Siberia and the Altai-mountains and being inherently "northern", made skiing the "quintessential example of social realist sport". [41] When the battle against the capitalist system was transferred to international sports competitions, skiing therefore became a central arena for exhibiting Soviet mastery. Training was a crucial weapon in this international battle, and a lot of resources were invested in scientific research into training methods in a broad range of sports.

The goal of the Central Committee in 1948 was two-fold: for the "mastery of Soviet skiers" to increase, and for Soviet skiers to reach a leading position internationally.[42] The committee also asked especially for a sharing of knowledge between the generations so that older ski champions could teach and inspire the younger ones, and at least two books were published in 1951 and 1953 with this goal in mind.[43] This way of teaching skiing and training seems to have been widespread, at least according to authors who in part came to criticize what they considered an uncritical transfer of knowledge and style from one generation to another, as we will see below.

However, there was also a longer scientific research tradition of sports and training, with roots in pre-revolutionary Russia.[44] Thus, the bases of ski training proposed in the late 1940s and early 1950s when our period of analysis starts, were already established before the war. These base presumptions can be

---

40 Frank. *Everyone to Skis!: Skiing in Russia and the Rise of Soviet Biathlon*, 117.
41 O'Mahony. *Sport in the USSR: Physical Culture – Visual Culture*, 165; Frank. *Everyone to Skis!: Skiing in Russia and the Rise of Soviet Biathlon*, 5–6, 114–118. For examples see Harlamov and Krivcov. Обучение и тренировка лыжника, 3; Serebrjakov, V. A. Лыжный спорт: Обучение и тренировка [Skiing: Teaching and Training]. Moscow: Fizkul'tura i Sport, 1952, here 4.
42 Serebrjakov. Лыжный спорт: Обучение и тренировка, 4.
43 Drugov, V. (ed.). Мастера лыжного спорта делятся опытом: Сборник статей. [Masters of Sports Share their Experience: Collection of Articles] Moscow: Voennoe Izdatel'stvo, 1951; Nemuhin, I. A. На спортивной лыжне: Очерки об опыте мастеров лыжного спорта [In the Ski Racing Track: Remarks on the Experience of Masters of Skiing]. Moscow: Fizkul'tura i Sport, 1953.
44 For example, Zamjatin, A. M. Развитие методики обучения и тренировки лыжников в России [The Development of Instruction and Training Methods for Skiers in Russia]. In Лыжный спорт: Сборник научных работ. Выпуск 1 [Skiing: Collected Scientific Work. First Edition], M. A. Agranovskij (ed.), 26–48. Moscow: Fizkul'tura i Sport, 1957, here 37–38.

found for example in Lieutenant Colonel Harlamov and Major Krivcov's manual from 1949 aimed at army coaches and skiers. The authors cite systematic exercises, a constant but slow increase of workload, a diversified training, a correct balance between training and rest, and a correct intensity of workload as the basic principles of training.[45] Another basic principle of Soviet sport that can be traced back to pre-revolutionary authors was periodic year-round training also for those sports with a very clear seasonal cycle, such as skiing.[46] Although details of the planning of these periods were discussed and developed over time, the idea and practice of year-round training as well as its basic principles seems to have been completely undisputed from the very beginning of the postwar period onwards.

Periodic training in skiing was organized in three periods: the preparatory period, the main period (when competitions take place, sometimes called the competition period), and the transitional period.[47] Of these, the preparatory period was the longest and most important one. From the beginning, the aim of training in the preparatory period was simply to train endurance, flexibility, strength, coordination of movement as well as what was called "will qualities", such as courage, willpower and decisiveness. The point was for the athlete to be in as good condition as possible before the first snowfall so that all snow time could be spent competing and training on skis.[48] Over time, technique became more and more important during the preparatory period, and in 1971 D. D. Donskoi and H. H. Gross, researchers in biomechanics at the State Central Institute of Physical Culture in Moscow, pointed out that the times when skiers train technique only on snow are long gone, since skiers simply do not have the time to prac-

---

45 Harlamov and Krivcov. *Обучение и тренировка лыжника*, 160.
46 Zamjatin. *Развитие методики обучения и тренировки лыжников в России*, 42–43; Matveev, L. P. *Проблема периодизации спортивной тренировки, 2-е издание* [The Issue of Periodization of Sports Training]. Moscow: Fizkul'tura i Sport, 1965, here 5–7.
47 Bergman, B. I. *Лыжный спорт: Тренировка лыжников- гонщиков, слаломистов, прыгунов с трамплина и двоеборцев* [Skiing: Training Skiers in Cross Country, Downhill, Ski Jumping and Biathlon]. Moscow: Fizkul'tura i Sport, 1959, here 8–12; Zamjatin. *Развитие методики обучения и тренировки лыжников в России*, 43–44; Koškin, A. A. *Исследование некоторых вопросов методики тренировки лыжников-гонщиков в подготовительном периоде* [Research on Issues of Training Methods for Cross-country Skiers in the Preparatory Period]. In *Лыжный спорт: Сборник научных трудов* [Skiing: Collected Scientific Works], V. S. Martynov (ed.), 2–7. Moscow: VNIIFK, 1978; Harlamov and Krivcov. *Обучение и тренировка лыжника*, 162.
48 For example, Donskoj, A. *Тренировка лыжниц* [Training Female Skiers]. In *Сборник методических писем по лыжному спорту и зимней тренировке легкоатлета* [Collection of Methodological Letters on Skiing and Winter Training of Track and Field Athletes], L. Rubanova (ed.), 4–8. Saransk: Komitet Po Delam Fizičeskoj Kul'tury i Sporta pri Sovete Ministrov Mordovskoj ASSR, 1952; Harlamov and Krivcov. *Обучение и тренировка лыжника*, 167.

tice technique during the winter any more.[49] The main period started when the first snow fell, and the goal during this period was to get back onto the skis and train technique and endurance, while reaching peak performance and work capacity. Then competitions would start, as well as a strict regime of competition and rest in order to keep performance up during the whole season. The transition period was a period of less training and so called active rest. Already in 1954 V. M. Naumov, a master of sports at the skiing faculty of the Moscow State Central Institute of Physical Culture, argued that professional athletes should never stop training completely, unless there were medical reasons.[50]

The main tool used to fulfil these basic principles of training was rigorous and correct planning of work and workload. Already in Kharlamov's manual there is a daily training plan for the month before races of different distances, and from the early 1950s exact plans for the whole year are elaborated.[51] Several authors write specifically about training women, and in the plans for activities in the manuals there are always parallel plans for women.[52] In the late 1940s and early 1950s, other sports were encouraged as training methods outside of the main period, and it seems to have been common that athletes competed both in a summer sport and a winter sport.[53] Over time, however, as more and more time during the preparatory period came to be dedicated to specialized exercises in skiing technique, professional athletes were discouraged from competition in other sports.[54]

This strict periodization and planning was paired with scientific research on specific training activities. Advanced formulas for calculating the angles of track topography as well as the skier's body parts in movement, were combined with physiological research on muscles and nerves as well as sports psychology. The Soviet Union was at the forefront of the field of sports psychology during this time, while the field was not very active in the West.[55]

Although biomechanical studies of technique had been a part of skiing research for some time, biomechanical analysis of skiing technique became an

---

[49] Donskoj, D. D. and H. H Gross. *Техника лыжника-гонщика: Техническое мастерство.* [The Technique of the Cross-country Skier: Technical Mastery] Moscow: Fizkul'tura i Sport, 1971, here 90.
[50] Naumov. Тренировка лыжника-гонщика, 47.
[51] Harlamov and Krivcov. *Обучение и тренировка лыжника,* 179–180; Naumov. Тренировка лыжника-гонщика, 34–43.
[52] For example, Bergman. *Лыжный спорт,* 141–143; Donskoj. Тренировка лыжниц.
[53] Harlamov and Krivcov. *Обучение и тренировка лыжника,* 52.
[54] Naumov. Тренировка лыжника-гонщика, 24.
[55] Frank. *Everyone to Skis!: Skiing in Russia and the Rise of Soviet Biathlon,* 127–128.

even sharper focus for the researchers and authors of the skiing manuals we have studied during the end of the 1950s and 1960s, and this seems to a large extent to be connected to the international context of competition.[56] After the goal set up by the Central Committee in 1948, Soviet skiers started to compete in international events. However, the big entry on the international stage was the world skiing championships in Falun 1954, where Soviet skiers performed well, taking first place in the 30- and 50-kilometre races, as well as a second place in the mens' relay, and first place in the 30 kilometre and the relay for women.[57] The positive results of this competition and others that followed paved the way for the first Soviet participation in the winter Olympic Games in 1956.[58] However, already in 1954, V. M. Naumov commented on the difficult terrains and high altitudes of contemporary international competition tracks, pointing out that Soviet skiers needed to practice more thorough competition training and under different terrain conditions.[59] In 1957, after the Olympic Games in Cortina d'Ampezzo where the Soviet team won the most medals in total, albeit only one gold in skiing for the male skiers, in the relay, Naumov exhibited a clear annoyance regarding what he considered the technical problems of the Soviet skiers. He claimed that the problems encountered by Soviet skiers during the Olympic Games in 1956 was due to their technique not being effective and flexible enough in difficult terrain and that they were not able to adapt their endurance and tempo in the long-distance races. Naumov concluded that Soviet competitions needed to be held in more difficult terrain, that more specific imitation exercises should be used during summer and autumn, and that in order to secure the future generations of skiers, young skiers need to specialize earlier.[60] The fe-

---

[56] Donskoj, D. D. К вопросу о биодинамическом анализе лыжника-гонщика [On the Issue of Biodynamic Analysis of the Technique of the Cross-country Skier]. In Лыжный спорт: Сборник научных работ. Выпуск 1 [Skiing: Collected Scientific Work. First Edition], M. A. Agranovskij (ed.), 151–156. Moscow: Fizkul'tura i Sport, 1957, here 152.

[57] Frank. *Everyone to Skis!: Skiing in Russia and the Rise of Soviet Biathlon*, 129.

[58] Riordan. *Sport in Soviet Society*, 367.

[59] Naumov. Тренировка лыжника-гонщика, 44.

[60] Naumov, V. M. Анализ подготовки советских лыжников-гонщиков к VII зимним олимпийским играм [Analysis of the Preparations of the Soviet Cross-country Skiers for the 7th Winter Olympics]. In Лыжный спорт: Сборник научных работ. Выпуск 1 [Skiing: Collected Scientific Work. First Edition], M. A. Agranovskij (ed.), 49–66. Moscow: Fizkul'tura i Sport, 1957, here 62–66; Donskoj, D. D. and V. M. Naumov. Гонки на лыжах: Методические материалы по технике и тренировке [Racing on Skis, Methodological Material on Technique and Training]. Moscow: Москва: Komitet po Fizičeskoj Kul'ture i Sportu RSFSR, 1957, here 13–15; Donskoj, D. D. and V. M. Naumov. Лыжные гонки: Методические материалы по технике и тренировке [Ski Racing: Methodological Material on Technique and Training]. Moscow: Sovetskaja Rossia, 1957, here 3–4.

male skiers, on the other hand excelled in Cortina D'Ampezzo, and this was a pattern that would continue all through the 1960s and 1970s, with the Soviet male skiers performing unevenly, while the women were virtually unstoppable.[61] This, however, did not stop Naumov from specifically criticizing the technical inefficiency of the female skiers.[62]

In a collection of articles from 1964, written by a group of sport researchers from different disciplines, Naumov's critique of Soviet training was repeated almost word for word, although this time concerning the 1960 Olympic Games, in Squaw Valley, California, and the World Cup, in 1962 in Zakopane, Poland. Both events were surrounded by Cold War politics and were symbolic, not least the 1962 World Cup; they took place in locations on either side of the Iron Curtain, and both held great expectations of Soviet victories. However, in the end these events had proved disappointments in regards to the male cross-country skiers who despite having a stable team with all members in the top group, won no gold or silver medals.[63] The authors of the 1964 collection attribute the problems to one-sided training and a "dismissive attitude" towards specific imitation exercises during the preparatory period, as well as a lack of systematic year-round training.[64] Although we have no means at this time to know anything about the realities of ski training, as opposed to the theory of these manuals and articles, we may speculate from this recurring critique that getting coaches and skiers to comply with the proposed methods of training was not a completely smooth process.

In the cross-country skiing arena, the main rivals were Finland, Norway and Sweden and the Scandinavian skiers were clearly the ones that the Soviet athletes were measured against in the reports from the Olympic Games.[65] However,

---

61 Frank. *Everyone to Skis!: Skiing in Russia and the Rise of Soviet Biathlon*, 129–130, 196, 204–205.
62 For example, Naumov. Анализ подготовки советских лыжников-гонщиков к VII зимним олимпийским играм; Donskoj and Naumov. *Гонки на лыжах*, 13–15.
63 Frank. *Everyone to Skis!: Skiing in Russia and the Rise of Soviet Biathlon*, 160–165.
64 Kamenskij, V. I. Планирование спортивной тренировки [Planning Sports Training]. In *Лыжные гонки: Учебное пособие для тренеров* [Ski Racing: Teaching Guide for Coaches], V. I. Kamenskij (ed.), 122–144. Moscow: Fizkul'tura i Sport, 1964, here 123; Spiridonov, K. N. Современная техника и ее совершенствование. [Contemporary Technique and its Perfection]. In *Лыжные гонки: Учебное пособие для тренеров* [Ski Racing: Teaching Guide for Coaches], V. I. Kamenskij (ed.), 7–81. Moscow: Fizkul'tura i Sport, 1964, here 7.
65 See for example, Agranovskij, M. A. *Зимние Олимпийские Игры (Лыжный Спорт)* [Winter Olympic Games (Skiing)]. Moscow: Gosudarstvennyj Central'nyj Ordena Lenina Institut Fizičeskoj Kul'tury im. I.V. Stalina, 1959; Dvorjašina, G. V. Об изменении длины и частоты шагов и среднеи скорости у лыжников на трассах зимних олимпийских игр [On the Changing

although observers followed the rival athletes at competitions, finding information about the everyday training of Scandinavian skiers seemed more difficult. For example, in an article about the preparations of Scandinavian skiers for the Olympic Games in 1962, the sources seem to be well informed about the Finnish skiers, where the author has consulted detailed daily training routines and other training material, whereas the Norwegian information is based on an interview book from 1956 portraying Hallgeir Brenden (*Gull i spor*). The information about the Swedish skiers is confessed to be sparse, and the few paragraphs about Swedish training seem to be taken from journal interviews with Swedish skiers Sonja Edström and Sixten Jernberg.[66]

Over time, training methods developed in what seems to be a rhythm at least partly decided after the Olympic Games, where Olympic results were evaluated and training regimes proposed specifically to remedy what seemed to be the biggest deficits. As an example, in 1964, V. I. Kamenskij proposed a new planning strategy, arguing that the most rational planning interval was on the basis of "perspective planning" over four years.[67] Technique was especially interesting in this regard, as well as difficult to assess and communicate to skiers. Over time the technology for assessing technique developed. Biomechanics was a central field to draw from, and new methods of measuring and analysing technique developed over this period.[68] The method of uncritically studying techniques of successful champions and directly transferring their style was criticized at quite an early stage for not taking into account the individual characteristics of the skiers.[69] In 1971, Donskoi and Gross commented that Soviet skiers and researchers now knew that the styles that were passed down during the early 1950s were

---

of Step Length and Interval and the Medium Speed of Skiers on the Tracks of the Winter Olympic Games]. In Лыжный спорт: Сборник научных работ. Выпуск 1 [Skiing: Collected Scientific Work. First Edition], M.A. Agranovskij (ed.), 203–209. Moscow: Fizkul'tura i Sport, 1957.

66 Šapošnikova, V. I. Подготовка скандинавских лыжников [Preparations of the Scandinavian Skiers]. In Лыжный спорт: Сборник методических материалов [Skiing: Collected Methodological Materials], 63–76. Moscow: Fizkul'tura i Sport, 1962.

67 Kamenskij. Планирование спортивной тренировки.

68 For a discussion of biomechanics and its influence on training see Braun, Hans-Joachim and Nikolaus Katzer. Training Methods and Soccer Tactics in the Late Soviet Union: Rational Systems of Bodies and Space. In *Euphoria and Exhaustion*, Katzer, Budy, Kohring and Zeller (eds.), 269–293.

69 Vzorov, B. N. and S. V. Jananis. Что дают публикуемые научные работы для теории, методики обучения и тренировки лыжника? [What can Published Scientific Work give to Theory, Methods of Education and Training of the Skier?]. *In Лыжный спорт: Вопросы научново изучения лыжного спорта: Сборник статей* [Skiing: Issues from the Scientific Study of Skiing], G. M. Krakovajak, A. N. Krestovnikov, A. C. Puni and S. V. Jananis (eds.), 5–11. Moscow-Leningrad: Fizkul'tura i Sport, 1948, here 5.

faulty, and subsequently technique was formulated as a tool to answer to a "system of specific demands", instead of just advice from individuals.[70] In 1957, Donskoi described biodynamic analysis of technique citing the study of kinematics (through the use of kinograms and films) of movement and measurement of strength using dynamometers, and different ways that these methods were being developed, for example through the invention of dynamographical skis.[71] Roller skis became an important addition to technique training and in the 1970s, other technologies of technique assessment were developed, such as dynamographical tracks and mathematical analysis of material on computers.[72] Physiological measurements such as oxygen uptake became increasingly important during the 1960s. This was an area where Sweden excelled, and in a publication from 1964, the Soviet authors consulted results of oxygen uptake assessments by the Swedish physiologist Per-Olof Åstrand from 1956–1961, and compared the results of the Swedish skiers with that of their own.[73] During the whole period, however, authors emphasized the importance of combining practical experience and scientific experimentation, as well as developing psychological and moral characteristics during training.[74]

---

70 Donskoj, Gross. Техника лыжника-гонщика,16.
71 Donskoj, Gross. Техника лыжника-гонщика, 3.
72 For example, Ermakov, V. V. and A. A. Makarov. Сравнительная характеристика техники передвижения попеременным двухшажным ходом на лыжах, лыжероллерах, роликовых коньках и при имитации [Comparative Technical Character of Movement by Rotation in the Double Step on Skis, Roller Skis, Roller Skates and through Imitation]. In *Лыжный спорт: Сборник статей* [Skiing, Collection of Articles], N. I. Kuz'min (ed.), 122–144. Moscow: Fizkul'tura i Sport, 1967; Ermakov, V. V., G. S. Lugovskoj, A. P. Kulešov, N. V. Matveeva, A. K. Kiričenko, A. V. Pirog, L. D. Ermakova, I. T. Jakovlev, V. A. Medvedev and L. F. Kobzeva. Динамографическая лыжня – установка для регистрации техники лыжных ходов [Dynamographic Skiing Tracks – Settings for the Registration of Skiing Techniques]. In *Сборник научно-методических статей по лыжным гонкам* [Collected Scientific-Methodological Articles on Cross-country Ski Racing], V. V. Ermakov (ed.), 9–11. Smolensk: Smolenskij Institut Fizičeskoj Kul'tury, 1973.
73 Mihailov, V. V. Физиологические особенности тренировки лыжника-гонщика [Physiological Particularities of Training for Cross-country Skiers]. In *Лыжные гонки: Учебное пособие для тренеров* [Ski Racing: Teaching Guide for Coaches], V. I. Kamenskij (ed.), 89–121. Moscow: Fizkul'tura i Sport, 1964, here 98–99. Åstrand's results were published internationally.
74 Bergman. *Лыжный спорт*, 5–6; Donskoj. Тренировка лыжниц, 50; Donskoj and Gross. Техника лыжника-гонщика, 3; Kamenskij. *Лыжные гонки*, 3, 142–143; Šapošnikova, V. I. Общие основы спортивной тренировки лыжника-гонщика [General Bases of Training of Cross-country Skiers]. In *Лыжные гонки: Учебное пособие для тренеров* [Ski Racing: Teaching Guide for Coaches], Kamenskij (ed.), 82–89, here 82–83; Martynov. *Лыжный спорт*, 1; Naumov. Тренировка лыжника-гонщика, 23.

Discussion

As we have seen, both Sweden and the Soviet Union have had extensive cooperation between cross-country skiing and science, mainly physiology but in the USSR also, for example, biomechanics. There is a clear and continuous process of scientization of training in both countries. In Sweden, this process began in 1954 when GCI physiologists were invited by the Swedish Ski Association. From the experiential training advice given by Gösta Olander in the 1940s to the scientific advice of the 1970s, Swedish cross-country skiing gradually became more and more influenced by physiology. In the Soviet Union, scientization had already started in the early years of the Soviet state.

During the Cold War, the role of sport in international politics deepened and it became a propaganda tool in many of the most successful sporting countries, including the US and the Soviet Union.[75] Totalitarian regimes such as Nazi Germany, East Germany or the Soviet Union have during the twentieth century been among the most ambitious in sport-related science, and in using international sport for political purposes.[76] In the Soviet material this is seen through the orders and aims regarding Soviet athletes' training and results in international competition, as well as through the way authors refer to political structures and the communist agenda.[77] In the Soviet Union, the political aspects of sport were explicit, as good performance was understood as a way to underline the superiority of the Soviet working class.

In countries like Sweden and Switzerland with a tradition of neutrality sport was apolitical, a view which in Sweden was upheld even in relation to Nazi Germany resulting in controversies between the Norwegian and Swedish Ski Associations during and after the Second World War.[78] The Swedish approach was

---

[75] Rider, Toby C. *Cold War Games: Propaganda, the Olympics, and US Foreign Policy*. Urbana: University of Illinois Press, 2016.
[76] Krüger, Arnd. Breeding, Rearing and Preparing the Aryan Body: Creating Supermen the Nazi Way. *The International Journal of the History of Sport* 16 (1999): 42–68; Hoberman, John M. *Mortal Engines: the Science of Performance and the Dehumanization of Sport*. New York: Free Press, 1992.
[77] For example, Bergman. Лыжный спорт, 5; Serebrjakov. Лыжный спорт, 4; Kamenskij. Лыжные гонки, 3; Šapošnikova. Общие основы спортивной тренировки лыжника-гонщика, 82–83.
[78] Yttergren, Leif. *I och ur spår!: en studie om konflikter och hjältar i svensk skidsport under 1900-talet*. Lund: KFS i Lund, 2006. See also: Holmäng, Per Olof. *Idrott och utrikespolitik: den svenska idrottsrörelsens internationella förbindelser 1919–1945*. Gothenburg: University of Gothenburg Press, 1988.

in line with the Olympic ideal as laid out by Pierre de Coubertin.[79] In the Swedish material there is the occasional reference to national pride, but apart from that there are no explicitly political statements. However, the scientization of training was political in Sweden as well. It was part of a larger rationalization movement connected to the expanding Swedish welfare state and its firm belief in the potential of science in most areas of society.[80] In Sweden, rational training was a tool to rationalize the entire population and make people more productive. Even in a neutral country like Sweden good performances in international ski competitions were related to national pride.[81] This is also suggested in Briandt's 1962 training instructions.[82] So, while the neutrality of Sweden prevented an explicitly politicized sport discourse like the one seen in the Soviet Union, there were still political dimensions to sport and sport science which should be understood in the political context of the Cold War and international sport exchange.

The Soviet Union was in some areas way ahead of Sweden. A big difference was the degree of scientific planning and structure in the earlier period. When Sweden still relied mainly on experiential methods, the Soviet Union already had advanced interaction between skiers and scientists. To summarize, there were similar ideas of experience exchange in the early period, then slow movement towards scientization in both countries. However, the importance of practical experience in relation to scientific research is emphasized in the Soviet Union by authors throughout the period, while in Sweden this is rather less emphasized after Olander. The overall developments in both countries can be seen as an example of sportification, where *technologies of sportification*[83] (not least the manuals studied here) were important tools as scientists and sport leaders tried to advance scientific training methods.

Gender is another area where differences are clear. The Soviet texts on training and sport physiology explicitly discuss the physiology and training of female skiers at least from 1952 (the effect of menstruation on female skiers had already been researched in 1948), and there are a few female authors in the article collections we have studied.[84] In the Swedish context, such issues are discussed by

---

[79] Chatziefstathiou, Dikaia and Ian P. Henry, *Discourses of Olympism: from the Sorbonne 1894 to London 2012*. Basingstoke: Palgrave Macmillan, 2012.
[80] Svensson. How Much Sport is there in Sport Physiology?
[81] Sörlin, Sverker. Nature, Skiing and Swedish Nationalism, *International Journal of the History of Sport* 12 (1995): 147–163.
[82] Briandt, *Träningsråd i längdlöpning*, 3.
[83] Svensson. Technologies of Sportification.
[84] See for example Donskoj. Тренировка лыжниц; Jackobskij, V. V. Спортивная работоспособность женщин при занятиях лыжным спортом в различные фазы менструального

physiologists in their scientific publications but not in the manuals studied here. Women already had a larger role in Soviet society before the war, and were specifically encouraged to take up sport as well as science during the 1920s and 1930s.[85] Still, the majority of the books have men as the norm and as authors. In the Swedish material this is even more pronounced, especially in Olander's book. The first mention of the possibility of a female skier is in the 1958 book by Briandt.[86]

The role of coaches is also different. Sweden more or less lacked specialized coaches (an important part of the sportification criteria of specialization and professionalization) up until the 1970s, while such coaches were not uncommon in the Soviet Union from the 1950s.

Conclusion

This comparison has shown both similarities and differences in the impact of the Cold War on national and international sport and sport science. While we have pointed out some important developments, much remains to be done. The role of the Cold War (and international sport relations in general) in the accelerating scientization of sports during the twentieth century deserves more attention. The Swedish case suggests that sport organizations even in neutral countries will be affected by political context on the international level. Sport has historically had a political role, not least for imperialistic reasons.[87] The apolitical ideal of international sport (and sport science!) is not easily upheld in geopolitical contexts of high tension, like the Cold War.

This is a quite limited study, with material that differs greatly on each side in regards to audience and publication context. However, this study has allowed us to identify a broader array of research questions within the field of sport history, especially relating to training exchange.

цикла [Working Capacity of Women Doing Skiing Exercises During Different Phases of the Menstruation Cycle]. In *Лыжный спорт: Вопросы научново изучения лыжного спорта: Сборник статей* [Skiing: Issues from the Scientific Study of Skiing]. In Krakovajak, Krestovnikov, Puni, and Jananis (eds.), 123–127. The author comes to the conclusion that women should not compete during the menstruation period, and that female athletes performed best during the secretion period. The idea that women should not train or compete during menstruation was held at least up until 1959.

85 Grant. *Physical Culture and Sport in Soviet Society*, 72–98.
86 Briandt, *Träningsråd i längdlöpning*, 35.
87 Dichter, Heather. Sport History and Diplomatic History, *H-Diplo Essay* 122 (2014): 1–17, here 2–3.

There is a lack of research regarding how international knowledge transfer within the field of elite training (not least scientific training models) has spread and been interpreted within different political and national contexts. Even though the Soviet authors had knowledge about the training of Swedish, Norwegian, and Finnish skiers and the theory behind it, they did not always appropriate their models. As earlier research indicates, transfers within the realm of sport are complex and there is no standard explanatory model of diffusion.[88] This is underlined in our study. There are national differences despite a continuous international standardization, not least illustrated by the different views on asthma medication among leading ski nations today.

Other questions that would be interesting to explore are the connections to research fields other than physiology, such as cybernetics and biomechanics. In Sweden, physiology had a dominant role as the leading sport-related science well into the 1970s, while in the Soviet Union (although physiology was a leading field there as well) other scientific fields were more visible according to our material.

The gender aspects also deserve further attention, especially the training practice and theory of the Soviet women's skiing team who were the leading athletes in their field for over 30 years, starting in the 1950s.

Further studies, based on a broader material, could analyse the complex relationships between scientists, athletes and coaches in the Soviet Union, in similar ways that have been used for other countries, such as Sweden and Norway.

The sportification process accelerated during the Cold War period in both the Soviet Union and Sweden, despite their many differences in political system, international relations, tradition and economy. It is also clear that the scientific contribution to sport, not least skiing, was vital in both countries. As the knowledge about Soviet sport science and training development increases, this also sheds new light on the Cold War era and its impact on sport. For the developments in cross-country skiing as well as sport science, the conscious effort by the Soviet Union to be the avant-garde of scientized training directly affected other countries such as Sweden into accelerating their own efforts. The Cold War was therefore not only fought in space or by military means, but also in labs and on skiing tracks. What is particularly interesting is that similar research on athletes was motivated in radically different ways. In the Soviet Union, sports and thus also sport science was highly political. In Sweden, it was framed as neutral, relating more to rationality and scientific ideals than to sport performance.

---

88 Naha, Souvik. "Over the Border and the Gates?" Global and Transnational Sport. *Sport in Society* 20 (2016): 1347–1353.

Juan Antonio Simón
Athletes of Diplomacy:

Francoism, Sport and the Cold War during the 1960s

Introduction

From before the end of the Civil War in April 1939, Francoism started to implement a new model of sporting policy that Franco's "New Spain" would employ, using the political-sporting structure that Mussolini had developed from 1922 onwards in Italy as a reference point. To this end, in 1941 they created the Delegación Nacional de Deportes (National Sports Delegation, DND) of the Falange Española Tradicionalista y de las Juntas de Ofensiva Nacional Sindicalista (Traditional Spanish Falange, FET de las JONS), the chief organization charged with controlling the numerous spheres of influence that sport encompassed.[1] This decision was meant to keep all sporting activity under the absolute control of the sole political party, the Falange, and more specifically the control of the apex of power, the Secretary General of the National Movement. The Franco regime understood that sport could be turned into the ideal tool to engender conformity amongst Spanish youth, while at the same time helping to achieve the international legitimization that it so desired. For this reason, the diplomatic battle between the Republican government and the Francoist faction found a new battleground in sport. The Franco regime's diplomatic service tried by any means necessary to gain the recognition of the main institutions of international sport, such as the International Olympic Committee (IOC) and the Fédération Internationale de Football Association (FIFA), even before the war had ended. Similarly, the Francoist rearguard started to organize sporting federations to parallel those that officially existed in the republican zone, sports competitions and even international matches, mainly with Portugal, which were made possible by the ideological affinity between the Franco regime and Salazar's dictatorship.[2]

---

[1] Head of State. Official Spanish Gazette (Boletín Oficial del Estado, BOE). Decree of 22 February 1941. *Creación de la Delegación Nacional de Deportes*, n. 64 of 5 March 1941, 1551–1553.
[2] Reconocimiento de la Federación Española de Fútbol en el territorio nacional. *ABC* (ed. Sevilla), 13 November 1937, 26. In the case of Spain, see Pujadas i Martí, Xavier. Del barrio al estadio: Deporte, mujeres y clases populares en la segunda república, 1931–1936. In *Atletas y ciudadanos: historia social del deporte en España (1870–2010)*, Xavier Pujadas i Martí (ed.), 125–167. Madrid: Alianza Editorial, 2011. At an international level, one of the many examples of studies

The Franco regime's victory in the Civil War meant that sport stopped being privately organized, and instead was moved under the complete control of the state and into a hierarchical and pyramidal system, copying the former totalitarian experiments of Germany and Italy. The DND would directly intervene in the management of federated sport, military sport and sporting and physical activities of the movement's youth organizations; at the same time this body would have a wide number of departments, which would oversee everything from the appointment of the presidents and vice-presidents of the various different national and regional federations, to the president of the Spanish Olympic Committee (COE), a man who was also the national delegate, despite this clearly contravening IOC regulations.[3]

It is indubitable that sport became a tool for social control, and nowadays there are a number of interesting studies that have brilliantly analysed this aspect of the Franco regime's sporting policy.[4] However, this article aims to open new lines of argument with regard to the relationship between sport and international relations during Francoism, and as such ensure that in the future we will be able to answer questions of great historical importance. In particular there is a need for research that includes the use of primary sources, which is one of the main deficiencies evident in the few investigations that have tried to address these aspects up till now.

The aim of this study is to analyse how the international context of the Cold War influenced Francoism's foreign policy, and how at the same time this transformed the sporting policy of the Franco regime. This research intends to demonstrate how the beginning of the 1960s was a clear turning point in the use of sport as a diplomatic tool, caused by a radical change in Franco's foreign policy strategy. This chapter will consist of a first section which will review the period in question, between 1939 and 1969, and will look at the role played by sport within a first phase of isolation that the Franco regime experienced after the Second World War and the subsequent incorporation of Spain as an ally of the Unit-

---

about the politicization of sport during the 1930s is Beck, Peter J. *Scoring for Britain: International Football and International Politics 1900–1939*. London: Frank Cass, 1999.

3 González Aja, Teresa. La política deportiva en España durante la República y el Franquismo. In *Sport y autoritarismos: la utilización del deporte por el comunismo y el fascismo*, Teresa González Aja (ed.), 169–202. Madrid: Alianza, 2002.

4 See as an example, Morcillo, Aurora G. Uno, don, tres, cuatro: modern women, docile bodies. *Sport in Society: Cultures, Commerce, Media, Politics* 11 (2008): 673–684; González Aja, Teresa. From Dictatorship to Democracy in Spain: The Iconography of Motorcyclist Angel Nieto. *The International Journal of the History of Sport* 28 (2011): 240–252; Viuda Serrano, Alejandro. Deporte, censura y represión bajo el franquismo, 1939–1961. In *Atletas y ciudadanos*, Pujadas i Martí, 273–321.

ed States in the accords of 1953. Next, the study will present the transformation of Francoism's sporting policy as of 1960, in clear relation to the change in the international political interests of Spain. As examples of this change during the 1960s, I will discuss the influence that the Olympic Games in Rome (1960) and Tokyo (1964) had, the first game between Real Madrid's basketball team and CSKA Moscow that took place in 1963, and finally in 1965 the presentation of Madrid's Olympic bid for the 1972 games.

Playing with our friends: autarchy and anticommunism, 1939 – 1959

Following the chronological division proposed by authors such as Jesús A. Martínez and Pastor Pradillo for analysing Francoism, we could define two long and clearly different phases up until the 1960s.[5] The first phase from 1939 to 1951 is defined by isolation, autarchy and the strong international pressure that Spain was subject to, a result of the ideological closeness to the Axis powers that Franco had demonstrated during the Second World War. From 1943 onwards, with the changing course of the armed conflict, the Spanish state decided to soften its fascist tone, trying to place itself in a position of strict neutrality; despite this, it could not avoid the condemnation of the Allied Forces.[6] In 1946 the UN General Assembly refused to recognize Franco's government, provoking the immediate withdrawal of the majority of ambassadors from Spanish territory, with the only diplomatic representatives remaining in the country during this period being those from Portugal, Argentina, the Holy See and the Dominican Republic.

This political context also directly influenced the world of sport, causing Spain to experience a phase of sporting autarchy in which international relations were almost entirely limited to a range of countries that were deemed ideologically close to the Franco regime, such as Germany, Italy and Portugal.[7] Despite the mistrust towards France and its dictatorship on the part of many states in

---

5 Pastor Pradillo, José Luis *El espacio profesional de la Educación Física en España: génesis y formación (1883–1961)*. Madrid: Universidad Alcalá de Henares, 1997, here 433–442; Martínez, Jesús A. (Coord.). *Historia de España siglo XX, 1939–1996*. Madrid: Cátedra, 1999.
6 Huguet Santos, Montserrat. La política exterior del franquismo (1939–1975). In *La política exterior de España (1800–2003)*, Juan Carlos Pereira (ed.), 495–516. Barcelona: Ariel, 2003.
7 Fernández, Carlos. *El fútbol durante la guerra civil y el franquismo*. Madrid: San Martín, 1990, here 77–83.

the Western bloc, the development of the Cold War and, more specifically, the attitude of the Truman administration, started to favour the Spanish position. The proclamation of the People's Republic of China in 1949 and the start of the Korean War in June 1950 meant that the US government considered the reinforcement of the defensive-military structure throughout the world as an objective of utmost importance; it understood that in this context, it was necessary to end the isolation of the Spanish regime.[8] At the start of November 1950, the UN revoked its resolution, favouring the return of ambassadors to Madrid and allowing diplomatic relations to be resumed, something which was consolidated in 1953 with the accord with the United States and the signing of the concordat with the Holy See. During the month of June 1951, the United States opted to redirect its diplomatic rapprochement with Spain, dispensing with the other Western countries. The establishment of American military bases on Spanish soil would be linked to economic aid to the tune of 125 million dollars. This period of Francoist consolidation, which we could characterize as a second phase spanning from 1951–1953 until 1960, was aided by the new context of the Cold War, in which Franco's extreme anticommunism became a determining factor for his integration on an international level. Intolerance of the Franco regime progressively lost ground when faced with the geostrategic interests of the democratic powers. On a sporting level, throughout these years Franco's authorities tried to emphasize Spain's image as a "sentinel for the West" against the communist enemy, opening up its sporting relations with Western countries but depending upon their complete intolerance of countries on the other side of the "Iron Curtain".[9]

Within this discourse we must also add the Spanish government's decision to boycott the Melbourne Olympic Games in 1956, in opposition to the IOC's refusal to veto the participation of the Soviet team following the occupation of Budapest. Furthermore, this decision benefited the DND, who had found themselves in a dire economic situation, and allowed them to save the great expense that sending Spanish sportsmen and women to Australia would have entailed.[10]

---

8 McMahon, Robert J. *La Guerra Fría: una breve introducción*. Madrid: Alianza, 2009, here 67–97; Fernández García, Antonio and Juan Carlos Pereira Castañares. La percepción española de la ONU (1945–1962). *Cuadernos de Historia Contemporánea* 17 (1995): 121–146.
9 Pereira Castañares, Juan Carlos and Pedro A. Martínez Lillo. Política exterior, 1939–1975. In *Historia Contemporánea de España (siglo XX)*, Javier Paredes (ed.), 736–751, here 737, Barcelona: Ariel, 1998.
10 Official Bulletin National Sports Delegation, October 1956, here 3. As a response to the Soviet Union's repression of the Hungarian rebellion which started in November 1956, and due to the

Another example that reinforces this argument can be found through analysing the birth of the European basketball championship in the second half of the 1950s. When the International Basketball Federation (FIBA) contacted the Spanish Basketball Federation (FEB) to check their availability with regard to incorporating Spanish clubs into the new competition, the head of the Falange's Foreign Service, Sergio Cifuentes, contacted the Ministry of Foreign Affairs in 1956 to consult on the criteria that they should follow when it came to the participation of Soviet clubs, with which Spain had no sporting relations, in the competition. The Ministry was very clear in reminding him that "the organization of these sorts of appearance, in which the Iron Curtain countries would inevitably be in attendance, was not considered appropriate", given that these teams were made up of "uncontrollable people, liable to create aggravating incidents which could end badly, being as they were representatives of Iron Curtain countries".[11]

The 1960s and the change in sporting policy in Spain

As has already been mentioned, from the beginning of the 1960s a new strategy based on the international perspective in sporting policy was established, driven by various sectors from within the Franco regime who believed in the possibilities that sport could offer as a tool to help the country's foreign policy and as a way to build a more positive image of the dictatorship outside Spain.[12]

In 1957 Fernando María Castiella was named Minister of Foreign Affairs, a position which he would hold until 1969. He became a key figure in understanding the role that sport played within Francoist foreign policy during this period.

IOC's refusal to sanction the Soviet Olympic Committee for these actions, Spain, Switzerland and the Netherlands boycotted the Olympic Games.

11 Spanish Ministry of Foreign Affairs Archives (AMAE), R4251 E33, 1956. See Simón, Juan Antonio. L'homme de l'ombre Raimundo Saporta et le basket espagnol et européen. In *Le continent basket: L'Europe et le basket-ball au XX siècle*, Fabien Archambault, Loïc Artiaga and Gérard Bosc (eds.), 215–231, Belgique: Peter Lang, 2015.

12 Bahamonde, Ángel. *El Real Madrid en la historia de España*. Madrid: Taurus, 2002; Shaw, Duncan. *Fútbol y franquismo*. Madrid: Alianza, 1987; Santacana, Carles. Espejo de un régimen. Transformación de las estructuras deportivas y su uso político y propagandístico. In *Atletas y ciudadanos*, Pujadas (ed.), 205–232; González Aja, Teresa. Monje y soldado. La imagen masculina durante el Franquismo. *RICYDE Revista Internacional de Ciencias del Deporte* 1 (2005): 64–83.

His interest in trying to improve the international image of the country was united with the quest to bring about Spanish integration on an international level, and especially in Europe. At the same time, as of the late 1950s the Cold War entered into one of its most politically tense periods; various moments of crisis culminated in 1962, in the confrontation between Washington and Moscow over the presence of Soviet missiles in Cuba, with the threat of nuclear war at its most critical.[13]

It was during these years that negotiations with the European Economic Community (EEC) began, going from the initial contact in 1962 to the signing of a Preferential Trade Agreement with the EEC on 29 June 1970.[14] In the same way, events such as the first meetings between Spanish and Soviet ambassadors in 1958, the renegotiation of the agreements with the United States in 1963 or the strengthening of bilateral relations with France or West Germany illustrate the context in which an evident transformation of the function of sport at an international level took place.

A good example of this change was the Spanish national football team's first appearance in the European Nations Cup in 1960, a competition that is nowadays known as the UEFA European Championship. In the quarter-finals Spain was drawn against the Soviet Union. While the majority of European countries had already normalized their sporting relations with the countries of the Iron Curtain, the Franco regime still wanted to highlight their deep anticommunist stance, refusing to let their sportsmen and women play against Soviet teams. However it is true that certain changes were made evident, in the very fact of having permitted the encounter between the Spanish team and another country of the Communist bloc, Poland, in the first round of this competition. In their meeting on 2 May 1960, the Cabinet agreed that the Spanish national side could not play against the Soviet Union, despite the fact that such a refusal would entail Spain's automatic elimination from the competition.[15] In this decision we can discern the differences in attitude that existed amongst Franco's ministers when it came to the role that sport should play and, in particular, the opportunities that sport could offer in terms of changing Spain's international image. On one side of this, we can identify a more liberal sector within the government, including Castiella alongside the chief of the DND at that time, José An-

---

13 Gaddis, John Lewis. *Nueva historia de la Guerra Fría*. México: FCE, 2011, here 91–105.
14 Pardo Sanz, Rosa. La etapa Castiella y el final del Régimen, 1957–1975. In *La política exterior de España en el siglo XX*, Javier Tussell, Juan Avilés and Rosa Pardo (eds.), 341–369. Madrid: UNED/Biblioteca Nueva, 2000.
15 Ramos, Ramón. *¡Que vienen los rusos!: España renuncia a la Eurocopa de 1960 por decisión de Franco*. Granada: Comares, 2012.

tonio Elola-Olaso, and the regime's Secretary General, José Solís. Opposing this group were the more conservative members of Franco's government, those radically uncompromising in the face of communism and, at the same time, afraid of the dangers that the normalization of sporting relations might create for the security and image of the country. Such influential figures as the Minister of the Presidency, Carrero Blanco, and the Minister of the Interior, Camilo Alonso Vega, tried to hinder the process of sporting liberalization during the first half of the 1960s.

However, something strongly indicative of Francoism's radical change in political-sporting strategy occurred four years later, in 1964, when the final phase of the second European Nations Cup took place in Madrid. On this occasion, the factions most convinced of the possibilities that sport, and especially organizing international sporting events, could offer as a means of creating an idealized image of the Franco dictatorship prevailed over those who saw these competitions (with huge numbers of spectators) as the ideal stage for arguments or protests of a political nature to take place in the stands, something which could undermine national security. But in 1964, Spain finally accepted UEFA's offer, leaving ideological principles to one side in order to prioritize creating the image of a "more tolerant and hospitable" nation.[16] In the Santiago Bernabéu stadium and in the presence of Franco himself, the Spanish national side beat the Soviet Union 2–1. What had changed within the regime to bring about such a radical change in their sporting policy, so that in only four years they would go from banning matches against Soviet clubs and national sides to Franco's authorities agreeing to host the competition?

In order to answer this question, it is imperative that we resume our analysis from the beginning of the 1960s. This was a key moment in the country's political and social changes which would be reflected in the use of sport as a way of showing the rest of the world a fictitious image of "normality" in Franco's Spain. Both the DND and the Ministry of Foreign Affairs understood that the fascist-inspired sporting policy model that the Falange had dreamed of could never become reality if the political authorities did not increase investment. If the collectivization of physical and sporting activity amongst Spaniards had become a pipe-dream that existed only in formal speeches and press statements, then sport could perhaps be used in another way, and transformed into an instrument to serve the regime's foreign policy.

In line with this policy, there were attempts to win bids to host large sporting events of international importance, as was the case in the aforementioned Euro-

---

16 Shaw. *Fútbol y franquismo*, 168–170.

pean Nations Cup in 1964 and Madrid's bid to host the 1972 Olympic Games. Two things helped to foster the dream that a sector of the government harboured to one day host an Olympic Games in Franco's Spain: firstly, the success that organizing the 1955 Mediterranean Games in Barcelona had represented for Francoism;[17] and secondly, the impact of seeing the success that hosting the 1960 Olympic Games in Rome and the Tokyo Games four years later had brought to Italy and Japan (both countries with a totalitarian past).

From the model of Rome 1960 and Tokyo 1964 to Real Madrid's first visit to the Soviet Union

The Italian government's strategy of using the Olympic Games to show the world that democratic Italy had moved away from its fascist past was a tactic that did not go unnoticed by the Franco regime. Rome 1960 turned out to be a political and diplomatic success, proving to the rest of the world that Italy could be a main player on the international stage, as a modern country experiencing strong economic development.[18] Why not dream of "Franco's Olympic Games" which could definitively change Spain's international image, even if, in reality, nothing would change on an internal level?

The cultural advisor from the Spanish Embassy in Rome, Emilio Garrigues, was aware of the importance that these kinds of sporting events were gaining on a diplomatic level, and he did not hesitate in informing his superiors that if the country wished to reach the desired "normalization", it was essential that it participate in the great sporting events with a significant number of athletes, even if the results were not what it had wanted: "It is as important to be present in the cultural, economic and political fields as it is in the sporting one; in this sense, any absence counts, in reality, as a loss".[19]

Both the DND and the Ministry of Foreign Affairs remained extremely close to the preparation process of the Olympic Games in Rome. Despite the limitations of the Spanish sportsmen and women at an international level, the DND

---

17 Every four years since the year 1951, the National Olympic Committees of the Mediterranean countries have held a multi-sport event in Alexandria which is similar to the Olympic Games. See Pernas López, Juli. *Barcelona 1955: els Jocs Mediterranis*. Barcelona: CG Anmar, 2012.
18 Martin, Simon. *Sport Italia: The Italian Love Affair with Sport*. London: I.B. Tauris, 2011, here 150–161.
19 AMAE. La participación española en la VII Olimpiada Universal celebrada en Cortina d'Ampezzo 1956. R4250 E9.

managed, after the Melbourne boycott, to form a national team with the highest number of participants in Spanish Olympic history: specifically 147 athletes who competed in 17 disciplines, with the inclusion of 11 women. José Solís emphasized that these sports stars also had the role of ambassadors, reminding them that they carried "the name of Spain on their shoulders",[20] and adding to the statements of other political and sporting representatives of the Franco regime who were starting to demand better results from the Spanish athletes: "[...] we must ask of our representatives, in order to achieve the honour of being such, a guarantee of class and form which ensures, in normal conditions, respectable performances on the Olympic stage".[21]

The Olympic Games which took place in Tokyo four years later would be analysed from a very similar perspective. At the same time, it is important to highlight that in the Rome games, 18 European countries received the television signal live via Eurovision, and that Tokyo saw the first retransmission of the games via satellite, and the first experiences of colour television.[22] Once again, the enormous impact that organizing an Olympic Games had on the image of the country at a political level was clearly demonstrated, and we cannot deem it a mere coincidence that one year later, specifically in December 1965, the Spanish Olympic Committee decided to put forward Madrid's candidacy in a bid to host the 1972 Olympic Games. As far as sport itself was concerned, Spain continued to seek further prominence from its athletes, even though the investment the government allocated to this area remained minimal. With the help of different Olympic sports federations, the DND tried to prepare a specific game plan which would allow the Spanish team to improve upon the results from the previous Olympics, given that the highest sporting authorities were aware of how important a good performance from Spanish athletes in these types of mega-events would be for the image of the country; as such, competitions such as the 1962 Football World Cup in Chile and the 1964 Olympic Games became critical objectives for the DND.[23]

Another of the events that highlighted the change in Francoist sporting strategy at an external level was the government's decision to finally allow Real Madrid's basketball team to play against their Soviet rivals. In 1961 the Spanish club

---

20 Official Bulletin National Sports Delegation, August 1956, here 3.
21 Official Bulletin National Sports Delegation, June 1956, here 10–11.
22 Peña, Emilio Fernández and Natividad Ramajo Hernández. La comunicación en el deporte global: los medios y los Juegos Olímpicos de verano (1894–2012). *Historia y Comunicación Social* 19 (2014): 703–714, here 708.
23 El ministro secretario del Movimiento clausuró ayer el pleno del Consejo Nacional de Deportes. *ABC*, 22 December 1960.

managed to get Franco's authorities to accept a double match against ASK Riga in Prague and Paris respectively. The following year, Real Madrid got to the final of the European Basketball Championship for the first time, coming up against Dinamo Tblisi along the way. Franco would not consent to the Spanish players travelling to the Soviet Union, but through the diplomatic abilities of the club's vice-president Raimundo Saporta, they managed to get permission to play the final in a single match in Geneva. One year later, Madrid would once again appear in the European competition, this time facing CSKA Moscow. The government finally accepted that the tie would take place over two matches, and for the first time they agreed to allow a Soviet team to enter Spain. In the same way, and with regard to the new liberal image that Francoism wished to portray, the Real Madrid players were also allowed to go to the Soviet Union for the first time.[24]

Madrid 1972: Francoism's Olympic bid and their diplomatic stance

In October 1965, the IOC chose Madrid to host its General Assembly. The Francoist authorities understood that this was a great opportunity to show the world a country that was open to international influences, and that welcomed all visitors without making political distinctions.[25]

Alongside the propaganda importance that the IOC Assembly had for the Franco regime, the political authorities made the most of this opportunity to grill the president of the IOC, Avery Brundage, on how the members of his organization would receive a Spanish Olympic bid. The head of the Olympic movement did not hesitate to encourage their spokespeople to propose a city. Once more, as had happened during the Civil War, the IOC endorsed and legitimized Francoism. But in order to completely understand this decision, it is necessary to bear in mind the context of the Cold War, which changed after the Cuban Missile Crisis in 1962, showing clear signs of a thawing in relations between the United States and the Soviet Union, threatened only by the Vietnam War. Both powers

---

24 See Simón, Juan Antonio. Jugando contra el enemigo: Raimundo Saporta y el primer viaje del equipo de baloncesto del Real Madrid CF a la Unión Soviética. *RICYDE Revista Internacional de Ciencias del Deporte* 28 (2013): 109–126.
25 Meléndez, Luis. Inicia el C.I.O. las sesiones de su 63 Congreso. *El Mundo Deportivo*, 6 October 1965.

tried to handle the conflict in a safer manner until the end of the 1970s, in order to minimize the possibility of an accidental war.[26]

At the end of December 1965, the Spanish Olympic Committee presented Madrid's bid to host the 1972 Olympic Games. From the isolation from the sporting world that had characterized the first years of the dictatorship, in two decades Franco's Spain had moved to validate the use of mega-events such as the Olympics from the political sphere, so as to try to achieve a radical change in the international image of the country; something that would be much more difficult to achieve in other fields. This strategy would help the government in its main foreign policy aim, which was simply to achieve integration into European institutions despite the unquestionable democratic deficiencies in their political system.

To bring this project into fruition, the Ministry of Foreign Affairs immediately put itself at the service of the Olympic bid. In March 1966, Director General Ramón Sedó, wrote to the 38 ambassadors of the countries in which members of the IOC resided, to request that they contact said members with a view to obtaining their support for the Spanish bid:

> Considering how greatly it would benefit Spain to have our bid accepted when up against those from West Germany, Canada and the USA, it would be advisable that, with the utmost tact and discretion given that Olympic regulations prohibit all types of official process, you privately contact: [a space is left to include the IOC member's name] Member of the International Olympic Committee in your country and try to secure their support for the Spanish bid.[27]

From this moment, an intense dialogue began between the diplomatic delegates and the ministry, looking to ensure the greatest possible support for the Madrid Olympic project in order to prevail over the prestigious bids from Munich, Detroit and Montreal. At the same time, the study of the Spanish Olympic bid once again allows us to identify the significant contradictions which, as previously stated, existed within Franco's government with regard to sporting policy and its courses of action. If on one side the Ministry of Foreign Affairs was putting all its diplomatic civil servants at the service of the Olympic bid, on the other, the Cabinet rejected the budget set aside for the Olympic project time and time again, forcing them to cut the funding on up to two different occasions and creating many

---

26 Lewis Gaddis. *Nueva historia de la Guerra Fría*, 239–241. Powaski, Ronald E. *The Cold War: The United States and the Soviet Union, 1917–1991*. New York: Oxford University Press, 1998.
27 AMAE. Letter from Ramón Sedó to the Spanish Ambassadors. R8410 E24, 14 May 1966.

doubts on an international level about Madrid's chances, something which was arguably the main cause for their loss of the bid to Munich.[28]

The initial figure of 29,335 million pesetas which had been estimated as a basic budget to be able to organize the Olympic Games in a respectable fashion had to be cut to 20,827 million pesetas, due to pressure from the group of ministers who radically opposed the expenses generated by the Olympic project. In no time at all this information was leaked to the international press, creating huge doubts for members of the IOC as to how secure the Spanish bid was.[29] Despite the support of the Ministry of Foreign Affairs and the DND, a significant group of Francoist politicians repeatedly withheld endorsement of the new sporting strategy, which the former organizations had tried to implement from the early 1960s in order to reap the benefits that organizing huge sporting events on Spanish soil would have for the country's image.[30]

Conclusion

Through the analysis of various political-sporting events that took place during the 1960s, this article has tried to demonstrate the role played by sport within Francoism's foreign policy, its evolution and its use as a tool to improve the dictatorship's damaged international image. While it is undeniable that sport was not the defining factor in the Franco dictatorship's foreign policy, I am convinced that we must continue to delve into the role played by this activity as a course of action within a wider global international relations strategy. In particular, it is vital that we improve the understanding of the role played by the Ministry of Foreign Affairs in this entire process, and I have tried to indicate this throughout this text.

In a totalitarian system like the Franco regime, in which sport, just as any other area of the lives of Spanish citizens, was subject to the political interests of the government, this activity allowed the state to transmit a more agreeable image of Franco's Spain which would encourage foreign investment and economic growth throughout this decade, as well as slowly getting closer to the European Economic Community and the United States without any apparent need to change the political regime. One aspect that remains to be examined in future

---

28 AMAE. R 8612, EXT 12. Simón, Juan Antonio. Fiscal follies of the "Franco Olympic Games" – Madrid's bid in 1972. *Journal of Olympic History* 201 (2013): 49–55.
29 Simón, Juan Antonio. Fiscal follies.
30 Simón, Juan Antonio. Madrid-72: relaciones diplomáticas y Juegos Olímpicos durante el Franquismo. *Revista Movimento* 19 (2013): 221–240.

is the attempt to go further in evaluating the success and the impact of this strategy, and the deficiencies in the implementation of these measures.

Finally, it is of interest to highlight that long before the establishment of consular relations with Eastern European countries such as Czechoslovakia, Hungary and Bulgaria, following the appointment of Gregoria López Bravo as Foreign Minister in 1969, and before the signing of trade deals with Poland, Romania, Yugoslavia and the Soviet Union itself, as we have seen, Spain had already normalized its sporting relations with these nations – and this was likely the first step towards their subsequent diplomatic rapprochement.

Second part. **A European space of exchanges. Crossing the Iron Curtain with sport**

Sylvain Dufraisse
The emergence of Europe-wide collaboration and competition:

Soviet sports interactions in Europe. 1945 – mid-1960s.

Introduction

A common narrative focusing on global sporting events is still dominating the history of Cold War sports. The "Blood in the Water" match in 1956, the Super series in ice hockey between Canada and the Soviet Union in 1972, the "Miracle on Ice" of 1980 and the boycotts of the Olympic Games: all these sports rivalries are well known and constitute major "battles" on sporting fields between the Superpowers and their allies. Many books and articles were written about "symbolic combats", opposing the United States and the Soviet Union, between the two blocs separated by the Iron Curtain. Direct oppositions on stadiums and on pitches played a major part in the struggle waged by the two countries to win hearts and minds. According to that research, the history of Cold War sports is composed of confrontations and oppositions. Consequently, it overemphasises the bipolar confrontational nature of the Cold War, using the superpower approach. Through reading archives and materials, other patterns are appearing. Sari Autio-Sarasmo and Katalin Mikossy remarked that the confrontational vision implies a simplified perception of the political blocs, and that the Iron Curtain was perceived, in consequence, as an impermeable barrier. Their studies of economic and cultural relations in Cold-War Europe recognized the existence of relations and collaboration between the West and the East. Lower-level actors experimented with cooperation and East-European states were much more independent than the literature has described. Two Finnish historians proposed a new paradigm to better analyse the developments of the Cold War in Europe: "multileveled-multipolar interaction"[1]. Sports are a good field to analyse these interactions as many common training programmes, many low-level competitions and bilateral games happened during the Cold War, not only between the two superpowers.

Thanks are due to Pauline Del Vechio and Susan Grant, whose comments and suggestions have strengthened this article.
1 Autio-Sarasmo, Sari and Katalin Miklossy (eds.). *Reassessing Cold War Europe*. New York: Routledge, 2011.

The history of the integration of the USSR in the global sports scene is now better known, thanks to James Riordan and Victor Peppard,[2] to André Gounot[3] and to Barbara Keys.[4] But these works focus on the 1920s and the 1930s. Barbara Keys, using Soviet archives, demonstrated that the development of closer ties between the USSR and the international sports institutions began during the mid-1930s, before the official Soviet entrance into international federations at the end of the 1940s and into the International Olympic Committee in 1951. "Bourgeois" sport was already observed and studied from the Soviet Union and even some encounters between Soviet and Occidental teams had already happened. Jenifer Parks in her dissertation used new material archives to study the Soviet entrance into the IOC. She demonstrated how the Soviet delegates were integrated in the IOC administration and how they came to lobby there during the 1960s and the 1970s.[5] In this article, we want to have a less institutional overview. We want to focus on interactions and contacts. Using materials and reports from the Soviet archives – from the Central Committee of the VKP(b), the Council of People's Commissars and the Physical Culture and Sports Committee,[6] this essay aims at going beyond a vision of internationalization based only on institutional integration. It seeks to reassess how Soviet sports authorities developed collaboration networks in many European countries soon after the Second World War, while entering international federations; how Soviet authorities developed a Europe-wide field of competition and collaboration.

---

[2] Peppard, Victor and James Riordan (eds.). *Playing Politics: Soviet Sport Diplomacy to 1992.* Greenwich: JAI Press, 1993.
[3] Gounot, André. Entre exigences révolutionnaires et nécessités diplomatiques: les rapports du sport soviétique avec le sport ouvrier et le sport bourgeois en Europe, 1920–1937. In *Sport et relations internationales (1900–1941): Les démocraties face au fascisme et au nazisme*, Pierre Arnaud and James Riordan (eds.), 241–276. Paris: L'Harmattan, 1998; Gounot, André. Sport or Political Organization? Structures and Characteristics of the Red Sport International, 1921–1937. *Journal of Sport History* 1 (2001): 23–39; Riordan, James. La politique sportive étrangère soviétique pendant l'entre-deux guerres. In *Sport et relations internationales (1900–1941)*, Arnaud and Riordan, 127–142.
[4] Keys, Barbara. *Globalizing Sport: National Rivalry and International Community in the 1930s.* Cambridge: Harvard University Press, 2006; Keys, Barbara. Soviet Sport and Transnational Mass Culture in the 1930s. *Journal of Contemporary History* 3 (2003): 413–434.
[5] Parks, Jenifer. Red Sport, Red Tape: The Olympic Games, the Soviet Sports Bureaucracy, and the Cold War, 1952–1980, PhD, University of North Carolina, 2009.
[6] Archives from the Central Committee of the VKP(b) (RGASPI – Rossijskij gosudarstvennyj arhiv social'no-političeskoj istorii), F. 17, Central'nyj komitet VKP (b), otdel propagandy i agitacij; Archives from the Physical Culture and Sports Committee (GARF – Gosudarstvennyj arhiv Rossijskoj Federacii – F. R7576, Komitet Fizičeskoj Kul'tury i sporta SSSR).

This article will focus on three aspects. First, it will demonstrate how the Soviet Union established ties with some European countries between the end of the Second World War and the beginning of the 1950s. Afterwards, it will describe how a Europe-wide collaboration and cooperation emerged with Western countries and then with People's Democracies from the 1950s to the middle of the 1960s.

Establishing ties

From October 1944, the All-Union Physical Culture and Sports Committee considered that it was necessary to follow international sports rules and that the Soviets had to take part in international sports, so as to compete with foreign teams, to enforce friendship between nations, to gain support among Western publics, to compare their standards of practice with opponents used to international competitions and to raise Soviet standards.[7] One year later, answering the physical culture committee president, K. E. Vorošilov, vice-president of the Council of the People's Commissars, insisted on the necessity to know more about Western sports performances, their forces and results before entering the world field of sports competition. Soon after, the Soviet Union began to take part in competitions with Western and "bourgeois" teams and to develop sports links with European countries.

The prestige of the victory against the nazi regime and the bonds established among the Allies during the war contributed to shaping new sports relationships. Many games took place between the European Allies: football games between British and Soviet soldiers' teams in Berlin and in Vienna,[8] a football tour by the triumphant Dinamo Moscow football team in England in November 1945[9] and successful basketball games in France in 1946.[10]

---

[7] GARF, f. R7576, o. 2, d. 251, 32.
[8] Hamelin, Guillaume. Le sport comme continuation de la politique: la tournée du Dinamo de Moscou en Grande-Bretagne, 1945. Master thesis, University of Quebec at Montreal, 2009.
[9] Kowalski, Ronald and Dilwyn Porter. Political Football: Moscow Dynamo in Britain, 1945. *The International Journal of the History of Sport* 14 (1997): 100–121; Kowalski, Ronald and Dilwyn Porter. Cold War Football: British-European Encounters in the 1940s and the 1950s. In *East Plays West. Essays on Sport and the Cold War*, David L. Andrews and Stephen Wagg (eds.), 64–81. London: Routledge, 2006.
[10] Spandarân, Stepan. *Sčet po pol'zu* [The score in our favour]. Moscow: Molodaâ Gvardiâ, 1953. 57. GARF, f. R7576, o. 1, d. 534, l. 21.

When frictions between the former Allies emerged and sporting exchanges decreased, the geography of sports circulations came to be modified. The frequency of relations between Soviet and Western teams shrank. The Soviet authorities confined sports relationships to the countries with whom they had developed tight links since the 1930s (Norway, Sweden and Finland).[11] The Soviets took part in rare events like the Cross de l'Humanité[12] in Western countries and in competitions in Eastern European People's Democracies,[13] which became "resource centres" for Soviet sportsmen and trainers.

The level of practice in the countries visited determined the exchanges. In January 1948, Soviet sports leaders decided to define which countries were to be visited. One of the members proposed to select countries according to results at a meeting with champions and trainers. In track and field, the Swedes and the Finns appeared to be good training partners and opponents. Hungarian water-polo teams seemed to be the best competitors to raise the Soviet level of practice in that sport. Another member of the audience proposed reducing the number of official sports meetings, to concentrate only on training and competitions with high-level athletes and to avoid unnecessary competitions. According to one of the participants, it was not necessary to compete with Czechoslovakians in gymnastics but training with French and Italian gymnasts could help the Soviets improve their technique.[14]

Destinations were chosen according to the sports talents of each country. The number of sports exchanges with Hungary grew in football, in fencing, in tennis, in water polo and in modern pentathlon. Exchanges between Soviet fencers, athletes, canoeists and Czechoslovakian sportsmen and women became more regular. Cyclists from the Soviet Union competed with Bulgarians and Rumanians. Finland became a common destination for weightlifters, athletes and skiers.

These exchanges had many goals: improving practice, assimilating new techniques, getting used to new tactics by competing or training with other teams. Training programmes with foreign teams followed the same patterns as those which were developed during the 1930s, like the Henri Cochet masterclass in 1937 and 1938 that included common trainings, debates and discussions on playing methods, games and private lessons.[15] Trainers, watching the games,

---

11 RGASPI, f. 17, o. 3, d. 1055, l. 8.
12 RGASPI, f. 17, o. 3, d. 1056, l. 39.
13 GARF, f. R7576, o. 29, l. 54.
14 GARF, f. R7576, o. 1, d. 654, l. 5.
15 Dufraisse, Sylvain. Les venues de Jules Ladoumègue, Marcel Thill, Henri Cochet: des séjours de spécialistes? In *Les Français dans la vie intellectuelle et scientifique en URSS au XXe siècle*,

had to learn new patterns of training, new gestures and new strategies. Players were able to assimilate them, playing with much stronger opponents.

Exchanges with Central European and Scandinavian countries could also be used to adapt the Soviet way of playing to international rules and standards and to get used to them. Russian ice hockey (bandy) was played in the Soviet Union. The rules were different from Canadian ice hockey (where the rink is much smaller and there are fewer players). As few countries in the world were playing bandy, the Soviet sports authorities decided to adopt Canadian ice-hockey rules so as to compete with the best teams. Czechoslovakian teams played a huge role in getting the Soviets accustomed to the Canadian game.[16] In March 1948, the hockey team from the Prague Lawn Tennis Club visited Moscow to take part in joint training. Twelve of them were part of the national Czech team, that was strong enough to resist the best hockey team in the world, Canada, in international games. The training programme was quite well known: joint training, matches behind closed doors before official games.[17] The Soviets might assimilate new strategies and new patterns of games by confronting the Prague team.

Between 1951 and the first six months of 1952, sports relationships with the People's Democracies increased. Even competitions gathering sportsmen from all the Eastern European countries were organized in various disciplines (rowing, cycling, track and field).[18] In 1952, Soviet sports delegations visited, in this descending order of importance, Hungary, the German Democratic Republic, Rumania, Czechoslovakia, Poland and Bulgaria. Only a few capitalist countries were visited by Soviet sportsmen. Most of them (Finland, Austria, Sweden, Switzerland) were not part of the North Atlantic Treaty Organization (NATO), but the Soviets did also visit American allies such as France, Italy and Belgium.[19]

Before the entrance into the Olympic arena in 1952 in Helsinki, the Soviet sports leaders established solid sports links with some of the European countries. The Helsinki victories, Stalin's death in 1953 and the new paradigm of pacific coexistence made new sports relationships possible.

Alexandre Tchoubarian, Francine-Dominique Liechtenhan, Sophie Coeuré and Olga Okouneva (eds.), 48–61. Moscow: IRI-RAN, 2013.
16 The Soviets were playing a variant of ice hockey named bandy: GARF, f. R7576, o. 29, d. 34, l. 197–199; and d. 43, l. 11–12.
17 Boivin-Chouinard, Mathieu: *Chaïbou! Histoire du hockey russe. 1. Des origines à la série du siècle*. Longueil: Kéruss, 2011, here 58–62; Prozumenŝlkov, Mihajl. Sport as a Mirror of Eastern Europe Crises. *Russian Studies in History* 49 (2010): 5–93, here 68; GARF, f. R7576, o. 2, d. 410, l. 60.
18 GARF, f. R7576, o. 1, d. 858; d. 859; d. 859, l. 114.
19 GARF, f. R7576, o. 29, d. 116, l. 2.

Intensifying ties with Western European countries

Soviet international sports relations evolved during the 1950s. This was the consequence of two factors. First, the numerous victories of the Soviet team at the Helsinki Olympic Games transformed the Soviet Union into a leading and respected sporting power. To Soviet leaders, this success showed that they could use sport to promote Soviet power and to demonstrate their achievements to a worldwide audience. A progressive change in Soviet foreign policy also led to less aggressive and tense relations. Therefore, the Soviet political authorities came to authorize more and more sports exchanges. This was also possible as exchanges abroad became easier.[20]

But the geography of sporting ties followed preexisting patterns and relied on well-established bonds. From 1953, Soviet delegations of sportsmen and women visited Scandinavian countries (Sweden, Norway, Finland) as well as France. Those countries hosted Soviet teams and also republic or city teams. Even if Norway belonged to the Western bloc and to NATO, it had developed contacts and exchanges in sports, even during the period of the Soviet sports exchange retraction between 1948 and 1951. Each year from 1953, dozens of sportsmen and women took part in competitions and common trainings. Winter sports were privileged, among them sports where the Norwegians fared best: ice skating, ice hockey or Nordic combined.[21] Friendly competitions happened in track and field and in football (Moscow CDSA in 1955, Stalino Šahter in 1956).[22]

The sporting relations with Sweden were similar. Sweden was one of the first sporting partners of the Soviet Union. After the Helsinki Olympic Games, sporting exchanges continued, increasing from 1954. Some sports dominated like wrestling, sailing, football and ice hockey.[23] Finland hosted many delegations of Soviet sportsmen for mutual trainings and for friendly games in a wide range of sports: skiing, ice skating, ice hockey, bandy, football, weightlifting, track and field, and gymnastics.[24]

---

20 Gorsuch, Anne. *All This is Your World, Soviet Tourism at Home and Abroad after Stalin.* Oxford: Oxford University Press, 2011, here 13.
21 GARF, f. R7576, o. 1, d. 919, l. 180; d. 937, l. 224; d. 1037, l. 145; d. 1037, l. 150; d. 1152, l. 121.
22 GARF, f. R7576, o. 1, d. 1066, l. 44; d. 1100, l. 28; d. 1174, l. 13.
23 GARF, f. R7576, o. 1, d. 936, l. 162; d. 972, l. 174; d. 1041, l. 158; d. 1061, l. 53; d. 1158, l. 12; d. 1161, l. 169; d. 1193, l. 29; d. 1203, l. 15; d. 1204, l. 162.
24 GARF, f. R7576, o. 1, d. 936, l. 162; d. 969, l. 133; d. 1037, l. 145; d. 1043, l. 31; d. 1091, l. 36; d. 1099, l. 43; d. 1099, l. 58; d. 1156, l. 3; d. 1163, l. 69; d. 1163, l. 123; d. 1163, l. 144; d. 1164, l.10; d. 1164, l. 243; d. 1170, l. 17; d. 1170, l. 125; d. 1172, l. 5; d. 1210, l. 55.

France was also one of the privileged partners. As with Scandinavian countries, exchanges between French and Soviet sportsmen had begun in the late 1930s and increased in the 1950s. But in the case of France, links with the Communist movement were determining and most of the sport relations with the Soviet Union happened in the framework of "worker sport". The Cross de l'Humanité, organized by the Communist newspaper *l'Humanité*, was an unmissable event for Soviet long-distance runners, men and women. Soviet gymnasts were invited by the French worker's federation (Fédération sportive et gymnastique du travail – FSGT) to take part in galas and in exhibitions.[25] French teams in collective sports like basketball or volleyball or in individual sports like fencing or boxing were well trained and had a good level of practice. In those sports, Soviet sportsmen came to France to improve standards of practice and were opposed to the "bourgeois" teams. Renowned teams like Moscow Torpedo[26] went to France, as well as less-well-known teams like the Moscow volleyball team.[27]

Sports came to be a field where new orientations of Soviet diplomacy were visible. Sporting events with the FRG began in October 1954 and preceded the restoration of official diplomatic relations and Adenauer's trip to Moscow in September 1955.[28] In 1954, collaboration between the Soviet Union and other West European countries (Italy, the United Kingdom, the Netherlands, the FRG) began. West Germany hosted 39 Soviet sportsmen in 1954, 145 in 1955 and 38 in 1956. 154 Soviet sportsmen visited the United Kingdom in 1954, 107 in 1955, 78 in 1956.[29] These states hosted newly funded European or international championships where Soviet teams were invited, as well as friendly games – basketball in Italy,[30] ice hockey, track and field, and boxing in the United Kingdom,[31] football and ice hockey in the FRG.[32]

Increasing sports exchanges set the stage for warmer relationships between those Western countries and the Soviet Union. They represented signs of an

---

25 GARF, f. R7576, o. 1, d. 980, l. 83; d. 1176, l. 8.
26 GARF, f. R7576, o. 1, d. 1174, l. 81.
27 GARF, f. R7576, o. 1, d. 1209, l. 16.
28 Rey, Marie-Pierre. *Le dilemme russe*. Paris: Flammarion, 2002, here 280–281.
29 GARF, f. R7576, o. 29, d. 151, l. 2–34; d. 169, l. 24–53; d. 185, l. 36–74.
30 GARF, f. R7576, o. 1, d. 1190, l. 18; d. 1190, l. 18.
31 GARF, f. R7576, o. 1, d. 1067, l. 24; d. 1096, l. 129; d. 1099, l. 65; d. 1157, l. 136; d. 1161, l. 29; d. 1163, l. 5; d. 1175, l. 68; d. 1198, l. 1; d. 1210, l. 71; d. 1212, l. 164.
32 GARF, f. R7576, o. 1, d. 1061, l. 65; d. 1067, l. 106; d. 1176, l. 5; d. 1199, l. 24; d. 1206, l. 149. On sports relations between the FRG and the Soviet Union, see Mertin, Evelyn. *Sowjetisch-deutsche Sportbeziehungen im Kalten Krieg*. Sankt Augustin: Akademia Verlag, 2009, here 154–156.

evolving diplomacy.³³ Relations were, however, determined by international current events. To protest against the Soviet repression after the Budapest uprising in 1956, the FRG sports authorities decided to reduce sports exchanges with Soviet teams.³⁴

In the context of the beginning of pacific coexistence, the Soviet Union multiplied sports exchanges first with Western countries with whom it already had close ties, and developed new bonds with Western countries, a sign of a more open diplomacy. Increasing exchanges were also visible in the Eastern bloc.

Developing and evolving bonds with European People's Democracies

As was the case for Western countries, the Krushchev Thaw period involved increasing exchanges with People's Democracies. But these exchanges adapted to new balances of power within the Eastern bloc. Thus, sports exchanges resumed with Yugoslavia. They preceded the official diplomatic rapprochement that culminated with Khrushchev's visit to Yugoslavia in May 1955 and the Belgrade declaration (2 June 1955). Exchanges with Yugoslavia grew rapidly:

Table 1. Number of members of Soviet delegations travelling to Yugoslavia³⁵

Year	Member of delegation
1954	29
1955	75
1956	92
1961	145
1964	183

During the 1950s, the geography of sporting exchanges evolved. Between 1947 and 1951, Czechoslovakia, Hungary and Rumania were the most visited countries in Eastern Europe. Between 1952 and 1956, Rumania, Poland and Hungary con-

---

33 Milza, Pierre. Sport et relations internationales. *Relations internationales* 38 (1984): 155–174, here 170.
34 Mertin. *Sowjetisch-deutsche Sportbeziehungen*, 156.
35 GARF, f. R7576, o. 29, d. 151, l. 2–34; d. 169, l. 24–53; d. 185, l. 36–74; GARF, f. R9570, o. 1, d. 693, l. 1–59; d. 1110, l. 12–68.

centrated most of the Soviet delegations. The number of Soviet visits to Czechoslovakia remained stable, while they grew substantially with the GDR and Bulgaria. In 1964, the map of Soviet sports exchanges within the Eastern bloc changed. The number of sports exchanges increased. The GDR was the principal destination of Soviet sportsmen (497), before Poland and Bulgaria. Sporting exchanges with Czechoslovakia and Hungary were not as popular (168 Soviet sportsmen visited those countries).

Exchanges from the Soviet Union and People's Democracies were varied including: common trainings, exhibitions, competitions, participation in local tournaments, in an Eastern-bloc competition, and in friendly games for the month of Soviet friendship. National teams as well as selections from republics, cities or sports societies took part in those sporting events. Bulgaria was visited in November 1955 by the freestyle wrestling RSFSR team, by the basketball Moscow selection in 1956, by Tbilissi Dinamo in October 1956, by the Odessa football team in 1957, by the Azerbaijan water polo team and by a selection of the best gymnasts from Ukraine in December 1957.[36]

Between 1948 and 1951, we have noticed that sports exchanges were concentrated in the few sports in which People's Democracies had the talent and a technical edge necessary to Soviet progression. During the 1950s, the range of disciplines practised during bilateral sports exchanges widened. Thus, between 1953 and 1958, Polish sportsmen trained or competed with Soviet shooters, weightlifters, cyclists, fencers, ice skaters, skiers, athletes, gymnasts and boxers, plus volleyball, football and ice hockey players.[37]

Common trainings with sportsmen from People's Democracies were organized to prepare for the Olympic Games. Ice skaters and skiers from the Soviet Union, Hungary, the GDR and Rumania were gathered in 1955.[38] Soviet figure skaters met their Hungarian, Polish and Czechoslovakian counterparts in January 1956 during a common training programme. In 1964, Soviet gymnasts were sent to the GDR from 1 to 29 February for a common month-long training programme. They trained with Germans six times a week, twice a day, three or four hours in the morning, one or two hours in the afternoon. Soviet trainers conducted common training.[39] In May 1964, Soviet wrestlers went to Bulgaria

---

36 GARF, f. R7576, o. 1, d. 979, l. 87; d. 1067, l. 103; d. 1094, l. 70; d. 1095, l. 41; d. 1101, l. 5; d. 1175, l. 76; d. 1171, l. 93, d. 1172, l. 6.
37 GARF, f. R7576, o. 1, d. 932, l. 213; d. 935, l. 55; d. 1041, l. 86; d. 1094, l. 88; d. 1100, l. 71; d. 1105, l. 1; d. 1093, l. 47; d. 1152, l. 113; d.1153, l. 26; d. 1156, l. 138; d. 1161, l. 158; d. 1163, l. 92; d. 1177, l. 41.
38 GARF, f. R7576, o. 1, d. 1068, l. 142.
39 GARF, f. R9570, o. 1, d. 1104, l. 29.

to compete and to train. During the major part of the programme, sportsmen, trainers and scientific workers shared methods and practices.⁴⁰

But relationships between Soviet athletes and sportsmen from People's Democracies were not as pacific and friendly as they might have been. While visiting countries from the Eastern bloc, Soviet sportsmen were perceived to be incarnations of a contemptible state. Consequently they were sometimes the victims of hostile reactions. Before their departure they were told that the states they would be visiting were young and less developed, with warm and fraternal relationships.⁴¹ Visiting People's Democracies, Soviet sportsmen could see the distortion between those narratives and everyday life, while they witnessed or while they were victims of manifestations of hostility. Thus, sporting events were also used in Socialist republics to express anti-Soviet feelings and slogans. It happened many times at the end of the 1950s and at the beginning of the 1960s in Hungary, Poland or Rumania.⁴² In 1954, during an international wrestling tournament, Hungarians supported their own wrestlers, even shouting anti-Soviet slogans. The report, written by a Soviet embassy official, which noted these outbursts was sent to Malenkov, Khrushchev, Vorošilov, Molotov, Bulganin, Kaganovič, Mikoân, Saburov, Pervuhin. It indicated that: 'Fortunately, Soviet wrestlers did not understand Hungarian language'.⁴³ In 1954, in Rumania, during the 4th World Youth Festival, Rumanians supported People's Democracies when Eastern European countries were opposed to the Soviet Union in sporting events.⁴⁴ In 1962, while Soviet table-tennis players were competing in Rumania, Rumanians applauded and supported their fellows, shouting, "Beat the Russians!".⁴⁵ These relations became more tense after the Hungarian and Polish crises in 1956. In October 1957, during a World Cup qualification match between Poland and the Soviet Union, Polish supporters insulted Soviet football players, throwing hostile slogans and projectiles at them.⁴⁶

Political tensions between the Soviet Union and People's Democracies even intruded on the pitch. In autumn 1955, during a game between the Hungarian and Soviet teams, the Magyars played a very offensive and impolite game and did not shake hands with their adversaries at the end of the game.⁴⁷ The best-

---

40 GARF, f. R9570, o. 1, d. 1104, l. 85.
41 Gorsuch. *All This is Your World*, 87–88.
42 Prozumenŝlkov. Sport as a Mirror, 53.
43 RGASPI, f. 5, o. 30, d. 81, l. 14–16.
44 RGASPI, f. 5, o. 30, d. 81, l. 50.
45 GARF, f. 9570, o. 1, d. 828, l. 34.
46 Prozumenŝlkov. Sport as a Mirror, 66.
47 Prozumenŝlkov. Sport as a Mirror, 60.

known example of strong opposition in a sporting event happened a few months later, at the Olympic Games in 1956 between Hungary and the USSR during the water polo tournament.

Conclusion

This article aims at understanding the new orientation of Soviet sports exchanges and their Europeanization during the beginning of the Cold War. One aspect is very clear. Between the end of the Second World War and the 1960s, sports exchanges increased and the Soviet Union increased sports delegations in Eastern and Western Europe, in various disciplines. The intensification of exchanges with European countries was a process that relied on traditions of contacts and evolving political links.

This is also a consequence of the Soviet Union's integration into international sports institutions (federations, the International Olympic Committee). USSR teams were now part of European and world championships and of the Olympic Games. But to perform well and to showcase Soviet successes and power, they needed more training, more competitions, more experience, thus more exchanges.

Table 2. Soviet sports delegations in European countries from 1946 to 1952

Year	Members of Soviet Sports delegations.	Albania	England	Austria	Belgium	Bulgaria	Denmark	England	Finland	France	Germany
1946	313	25	0	0	0	0	0	0	47	77	1
1947	286	1	16	0	0	0	0	16	49	27	3
1948	733	2	13	0	0	5	0	13	27	4	4
1949	318	2	0	0	0	10	0	0	12	6	2
1950	509	0	0	0	43	73	5	0	49	15	46
1951	890	29	2	21	0	29	4	2	53	82	–
1952	1242	0	0	14	4	25	0	0	791	26	–

Year	GDR	Netherlands	Hungary	Italia	Norway	Poland	Romania	Sweden	Switzerland	Czechoslovakia
1946	–	6	0	0	56	20	0	0	0	85
1947	–	4	29	0	28	35	0	26	0	68
1948	–	19	0	0	23	90	0	14	10	522
1949	–	4	207	0	17	0	4	7	0	51
1950	–	0	50	4	26	31	65	25	0	52
1951	379	0	24	12	8	43	170	0	23	69
1952	103	0	119	5	0	33	54	14	9	42

Sources:
GARF, f. R7576, o. 29, d. 17, l. 1–17; d. 29, l. 5; d. 42, l. 5; d. 56, l. 2; d. 74, l. 17; d. 91, l. 19; d. 116, l. 2.
GARF, f. R7576, o. 29, d. 17, l. 20–27; d. 29, l. 6–16; d. 42, l. 5–17; d. 56, l. 2–13; d. 74, l. 2–17; d. 91, l. 5–21; d. 116, l. 3–17.

Philippe Vonnard and Kevin Marston
Building bridges between separated Europeans:

The role of UEFA's competitions in East-West exchanges (1955–1964)

From the North, South, East and West of Europe, representatives of the Union of European Football Associations are gathered together here, in Lisbon, for the Congress of the Union and for the Congress of FIFA.[1]

Introduction

These words were pronounced by Ebbe Schwartz, president of UEFA (Union of European Football Associations), during his inaugural speech at the 1956 UEFA Congress held in Lisbon. The Dane highlighted that the representatives came "from the North, South, East and West of Europe". UEFA, the European body for football had been created two years prior and held its first general assembly in March 1955 in Vienna. In a certain sense, it was not all that surprising that a European organization in football was founded in this period. In fact, the context for this continental sporting movement was shaped by the development of European ideas in many different fields and by the creation of numerous European entities.

In fact, beyond the European integration process in the fields of economic relations (notably with the creation of the European Economic Community in 1957) and the wider political sphere (notably with the creation of the Council of Europe), Kiran Klaus Patel has rightly indicated that we must consider this process for the other fields.[2] Some authors have already made steps in this direction and have studied the exchanges, or the creation of organizations in the fields of culture,[3] infrastructure[4] or telecommunications.[5] One point of crucial

---

[1] Schwartz, Ebbe. Allocution du Président Schwartz à l'Assemblée Générale de l'UEFA tenue à Lisbonne. *Bulletin de l'UEFA* 2 (1956): 1.
[2] Patel, Kiran Klaus. Provincialising European Union: Co-operation and Integration in Europe in a Historical Perspective. *Contemporary European History* 22 (2013): 649–673.
[3] See notably: Fleury, Antoine and Lubor Jilek (eds.). *Une Europe malgré tout, 1945–1990*. Bruxelles: P.I.E. Peter Lang, 2009.

importance is the fact that at this time the European integration process generally concerned only the countries from the Western bloc. In fact, the confrontation between the United States and the Soviet Union impacted these efforts profoundly. If "we know now" that during all the period of the Cold War the two blocs did indeed maintain contacts and exchanges,[6] each bloc largely maintained its own separate organizations. Studying the integration of Europe means considering the Cold War in parallel because, as stressed by Piers Ludlow, the division of the European continent made it "impossible for any of the members of the Soviet bloc to consider or be considered for inclusion in the institutions of European co-operation".[7] Our argument here rests precisely on this point since UEFA was probably the sole European body that had countries from the two blocs as members since the crisis years of the Cold War.

Some authors have recounted football's unique situation under the umbrella of UEFA,[8] notably Jürgen Mittag who has posited that the confederation's congress was a unique platform for pan-European exchange between representatives from East and West especially in the Cold War years.[9] A common organization meant, of

---

[4] Badenoch, Alexander and Andreas Fickers (eds.). *Materializing Europe. Transnational Infrastructure and the Project of Europe*. Basingstoke: Palgrave Macmillan, 2010.

[5] See notably: Lévy, Marie-France and Marie-Noëlle Sicard (eds.). *Les lucarnes de l'Europe. Télévisions, cultures, identités, 1945–2000*. Paris: Publications de la Sorbonne, 2008; Laborie, Léonard. *L'Europe mise en réseaux. La France et la coopération internationale dans les postes et les télécommunications (années 1850–années 1950)*. Bruxelles: P.I.E. Peter Lang, 2010.

[6] On these East-West exchanges see notably: Hochscherf, Tobias, Laucht, Christopher and Andrew Plowman (eds.). *Divided, but not Disconnected: German Experiences of the Cold War*. New York, Berghahn Books, 2010; Romijn, Peter, Scott-Smith, Giles and Joes Segal (eds.). *Divided Dreamworlds? The Cultural Cold War in East and West*. Amsterdam: Amsterdam University Press, 2013; Bönker, Kirsten, Obertreis, Julia and Sven Gramp (eds.). *Television Beyond and Across the Iron Curtain*. Cambridge: Cambridge Scholars, 2016; Mikkonen, Simo and Pekka Suutari (eds.). *Music, Art and Diplomacy. East-West Cultural Interactions and the Cold War*. London: Routledge, 2016.

[7] Ludlow, N. Piers. European Integration and the Cold War. In *The Cambridge History of the Cold War*, Vol. 2, Melvyn Leffler and Odde Arne Westad (eds.), 179–197, 190. Cambridge: Cambridge University Press, 2010.

[8] Barcelo, Laurent. L'Europe des 52: L'Union Européenne de Football Association (UEFA). *Guerres mndiales et conflits contemporains* 228 (2007): 119–133; Maumon de Longevialle, Antoine. La Construction de l'Europe du football. Masters thesis, University of Strasbourg, 2009; Vonnard, Philippe and Grégory Quin. Did South America Foster European Football? Transnational Influences on the Continentalization of FIFA and the Creation of UEFA, 1926–1959, *Sport in Society* 20 (2016), 1424–1439.

[9] Mittag, Jürgen. Negotiating the Cold War? Perspectives in Memory Research on UEFA, the Early European Football Competitions and the European Nations Cups. In *European Football and Collective Memory*, Wolfram Pyta and Nils Havemann (eds.), 40–63. Basingstoke: Palgrave

course, common competitions, although competitions as such have not always been seen to be a favourable space for exchange. In their *longue durée* periodization of global football, Giulianotti and Robertson have argued that international matches served rather as "processes of 'relativization'" allowing nations to claim to be the best among as wide a range of competitors as possible.[10]

While the battle for the hierarchy of nations as seen through football results should not be downplayed entirely, we wish to advance the idea that the competitions themselves may also have had a role in rapprochement rather than solely being adversarial. Indeed, competitions were a bridge, a place of encounter and a forum for exchange in a divided postwar Europe. In this perspective, we focus on the launch and first developments of the European competitions organized by UEFA which coincided with some of the highest points of tension in the first decades of the Cold War. Thus, the aim of this paper is to underline that these tournaments probably gave UEFA a major, and still underestimated role in maintaining East-West connections during the height of the Cold War.

UEFA's competitions have been the object of limited discussion in the historiography of football, except for the case of the European Champion Clubs' Cup.[11] In this research, we highlight other competitions that were created by UEFA soon after the European Champion Clubs' Cup. The first one is the International Youth Tournament which was created in 1948 and taken over from FIFA (Fédération international de football association) by UEFA in 1956. The second is the European Cup of Nations (renamed European Championship in 1966 and now commonly called EURO). If Kevin Tallec Marston has already offered some perspectives about the International Youth Tournament[12] and some authors have focused

---

Macmillan, 2014; Mittag, Jürgen and Philippe Vonnard. The role of societal actors in shaping a pan-European consciousness. UEFA and the overcoming of Cold War tensions, 1954–1959. *Sport in history* (in press).

10 Giulianotti, Richard and Roland Robertson. *Globalization and Football*. London: Sage, 2009, here 19–20.

11 See notably: Vonnard, Philippe. *La genèse de la Coupe des clubs champions. Une histoire du football européen (1920–1960)*. Neuchâtel: CIES, 2012. For a summary see: Vonnard, Philippe. A Competition that Shook European Football! The Origins of the European Champion Clubs' Cup (1954–1955). *Sport in History* 34 (2014): 595–619.

12 Tallec Marston, Kevin. A Lost Legacy of Fraternity? The Case of European Youth Football. In *The Routledge Handbook of Sport and Legacy: Meeting the Challenge of Major Sport Events*, Richard Holt and Dino Ruta (eds.), 176–188. London: Routledge, 2015; Tallec Marston, Kevin. "Sincere Camaraderie": Professionalization, Politics and the Pursuit of the European Idea at the International Youth Tournament, 1948–57. In *Building Europe with the Ball. Turning Points in the Europeanization of Football, 1905–1999*, Philippe Vonnard, Grégory Quin and Nicolas Bancel (eds.), 137–161. Oxford: Peter Lang, 2016.

on the case of the European Championship,[13] these works did not really offer answers to one major question: how did these competitions help to engage more connections between increasingly divided European countries?

These competitions had three main effects on UEFA. Firstly, the competitions gave UEFA an organizational legitimacy with the creation of new committees and events. Secondly, it provided the confederation with new financial power to help to develop its activities as recent research has briefly shown in the case of European Champion Clubs' Cup.[14] Moreover, and this is the point that we emphasize particularly in this chapter, the competitions offered new opportunities to create links between UEFA members, and finally gave more reality to a truly European football sphere. In essence, we argue that these tournaments reinforced UEFA's position and gave the confederation an active role in pan-European rapprochement at a key and tense moment in political history.

To undertake this research we have used various new sources which came notably from the UEFA archives – still underexploited – (Minutes of the Congress, Executive Committee minutes and Special Commissions for the two competitions); the FIFA archives (notably the correspondence between UEFA and FIFA); personal archives (from Sir Stanley Rous); and national association archives (Belgium, France, England and Switzerland). To complete the studies a general reading of French newspapers *France football* and *L'Equipe* has been undertaken and one interview was also conducted with Pierre Delaunay, general secretary of UEFA from 1955 to 1959.

This chapter is divided into three parts and begins in 1955, when the European Champion Clubs' Cup was created and the year before UEFA took over the Youth Tournament, and ends in 1964, with the last playing of the European Cup of Nations before some major competition changes decided in 1966 as well as being the last year a country withdrew from the youth tournament due to the political context. Firstly, we briefly revisit the creation of UEFA and give information about the role of the European Champion Clubs' Cup in its first development. Secondly, we focus more specifically on the case of the International Youth Tournament and then on the European Cup for Nations.

---

[13] Schulze-Marmeling, Dietrich and Hubert Dahlkamp. *Die Geschichte der Fussball Europameisterschaft*, Göttingen: Verlag die Verkstatt, 2008. Notably pages 28–33. Mittag, Jürgen and Benjamin Legrand. Towards a Europeanization of Football? Historical Phases in the Evolution of the UEFA Football Championship. *Soccer & Society* 11 (2010): 709–722.

[14] Vonnard, Philippe. How did UEFA Govern the European Turning Point in Football? Reflexion Based on the Case of the Creation of European Champion Clubs' Cups and Inter-cities Fairs Cup. In *Building Europe with the Ball*, Vonnard, Quin and Bancel, 165–186.

UEFA: a pan-European organization across a divided Europe

UEFA was created in the middle of the 1950s at the same time as many other European organizations in the academic, cultural, economic, scientific and technical fields. Alan Tomlinson and John Sudgen have noted[15] that the creation of a European body has to be understood in regard to FIFA's reorganization[16] as decided during a FIFA Extraordinary Congress held in Paris in 1953. If the beginning of what historians have called an "integration process" probably played a role in the actions of European football leaders,[17] this agreement to "continentalize" FIFA helped answer the claims of South American football leaders who had argued since the interwar period for more recognition inside the organization.[18] Moreover, it was also a pragmatic decision due to the increase in FIFA's internationalization (more than 80 national football associations were now FIFA members) that brought some difficulties for administrative reasons.

The decision taken in Paris had a crucial implication for the European associations because article 17 of the new FIFA statutes, printed in February 1954, indicated that the executive committee of the international federation of football now had to be composed of members elected directly by continental bodies (except for the president).[19] Thus, this decision obliged Europe to create an organization. In the minds of FIFA's leaders, Europe's football territory was composed of about 30 countries.[20] This vision followed the geographical border determined for World Cup qualifications during the 1930s. Thus, countries from the Eastern and Western blocs had to be involved in the same body. Considering the Cold War context at the time, gathering all the European football associations togeth-

---

15 Sudgen, John and Alan Tomlinson. *FIFA and the Contest for World Football: Who Rules the Peoples' Game?* Cambridge: Polity Press, 1998.
16 Created in 1904, FIFA is composed of national football associations, one per country.
17 On this point see: Vonnard, Philippe. Œuvrer en faveur du football européen. Jalons biographiques sur les précurseurs de l'Uefa (1920–1950). In *L'Europe du football. Sociohistoire d'une construction européenne*, William Gasparini (ed.). Strasbourg: Presses universitaires de Strasbourg (in press).
18 Vonnard and Quin. Did South America Foster European Football?
19 Statutes of FIFA [1954 edition]. Fédération internationale de football association (FIFA) archives, folder: FIFA – Statutes 1904–1981.
20 Note préliminaire à l'examen des 124 propositions que le Congrès d'Helsinki a renvoyées devant la Commission de révisions des statuts et règlements de la FIFA, Nommée en 1950 au congrès de Rio de Janeiro, 19 December 1952. FIFA archives, box: Réorganisation 1950–1953, 2. Commission d'Etudes et Bureau (folder: séance Paris).

er under one roof was not simple. What the European football leaders sought was something totally innovative because no organization at this time with the name "European" crossed the Iron Curtain. Moreover, the Eastern Bloc associations were not in favour of the FIFA reform – they voted against it during the 1953 congress[21] – and the Soviet Union was barely involved in European football exchanges.[22] Indeed, both sides progressively organized themselves, the West with its Organization for European Economic Co-operation (OEEC) in 1948 and NATO the following year, while the East created the Council for Mutual Economic Assistance (Comecon) in 1949 and the Warsaw Pact in 1955.[23]

Here we do not delve into much detail about the creation of UEFA since some key elements of this have been treated elsewhere.[24] We do, however, wish to draw attention to several points about UEFA's foundation. After several months of discussion, on 15 June 1954, 25 European associations attended a conference in order to create a European body.

Most of the Soviet bloc members, especially the Soviet Union, were present at the meeting, which was held in Basel. There, the delegates present quickly accepted the creation of an organization and found a solution for the election of their representatives on FIFA's Executive Committee. They elected two experienced leaders in European football already members of FIFA's board as vice-presidents, the Swiss, Ernst Thommen, and the Dutchman, Karel Lotsy. They also decided to give the confederation a board, composed of members different from those representatives who had been elected to the board of the international federation. This point is important because it helped to create some autonomy for the organization vis-à-vis FIFA. Moreover, the leaders present did not vote but chose people who could be seen as a consensual selection; their chosen repre-

---

21 FIFA, General Assembly Minutes, 14 and 15 November 1953. FIFA archives, box: classeur 29th – 30th Congress, 1953–1959, Activity Report/Financial Report Minutes.

22 The USSR largely withdrew from international football between 1948 until 1952 when it did send a team to the Helsinki Olympic Games and returned to the scene in 1958, entering the World Cup for the first time. See Edelman, Robert. *Serious Fun: A History of Spectator Sport in the USSR*. New York: Oxford University Press, 1993, here 91–110.

23 Comecon was in a certain sense leading by the same idea as did the EEC for the Western countries. However, as Simon Godard has shown, the exchanges were not so easy and were dominated by the Soviet Union. See: Godard, Simon. Construire le bloc de l'Est par l'économie? La délicate émergence d'une solidarité internationale socialiste au sein du Conseil d'aide économique mutuelle. *Vingtième siècle* 109 (2011): 45–58. Concerning the Warsaw Pact, it was signed in 1955 after the recreation of an army for Western Germany. It incorporated all the Eastern bloc countries except Yugoslavia.

24 See: Vonnard, Philippe. Genèse du football européen. De la FIFA à l'UEFA (1930–1960). PhD, University of Lausanne, December 2016.

sentatives had taken an important part in the FIFA reorganization and represented different sectors of the regional football powers (the British, Latin, Scandinavian and Soviet areas) inside the European organization. The leaders chosen were (in alphabetical order): José Crahay (Belgium); Henry Delaunay (France); George Graham (Scotland); Joseph Gerö (Austria); Ebbe Schwartz (Denmark); and Gustav Sebes (Hungary). This process shows the strong will of European football leaders to mitigate the possible Cold War effects inside UEFA, a policy that continued in the following years and notably was emphasized by the leaders of the executive board in UEFA's official publications (annual report of general secretary and official bulletin of UEFA published from 1956). The choice of the president, the day after the congress, also revealed this trend.

In fact, the board nominated Ebbe Schwartz as president. The choice of the Danish leader was significant given the intention to create more unity inside UEFA. In fact, if Denmark was in a certain sense a member of Western Europe, for example, it was a founding member of NATO, it was part of what Jussi Hahnimäki has called the "Western neutral".[25] Given its absence from key organizations of the time such as the European Coal and Steel Community (ECSC), which the Danes never joined, and the European Economic Community, which it joined only in 1973, Denmark could be seen as a neutral country. Thus, electing a leader from this country was an opportunity for the delegates to show that they would not explicitly position themselves in either the Eastern or Western camp and preferred to follow the apolitical approach created by FIFA's football leaders during the interwar period.[26] Thus, in the summer of 1954, a European body – renamed UEFA in October 1954 – was created and began a new step in the development of football on a European geographic scale.

The organization went on to structure itself at the first General Assembly held in Vienna in March 1955. There, the delegates accepted the draft statutes presented. From this point onwards, the organization was able "to study all

---

[25] Hanhimäki, Jussi. Non-Aligned to What? European Neutrality and the Cold War. In *Neutrality and Neutralisme in the Global War. Between or Within the Blocs?* Sandra Bott, Jussi M. Hanhimaki, Janick Schaufelbuehl and Marco Wyss (eds.), 17–32. London: Routledge, 2015.

[26] Quin, Grégory. La reconstruction de la Fédération Internationale de Football Association (FIFA) après la Seconde Guerre mondiale (1944–1950). Jalons pour une histoire des relations sportives internationales. *STAPS* 106 (2014): 21–35. More generally about the apolitism of sport leaders see: Defrance, Jacques. La politique de l'apolitisme. Sur l'autonomisation du champ sportif. *Politix* 50 (2000): 13–27; Schotté, Manuel. La structuration du football professionnel européen. Les fondements sociaux de la prévalence de la "spécificité sportive". *Revue française de Socio-Economie* 13 (2014): 85–106.

the questions concerning the football in Europe".[27] Moreover, it was also imagined that in the near future it could organize a European tournament for nations. But these tasks were seen as secondary because the major activity of UEFA was to discuss the issues for the FIFA congress and eventually to arrive at some form of consensus about the congress agenda and specifically to discuss the question of European football with FIFA's board, as well as to elect the six European representatives (two vice-presidents and four members) on that board. At the end of the sessions, a project led by French journalists from *L'Equipe* for a European cup for clubs was presented.

The delegates decided not to support it following the recommendations of the Executive Board. But, some weeks later, UEFA's leadership returned to the question, because journalists and 15 clubs decided to create the competition and elaborated the first draft rules.[28] Finally, UEFA decided to take over the competition during the summer of 1955 because it jeopardized its still weak and nascent authority to let these private actors create this tournament.

The European Champion Clubs' Cup: a turning point for European football

Organizing the competition had a huge impact on UEFA in three ways. Firstly, this competition offered a new important task – to create and develop competitions – and, as a result, empowered UEFA with organizational legitimacy. In fact, at this moment of its nascent history, UEFA had still not yet been involved in this task. Although the first draft statutes included the idea to organize a European championship for nations, this project was refused by the first UEFA general assembly held in Vienna in March 1955.[29] In fact, the members of the Executive Committee (such as Henri Delaunay or José Crahay) who would later develop European competitions were a minority inside the Union. Thus, the takeover of the European cup changed this situation. After a first successful cup during the 1955–1956 season, a second competition was organized; more than 20 clubs took part and a special committee was created inside UEFA in 1956.

---

27 Statutes of UEFA, 1956 edition ["Goal"]. Union of European Football Associations (UEFA), box: Statutes of UEFA, 1954–1976 (RM00005779).
28 Vonnard. A Competition that Shook European Football!
29 UEFA, General Assembly Minutes, 2 March 1955. UEFA archives, box: Founding Congress, 1954. I-III. Ordinary Congress, 1955–1957 (RM0005986).

After the Executive Committee, it was the first permanent committee inside the continental body.

Secondly, the competition gave UEFA new financial possibilities. At the beginning, the Union had no budget. If the financial question began to be more important from the spring of 1955, the creation of European Champion Clubs' Cup was an obvious step forward since UEFA received a 1 per cent levy on the general receipts for each match and 5 per cent for the final.[30] This new financial support notably helped to sponsor youth football – especially within small associations – because from 1957 a special account was created and directly financed with money from the European Champion Clubs' Cup.[31]

In addition to these two effects on UEFA's structure, the tournament offered opportunities to create new links between the confederation's members. In fact, all the European countries were quickly involved in the tournament. When UEFA decided officially to take over the competition in June 1955, Bulgaria, Czechoslovakia and East Germany – countries that had not been initially invited by the journalists of *L'Equipe* – asked to be integrated in the tournament.[32] Moreover, the first competition – that knew a great public success (gathering an average of 25'000 spectators per games) – was a wonderful opportunity to create links between countries that were politically divided.

The quarter-final draw of the first competition presented a rather unlikely fixture between Real Madrid and Partizan Belgrade. In fact, the two countries had no diplomatic relations at that time, and the symbolic aspect of the game was clearly reinforced by the fact that these two clubs were the flagship football teams of their respective political regimes. After discussions between the two governments, UEFA and even French journalists at *L'Equipe* (the details of which have not yet been researched)[33] the two games (one in Madrid, one in Belgrade) were finally organized without problems (in front of 120'000 spectators in the Spanish capital and 60'000 in the Yugoslavian capital), at least according to the reports given in the articles written about the games in the French newspapers *L'Equipe* and *France*

---

30 EEEC Regulations 1956–1957. UEFA archives, box: Publication Department. European Champion Clubs' Cup. Règlements (RM00005391).
31 UEFA, General Assembly Minutes, 28 and 29 June 1957. UEFA archives, box: Founding Congress, 1954. I-III. Ordinary Congress, 1955–1957 (RM0005986).
32 Finally, due to the lack of time, UEFA did not accept this request but from the second Champions Clubs' Cup these countries were invited to send their national champions. Vonnard, How did UEFA Govern the European Turning Point in Football?
33 These games have never been studied. It would be very helpful to look in the Spanish and former-Yugoslavian archives to see if documents exist about this topic.

Football.³⁴ During the following Champions Clubs' Cup, other games between East and West were organized and offered UEFA a unique opportunity, namely to organize regular and official exchanges between the two blocs.

Table 1. East and West opposition during the European Champions Clubs' Cup (season 1955–1956/1963–1964)

Season	Round	Team 1 (East)	Team 2 (West)
1955-56	First (1/8)	Partizan Belgrade (Yug.)	Sporting Portugal (Por.)
1955-56	First (1/8)	Gwardia Warsaw (Pol.)	Djurgårdens IF (Swe.)
1955-56	First (1/8)	Voros Lobogos (Hung.)	Anderlecht (Bel.)
1955-56	Second (1/4)	Partizan Belgrade (Yug.)	Real Madrid (Spain)
1955-56	First (1/8)	Voros Lobogos (Hung.)	Stade de Reims (Fra.)
1963-64	First (1/16)	Honved Budapest (Hung.)	Athletic Bilbao (Spain.)
1963-64	First (1/16)	Gornil Zabrze (Pol.)	Austria Vienna (Aus)
1963-64	First (1/16)	Dukla Prag (Cze.)	Valetta (Malta)
1963-64	First (1/16)	Ferencvaros Budapest (Hung.)	Galatasaray Istanbul (Tur.)
1963-64	First (1/16)	Partizan Belgrade (Yug.)	Jeuness d'Esch (Lux.)
1963-64	First (1/16)	Spartak Polvdiv (Bulg.)	PSV Eindhoven (Neth.)
1963-64	First (1/16)	Dinamo Bucarest (Rum.)	Real Madrid (Spain)
1963-64	Third (1/4)	Partizan Belgrade (Yug.)	Inter Milan (Ita.)
1963-64	Third (1/4)	Dukla Prag (Cze.)	Borussia Dortmund (W.Ger)

In total, from 1955 to 1964, there were 50 East-West oppositions (a number that did not take into account the preliminary rounds) that involved more than 100 actual matches because the competition was played in two legs, at home and away. Undeniably, the competition created more links between East and West even if the sporting results were clearly in favour of Western countries – in the period studied here, no team from the Eastern bloc reached the final and only one played a semi-final (Vasas Budapest during the 1957–1958 season). Thus, the competition aspect prevented even more exchanges in the final, and undoubtedly most important rounds due to the weakness of the Eastern bloc clubs. An example of this new European unity in football through the tournament was symbolized by the aircraft crash that happened to the team of Manchester United in February 1958 after a game in Belgrade.³⁵

---

34 Notably in an article entitled, Le football a donné une leçon à l'ONU, quoted by Maumon de Longevialle in his Master thesis. Longevialle. La Construction de l'Europe du football. Also in the article, Quand Tito rime avec Franco. *France football*, 27 December 1955.
35 On this event see: Mellor, Gavin. "The Flowers of Manchester": The Munich Disaster and the Discursive Creation of Manchester United Football Club. *Soccer and Society* 5 (2004): 265–284.

As had happened with the Torino team ten years before,[36] this event shocked the European football sphere and many messages from all parts of Europe were sent to the English club and national associations. In this sense, this dramatic event could perhaps give other insights into what scholars like Michael Groll have advanced in calling this tournament a European site of memory.[37]

Of course the Cold War effect was not absent from these confrontations since football – like sport in general – was clearly a tool for the state in this period where all societal areas were engaged in an ideological battle.[38] Moreover, some problems arose with the difficulties of travel or with the delivery of visas. That is why, in the beginning of the 1960s UEFA's board decided to create geographical groups for the preliminary and first rounds and to do the draw accordingly – in addition, this decision also had the benefit of limiting travel costs for clubs.

Although they had some problems, the tournament was played each year on a regular basis. Thus, it offered UEFA the opportunity to be an actor in the creation of more links between European football associations. These aspects were reinforced in 1961 with the creation of what journalists called the "little sister" of the European Champions' Club Cup: the European Cup Winners' Cup. However, these two competitions remained tournaments between clubs from cities and the national prestige at stake was not the same as for national teams. Once UEFA took on a national team tournament a few years later, notably at youth and senior level, national prestige took centre stage. Together, these competitions were where football preceded some other areas (politics, economics and even culture) in creating European interaction between East and West. Two national team competitions furthered these links, even if not always without difficulty, beginning with the International Youth Tournament and then the European Cup of nations.

The International Youth Tournament: bridging tensions across Europe through youth football

The second tournament organized by UEFA was a youth national team event and it contributed to UEFA's growth as an autonomous confederation and also to its role

---

[36] Dietschy, Paul. The Superga Disaster and the Death of the "Great Torino". *Soccer and Society* 5 (2004): 298–310.
[37] Groll, Michael. UEFA Football Competition as European Site of Memory – Cups of Identity. In *European Football and Collective Memory*, Pyta and Havemann, 63–84.
[38] Shaw, Tony. The Politics of Cold War Culture. *Journal of Cold War Studies* 3 (2001): 59–76.

in bridging across Europe during the height of the Cold War. Encapsulated in his address to the 1958 youth event's participants, UEFA president Ebbe Schwartz exhorted the "magnificent example of what football can do for the bringing together of peoples".[39] Indeed, the first ever International Youth Tournament in 1948 was largely the brainchild of Englishman Sir Stanley Rous and the early years were anchored in a hope of postwar universal peace personified in the "fraternal spirit" of the leaders of the day, as has been argued elsewhere.[40] Originated by FIFA in 1949, the event had grown in stature by the time UEFA was charged with its organization in 1956. Over the period 1956 to 1964, the committee responsible included Rous, Frenchman Louis Pelletier, Josef Vogl from Czechoslovakia, Karl Zimmermann from West Germany, the aforementioned José Crahay, Benito Pico from Spain and Lo Brunt from Denmark. The establishment of this committee continued the organizational development of UEFA because it was the third one to be created in the organization's history.

It went from a modest participant-focused event of no more than eight teams over a two-day Easter weekend to a significant 16-team (or more) event played over almost a full week and drawing large crowds. The FIFA Executive Committee responsible for the event balanced the forces of competition and commercialization with aims of fraternal exchange through sport. By 1952 Rous was arguing that "it seems that each federation seeks above all to make money" from the event, a comment which resulted in steering the committee to lower the age limit back to 18 for future tournaments in hopes of curbing excessive competition.[41] Karel Lotsy, another FIFA Executive Committee member and longtime supporter of the tournament, recalled the 70,000 crowd at the 1954 final and lamented the change in his report.[42] The growth of the event did, however, offer opportunities to include more countries and not just those from the initial Western associations. Yugoslavia and Hungary joined in several tournaments prior to 1954 when East Germany first sent a team, and the 1955 event in Italy was attended by a number of other Comecon countries (Bulgaria, Poland, Rumania, Czechoslovakia); the USSR, however, did not send a team until 1962. So by the

---

39 Freely translated from French. Allocution du Président Ebbe Schwartz avant la finale du Tournoi international des juniors. *UEFA Bulletin* 8 (1958): 1.
40 Tallec Marston. "Sincere Camaraderie".
41 The French and English versions of the minutes present minor differences in tone. The English version makes no mention of the money-making objective. FIFA, Executive Committee Minutes, 9–10 March 1952. FIFA archives, box: Executive Commitee Meeting, Agenda Minutes, 1951–1952.
42 FIFA, Comments on Agenda of the Executive Committee Minutes, 18 November 1954. FIFA archives, box: Executive Committee Meeting, Agenda Minutes, 1953–1954.

time the tournament came to UEFA in 1957, it had become an important event in terms of organization, resources and an inclusive forum creating links between countries on both sides of the Cold War divide. It was not immune to some problems, however.

Despite growing political tensions towards the end of the 1950s, there had been almost no issues with youth players travelling across Europe to attend the tournament. Teams from Eastern countries had travelled to Italy in 1955 – several weeks prior to the Warsaw Pact's signing – to Spain in 1957 and Luxembourg in 1958. Equally, teams from NATO countries in the West played in Hungary in 1956 and Bulgaria in 1959. It was at the UEFA Youth Tournament that East and West Germany played their first official football match in 1960 in Austria, four years before their respective Olympic sides met and 14 years before the 1974 World Cup encounter.[43] The choices for hosting the tournament and the presence of teams were a strong message through football for links across Europe no matter the political ideology. In fact, during the five first years under UEFA's supervision two tournaments were played in Eastern countries. The organization of a "European" event in the communist bloc in this era was still an exception. Moreover, the tournament was also the opportunity for little national associations in UEFA – like Luxembourg and Bulgaria – to organize an important football event and to be actors inside the body. In this regard, the tournament appears to have contributed to the pan-European policy developed by the Executive Board of UEFA since its beginning. Nevertheless, international policy could sometimes be stopped or limited, for example during the crises in Berlin between 1958 and 1961, which reinforced a dilemma in which the city both "symbolised the Cold War division" while remaining "a beacon of hope for German reunification".[44]

The situation between 1960 and 1964 became more complex for football due to the Hallstein Doctrine and NATO's non-recognition of the German Democratic Republic which required countries to recognize West Germany as the sole German state or risk breaking relations with the Federal Republic. The political situation had an impact not only on football exchanges; it created various diplomatic incidents in international sporting relations because it was obviously contradictory to the football world which had to deal with two FIFA-recognized German associations. For example, delegations were asked to provide national flags at the UEFA youth tourney, but showing state symbols was generally limited since the

---

[43] UEFA. *Les 25 ans du Tournoi des Juniors de l'UEFA*. Bern: UEFA, 1973, 230.
[44] Gearson, John. Origins of the Berlin Crisis of 1958–62. In *The Berlin Wall Crisis: Perspectives on Cold War Alliances*, John Gearson and Kori Schake (eds.), 10–21, here 18. New York: Palgrave Macmillan, 2002.

confederation actively worked to minimize overt nationalism. However, the issue came to a head at the 1960 event – in which both Germanys were drawn in the same group – the tension forced the point to be raised at FIFA's Executive Committee during the planning before the tournament.[45] UEFA's youth committee, through the pragmatic leadership of its chair Rous, avoided a "flag war"[46] of the kind that was indeed witnessed at full senior level at the following year's ice hockey world championships as recounted by Heather Dichter.[47]

The effects of the Hallstein doctrine were far reaching and caused all sorts of problems for travel to and from the Youth Tournament. For any travel all East Germans were required to obtain "temporary travel documents" or TTDs from the Allied Travel Office (ATO) based in Berlin; only then could they apply for a visa from the respective NATO country since no East German travel document would be officially recognized.[48] In the midst of the Berlin Crisis towards the autumn of 1960, the ATO suspended issuing TTDs except for specific cases. This had a direct and unfortunate impact on the organization of the 1961 UEFA Youth Tournament in Portugal. In December 1960 at the Junior Committee meeting, the Portuguese representatives indicated it would be "unlikely for Eastern Germany to get the necessary visas" because of Portugal's NATO membership.[49] This caused the committee to have Hans Bangerter, UEFA general secretary since January that year, write and advise the East German federation to apply for visas immediately. Interestingly, the UEFA Junior Committee minutes in late March the following year mentioned that the restrictions on TTDs had been lifted at the start of the month in part thanks to the efforts of Rous and UEFA Executive Committee members, West German Dr Peco Bauwens and Dane Lo Brunt, although it is unknown to what extent they actually influenced the matter. Despite the good news, the Portuguese authorities were "exceedingly slow in issuing the necessary visas" for both the DDR and Yugoslavia ultimately causing the Yugoslavian

---

45 FIFA, Executive Committee Minutes, Sir Stanley Rous collection, UEFA Junior Committee Minutes, 10 March 1960, Folder Executive Committee Minutes 1958–1964.
46 UEFA, Junior Committee Minutes, 15 April 1960, Sir Stanley Rous collection, Folder International Youth Committee Minutes 1957–1961.
47 Dichter, Heather. "A Game of Political Ice Hockey". NATO Restrictions on East German Sport Travel in the Aftermath of the Berlin Wall. In *Diplomatic Games. Sport, Statecraft, and International Relations since 1945*, Heather Dichter and Andrew John (eds.), 19–51. Lexington: University Press of Kentucky, 2014.
48 Turack, Daniel. Selected Aspects of International and Municipal Law Concerning Passports. *William and Mary Law Review* 12 (1971): 805–837, here 827.
49 UEFA, Junior Committee Minutes, 28–29 December 1960. Sir Stanley Rous collection (SRC), box: Folder International Youth Committee Minutes 1957–1961.

team to withdraw followed shortly thereafter by East Germany (in solidarity with Yugoslavia) and Hungary (for "technical reasons").[50]

The Portuguese organizers and UEFA stressed the significant loss in gate revenue and went as far as sending a harsh communiqué to the three withdrawing associations holding them responsible for one-third of the loss of gate receipts.[51] The interesting point here is that the sole voice against the financial sanctions was journalist and Czech representative, Josef Vogl, the only Eastern European member of the UEFA Junior Committee at the time.[52] It is impossible to discern the individual motivations of each committee member, but it is hard to imagine them being entirely partial given their support for the reimbursement of the last-minute expenses for a charter to bring another Eastern team – the Rumanians – to Lisbon for the tournament.[53]

Similarly, the choice for the 1962 host country was made just weeks following the events of Operation Rose which began to close the borders separating the two sides of Berlin on the night of 12–13 August. In this tense political climate, a UEFA Junior Committee composed of a majority of Western Europeans opted for Eastern European Rumania as host for 1962 over Spain – provided they could guarantee visas for all participants. It could be interpreted as a strong symbolic gesture by UEFA to maintain an open hand towards the East but also advancing its vision of an apolitical and unrestricted Europe in which youth tournament hosts would be chosen only if they "engage themselves to ensure free entry to all the participants into their country and where no restriction whatsoever exists".[54]

Despite UEFA's attempts to solve political issues, the travel problems did not go away. After not obtaining visas for the 1963 tournament in England, things appeared glum once again for the East German Federation which looked ready to withdraw again for the 1964 event in Holland. Once more, the members of the UEFA Junior Committee worked to find a solution and efforts were made at the Foreign Office in London and with the Dutch Ministry of Foreign Affairs. After he spent a day pleading the East German case in London, Rous wrote to

---

50 UEFA, Junior Committee Minutes, 28 March 1961. UEFA archives, box: Youth Committee, 1960–1971, meetings (RM00009008).
51 UEFA, Communication to the Football Associations of Yugoslavia, Hungary, Eastern Germany, 4 April 1961. SRC, box: Folder International Youth Committee Minutes 1957–1961.
52 UEFA, Junior Committee Minutes, 5 April 1961. SRC, box: Folder International Youth Committee Minutes 1957–1961.
53 UEFA, Junior Committee Minutes, 31 August 1961. SRC, box: Folder International Youth Committee Minutes 1957–1961.
54 UEFA, Junior Committee Minutes, 31 August 1961. SRC, box: Folder International Youth Committee Minutes 1957–1961.

Committee Chair, the Dane Lo Brunt, asking for news and noting that the Foreign Office hinted at a possible change to the ATO regulations "in the foreseeable future but they fear not in time for the Youth Tournament".[55] On the same day UEFA president Gustav Wiederkehr – elected in 1962 – and General Secretary Hans Bangerter co-wrote to the Dutch government again lobbying for travel authorization so that the East Germans could participate in "friendly rivalry, on the football fields of your country".[56] An official reply came via the Dutch embassy in Bern once again illustrating the impossible situation. Just as the Dutch Ministry of Foreign Affairs had already told Brunt, the embassy in Bern explained that unless the East German youth had TTDs issued by the ATO in Berlin they could not be granted visas.[57]

As expected the East German delegation were unable to obtain TTDs and withdrew for the third time in four years. Despite a record 23 European teams, the absence of the East German youngsters was a source of disappointment. The UEFA Junior Committee sent a telegram to the Dutch Foreign Office regretting the situation:

This refusal is all the more regrettable as one of the main aims of UEFA is to promote international friendship and understanding among people – It is also against the spirit of sport – The official representative of the world Federation (FIFA) to the Tournament present in Amsterdam joins us in expressing the hope that you take the matter up again.[58]

The 1964 event was the last time there were significant issues for teams withdrawing because of political reasons. Over the period 1957–1964 at the Youth Tournament, UEFA weathered a number of political storms and ensured, albeit not always perfectly, connections across the East-West divide. At times, UEFA went as far as taking the moral high ground in order to pursue its own aims at bridging the political divides in Europe through football.

By 1964, with its increased autonomy and responsibility – the confederation organized courses for trainers, referees and coaches along with running many competitions – UEFA was a stronger entity and its leaders endeavoured to play

---

55 Rous, Stanley, Letter to Lo Brunt, 27 February 1964. SRC, box: Folder International Youth Committee Minutes 1957–1961.
56 UEFA, Letter to the Dutch Ministry of Foreign Affairs, 27 February 1964. SRC, box: Folder International Youth Committee Minutes 1957–1961.
57 Royal Netherlands Embassy, Letter to UEFA, 11 March 1964. SRC, box: Folder International Youth Committee Minutes 1957–1961.
58 Report of the UEFA Youth Tournament in Holland 1964. FIFA, Emergency Committee Agenda, 19 June 1964. FIFA Archives, box: Emergency Committee Meeting, Agenda Minutes, 1961–1964.

an active role at the international level by engaging directly with governments on the topic of youth football, a priori not a key issue for the state but with a rhetoric that surpassed the activity itself and echoed a vision of an apolitical and united Europe. In this sense, we could consider that from this period onwards, the Union began to be a veritable actor in international relations following the example – albeit certainly not in the same way and with less power – of the International Olympic Committee (IOC) studied in particular by Gabriel Bernasconi.[59] Another notable competition which served as a forum for UEFA's active role in East-West exchanges was the European Cup for nations.

A crucial step in European exchanges: graduating from youth to senior and the creation of European Cup for nations

The idea of a European Cup for nations had existed since the interwar period[60] and was present in the first draft of the European body's statutes.[61] A study commission was created in October 1955 to develop a project. However, it suffered from the limited interest of the national federations and was finally refused by the delegates at the UEFA Congress both in 1955 and 1956. The arguments against the idea were that UEFA did not have strength enough to organize this kind of tournament and that such an event might compete with the FIFA World Cup. However, around 1957, a change was in the air.

In fact, the success of the European Champion Clubs' Cup and the take over of the International Youth Tournament put UEFA clearly on the road to organize a senior national team European tournament. Inside the Executive Committee, the idea benefited from a strong supporter. First, the new General Secretary, Pierre Delaunay saw the creation of this competition as a personal affair – he wanted to create it in honour of the first promoter of the project, his father Henry Delaunay, who had died in 1955.[62] Secondly, UEFA president Ebbe

---

[59] Bernasconi, Gabriel. De l'Universalisme au transnational: le Comité international olympique, acteur atypique des relations internationales. *Bulletin de l'Institut Pierre Renouvin* 31 (2010): 151–159.
[60] Quin, Grégory. La Coupe de l'Europe Centrale (1927–1938), une compétition internationale oubliée? *Stadion. Revue Internationale d'Histoire du Sport* 37 (2013): 285–304.
[61] We found this document in the German national archives. Bundesarchives (BDA), box. DY 12 Deutscher Turn und Sportbund (DTSB) (folder: 2.081 Zusammenarbeit mit der FIFA).
[62] Interview with Pierre Delaunay, 18 September 2012.

Schwartz thought that the competition could be a good tool to create more connections between UEFA's members. But major European countries were still against the project, like England, Italy and Germany which argued that this new tournament would disrupt the preparations for the World Cup and hinder the formation of new teams during the period between World Cups. Additionally, they did not want to give up on friendly matches, as these were a lucrative source of income for the national associations.

To answer the critics, the special commission that had studied the project since 1955 developed a new system for a single tournament played over two years with a short final stage, although this met renewed and heavy scepticism. New discussions happened during the 1957 UEFA Congress held in Copenhagen. There, the strong opposition of important leaders like Ottorino Barassi (Italy), Stanley Rous (England) or Ernst Thommen (Switzerland) obliged the Executive Committee to work on the project again.[63] Nevertheless, other countries showed their wish for the competition and the delegates decided to create the tournament at the next UEFA Congress in 1958 with above 16 countries registered.[64] It is interesting to note that on this point, Spain and countries from the Eastern bloc were agreed on this question. We could hypothesize that these positions revealed how these governments used football,[65] notably because they were not party to many other areas of the European integration process and sport.

The creation of this tournament was important for UEFA because it offered the body a new important task which further reinforced its legitimacy. Some months later, UEFA's executive members took a decision to gain more autonomy from FIFA. They decided to remove the name of FIFA which still existed on UEFA's statutes,[66] to create UEFA's own administrative headquarters and finally to hire a permanent secretary.[67] At the end of the 1950s, UEFA could be consid-

---

[63] UEFA, General Assembly Minutes, 28 and 29 June 1957. UEFA archives, box: Founding Congress, 1954. I-III. Ordinary Congress, 1955–1957 (RM0005986).

[64] UEFA, General Assembly Minutes, 4 June 1958. UEFA archives, box: IV Ordinary Congress, 1958. I Extraordinary Congress, 1959 (RM0005987).

[65] For Spain see: Simon, Juan Antonio. La diplomacia del Balón. Deporte y relaciones internacionales durante el franquismo. *História e Cultura* 4 (2012): 165–189. For the case of the Soviet Union, to our knowledge it seems that there is not an effective study of this point. Some information can be found in: Veth, Manuel. La Sbornaya, de l'URSS à la Russie de Poutine. In *Le football des nations. Des terrains de jeu aux communautés imaginées*. Fabien Archambault, Stéphane Beaud and William Gasparini (eds.), 121–131. Paris: Publications de la Sorbonne, 2016.

[66] UEFA, Executive Committee Minutes, 28 October 1958. UEFA archives, box: ExCo meetings, 1954–1959 (RM00000749) folder: 1958.10.28.

[67] UEFA, Extraordinary General Assembly Minutes, 11 December 1959. UEFA archives, Box: Extraordinary Assembly held in Paris, November 1959 (RM0005986).

ered as an independent established organization. The creation of this tournament was not only an important task for UEFA but it also gave a new opportunity to boost exchanges between the European national associations.

Table 2. Games during the First European Cup for Nations (1958–1960)

Round	Countries	Countries	Games between same countries before 1948*	Games between same countries after 1952*
Preliminary round	Ireland	Czechoslovakia	1	0
First (1/8)	Soviet Union	Hungary	0	4
First (1/8)	Poland	Spain	0	0
First (1/8)	Rumania	Turkey	4	1
First (1/8)	Denmark	Czechoslovakia	0	3
First (1/8)	France	Greece	0	0
First (1/8)	Norway	Austria	0	1
First (1/8)	Eastern Germany	Portugal	0	0
First (1/8)	Yugoslavia	Bulgaria	2	0
Second (1/4)	Soviet Union	Spain	0	0
Second (1/4)	Rumania	Czechoslovakia	7	6
Second (1/4)	France	Austria	5	6
Second (1/4)	Portugal	Yugoslavia	2	0
Third (1/2)	Soviet Union	Czechoslovakia	0	2
Third (1/2)	Yugoslavia	France	5	8
Third place	Czechoslovakia	France	10	1
Final	Soviet Union	Yugoslavia	0	3

This table illustrates international matches played before 1948 and after 1952 once the division of Europe was confirmed. Football, of course, mirrored society and no international matches between East and West occurred between 1948 to 1952 (except for Italy-Yugoslavia but it was the only match and Yugoslavia could be considered as somewhat of an "insider-outsider"). The table shows us that the first European Cup offered a fixture opposing Spain and Poland. It was the first game in the history of football between these two countries, at this time politically divided. The same observation could be made for the match between East Germany and Portugal. Moreover, it was only the second time that Czechoslovakia played against Ireland and Austria played against Norway. Thus, despite the context of the Cold War after 1952, under UEFA's umbrella, new relationships in football were created during the second part of the 1950s. Moreover, we can also observe that this tournament recreated former links. For example, in the game for third place, France faced Czechoslovakia. Though the two countries had played five times during the 1930s, a situation that mirrored the close relationship that existed between the two countries,[68] they did not play any matches from 1948 until this third-place game, principally due to the Cold War. The participation in this tournament impacted the exchanges between national associations. At the same time, other countries that did not participate in the competition went on to play against their "traditional" opponents. For example, Switzerland played against Germany, Italy against Hungary, and Sweden was England's opponent. As with other UEFA competitions, the tournament was also coloured by the Cold War.

In fact, during the quarter-final, Spain met the Soviet Union. UEFA's board members felt that the match could pose some difficulties and they decided that president Schwartz would be present for the first game in Moscow as a sign of the unity of the European continent. But the Spanish refused to travel to the Soviet Union for the match. Despite the attempts at negotiation by UEFA's leaders, the game was finally cancelled. In a policy of compromise, UEFA gave a financial penalty to Spain – because this country did not want to play – and encouraged the organizing of a friendly game between the two countries to show that sport could surpass the political difficulties.[69]

The second European Cup for nations beginning in 1962 saw the majority of European countries decide to take part in the tournament. Thus, it created even more new connections between UEFA's members and started to minimize the friendly games that were up to then the most important events for European national teams save the games for World Cup qualification. For the first time, Bulgaria played against Portugal, Spain met Rumania and Poland faced Northern Ireland. Thus, three games between Eastern and Western blocs were organized just months after the building of the Berlin Wall began. The final game of the 1962 tournament revealed the new paradigm quite well.

This match in Madrid once again opposed Spain and the Soviet Union. Certainly, the progressive change in the foreign policy of Francoism, revealed by the first travel of Real Madrid to Moscow for a game in European inter-cities basketball competitions in 1962,[70] helped this situation. But, we could argue that the continued action by UEFA aiming to create regular connections between European countries also played a role in this shift.

---

68 On French-Czech relations see notably: Hnilica, Jiri. *Les nouvelles élites tchécoslovaques. Une formation française (1900–1950)*. Paris: Institut d'études slaves, 2015.
69 UEFA, Executif Committee Minutes, 3 October 1962. UEFA archives, box: ExCo meeting, 3 October 1962 (RM00000754); see also the paper of Juan Antonio Simon in this volume.
70 Simon, Juan Antonio. L'homme de l'ombre. Raimundo Sapporta et le basket espagnol et européen. In *Le continent basket. L'Europe et le basket-ball au XXe siècle*, Fabien Archambault, Loïc Artiaga and Gérard Bosc (eds.), 215–231. Bruxelles: Peter Lang, 2015.

Conclusion

While these two competitions were important for UEFA, reinforcing its structure and legitimacy as an independent sporting organization, they are examples of how the confederation created links between European associations across the East-West divide during the complex years of the Cold War. Some of these links were in the organization of matches and tournaments for which individuals from otherwise politically opposed countries met and even collaborated within UEFA committees. Not all the bridging attempts were successful as the trials of Eastern Europeans seeking travel documents demonstrates. However, the fact remains that through its competitions, UEFA provided a forum for exchanges and meeting for ideologically opposed countries. And when UEFA's efforts were unsuccessful, it conceded while still taking the moral high ground.

We have argued here that sporting competitions during the late 1950s and early 60s did not only serve as places to establish a hierarchy of nations but also as a rare meeting place between regimes and ideologies often diametrically opposed. As a result, this research has also forced us to consider further avenues to explore. Indeed, in comparison with other areas of culture where European exchanges at this time can be studied, such as music, football seems to be at the forefront. In addition, the organization of football competitions provided the platform for exchanges between individuals and the creation of networks of administrators who met regularly to plan, at times to argue, and to organize these tournaments.

Moreover, these competitions were also largely covered by both specialised and generalist newspapers (in Eastern and Western bloc). In the meantime, the tournaments were about to be broadcasted by radio and also by television, media that saw a great development during the 1950s and 1960s in Europe.[71] If football leaders were reluctant to embrace the television coverage of the games because they thought that it could have an impact on match attendance, discussions nevertheless took place between the European Broadcasting Union (EBU) and UEFA from 1956.[72] In fact, EBU wanted to broadcast European Champions' Cup

---

[71] On the development of television in Europe, see: Bignell, Jonathan and Andreas Fickers. *A European Television History*. Malden: Wiley-Blackwell.

[72] For some ideas about these connections see: Mittag, Jürgen and Jörg-Uwe Nieland. Auf der Suche nach Gesamteuropa: UEFA und EBU als Impulsgeber der Europäisierung des Sports. In *Freunde oder Feinde? Sportberichterstattung in Ost und West während des Kalten Kriegs*, Christoph Bertling and Evelyne Mertin (eds.), 208–229. Gütersloh: Medienfabrik Gütersloh, 2013.

games on its network of programme exchanges, Eurovision, created in 1954.[73] Thus, the tournament also allowed UEFA to show itself as the representative of European football vis-à-vis other European organizations. After five years of discussion and some preliminary tests (the first whole final to be showed in France was watched by two million of people), some games of the 1960 cup[74] were broadcast live and one year later a first contract was signed between the two organizations.[75] The 1963 final was followed by 16 million of people from different European countries.[76] From the beginning of the 1960's, the broadcast of national team games (and particularly the European cup of nations) became more and more popular, and some years laters, a new contract between UEFA and the International Broadcasting Union (IBU) was also signed. Thus, European citizens – through Eurovision network for the West and Intervision for the East – could sometimes 'meet' the other bloc through football from their sofas!

Looking first at the sport-culture parallel, the Eurovision Song Contest was founded about the same time, in 1956 in Lugano with seven countries and was essentially exclusively Western European until the merger of the Eastern broadcasting alliance IBU with EBU in 1993.[77] If some exchanges existed between the two organizations from the 1960s onwards,[78] the most popular event on the Eurovision network was not open to Eastern bloc countries except Yugoslavia – the only socialist state to shun IBU and participate in Eurovision beginning in 1961 due to the country's unique geopolitical position. Eastern European countries had their own competition – the Sopot International Song Festival – held

---

[73] About the creation of Eurovision: Fickers Andreas, The Birth of Eurovision. Transnational television as a challenge for Europe and contemporary media historiography. In *Transnational Television History. A Comparative Approach*, Andreas Fickers and Claire Johnson (eds.), 13–32. London: Routledge, 2012.

[74] En direct de Glasgow. Finale de la Coupe d'Europe. Di Stéfano, phénomène du football, est aussi un monstre d'égoïsme, *Tele-Magazine*, no. 238, 15–21 May, 1960.

[75] Bangerter, Hans. Rapport sur la deuxième Conférence des secrétaires généraux des 9/10 septembre 1965 à Hambourg, septembre 1965. Archives de l'UEFA, RM00010067: rapport conférence secrétaire généraux, 8–9.

[76] Vonnard, Philippe. A "European space of discussions"? UEFA-EBU interconnexions (1950's-1960's). Paper presented at the Congress: Competing Visions: European integration beyond the EC/EU, Helsinki, october 2017.

[77] Bolin, Göran. Visions of Europe: Cultural Technologies of Nation-states. *International Journal of Cultural Studies* 9 (2006), 189–206, here 194.

[78] Heinrich Franke, Christian. Curtains in the European Ether: Broadcasting and the Cold War. In *Airy Curtains in the European Ether: Broadcasting and the Cold War*, Alexander Badenoch, Andreas Fickers and Heinrich-Franke Christian (eds.), 183–219. Baden-Baden: Nomos, 2013.

in Poland from 1961.[79] The musical *clivage* between Eastern and Western Europe was reflected in this division of two parallel competitions, a stark contrast with football with its singular organization and unified competitive structure. While Raykoff has argued that the Eurovision contest "reflected the political zeitgeist of Europe", both anticipating certain developments and being behind the times, when juxtaposed with football, it would appear that music certainly took longer to bridge across Cold War Europe especially during the key early years.[80] To wit, the UEFA Youth Tournament included almost all Eastern countries as early as 1955 with the USSR finally joining in 1962 while the UEFA European Nations Cup counted 17 nations in the inaugural 1960 tournament and qualifying rounds. At a similar stage in 1961, the Eurovision song contest included 16 members but without any Eastern European representation – save Yugoslavia – until 1993; even Morocco participated in 1980. It would appear then that football bridged East and West more than other areas of culture. Was this because of an organized structure under a unified continental federation, something which music or ballet, for example, never benefited from?

The second avenue is that of the role of individual exchanges and networks. The competitions brought together athletes of course, but equally delegations of officials and administrators who corresponded, met and collaborated to organize the tournament. Just as there were opportunities in the Cold War for "kitchen debates" where ideological wars could be fought over apparently innocuous discussions over televisions and kitchen appliances, football also provided a space for regular interaction and exchange across the East-West divide.[81] For example, the UEFA Youth Committee which included mainly Western members from England, France, West Germany, Belgium, Denmark, as well as Spain and Czechoslovakia, had to work with host countries Hungary, Bulgaria and Rumania between 1956 and 1964 when the committee was renewed with members from Czechoslovakia, Yugoslavia, West Germany, Denmark and England. How

---

[79] Vuletic, Dean. Popular Culture. In *The Oxford Handbook of the History of Communism*, Stephen A. Smith (ed.), 571–584, here 575. Oxford: Oxford University Press, 2014.
[80] Raykoff, Ivan. Camping on the Borders of Europe. In *A Song for Europe: Popular Music and Politics in the Eurovision Song Contest*, Ivan Raykoff and Robert Deam Tobin (eds.), 1–13. Aldershot: Ashgate Publishing, 2007.
[81] For a discussion of the economic competition between Western capitalism and Eastern state socialism and a contextualization of the famous 1959 "kitchen debate" between Richard Nixon and Nikita Kruschchev, see Maier, Charles. The World Economy and the Cold War in the Middle of the Twentieth Century. In Leffler and Westad (eds.). *The Cambridge History of the Cold War*, Vol. 1, 44–66.

did these individual exchanges take place and what kind of relationships were created and nurtured over time?

We need to pursue more research into football exchanges in Europe during the Cold War, and on sport more generally, because these numerous and regular links may have played an as yet underestimated role in the fall of communism. In this connection, research must give particular consideration to both perspectives exploring primary sources from both sides since, as Jenifer Parks argues, these exchanges were not unidirectional. Parks explains the case of Soviet sport administrators during these key years around the Berlin crisis who used the Olympic arena to advance a "democratic" agenda against the Western and "Anglo-American" bloc which ultimately did – despite a failed overall reform proposal in 1961 – have some effect on the IOC's future expansion towards greater geographical representation.[82] Sport has often anticipated political changes in international relations and since football was largely led by Western capitalistic countries even under a pan-European UEFA, the participation of Eastern countries in these competitions was, in a certain sense, already an acceptance of this system and a finally "soft" preparation for the major changes two decades later through Gorbachev's glasnost policy reform and resulting perestroika.

Through regularity and popular success UEFA's tournaments offered a unique, and at times astonishing, meeting point for European countries during the Cold War, even if not without its own problems of nationalism or travel difficulties. In this sense, and with other competitions created during the 1960s (the Cup Winners' Cup and later the UEFA Cup), it allowed UEFA to actively participate in the creation of a "space for inter-European relations" to borrow from French historian, Gerard Bossuat.[83] In a way, UEFA navigated Miroslav Krleža's "Two Europes" indeed advancing the first one – a largely Western Europe unified across geography – but certainly fighting to include the second, Europe including the periphery, the East, Balkans and Baltics.[84] While stopping short of explicitly asserting one political ideology or religious identity, UEFA sought to gather together on the fields of its competitions the "Europes" from North, South, East and West.

---

[82] Parks, Jenifer. "Nothing but Trouble": The Soviet Union's Push to "Democratise" International Sports during the Cold War, 1959–1962. *The International Journal of the History of Sport* 30 (2013): 1554–1567.

[83] Bossuat, Gérard. Des identités européennes. In *Pour l'histoire des relations internationales*. Robert Frank (ed.), 663–686, here 664. Paris: Presses Universitaires de France 2012.

[84] For more on Krleža, see Hudabiunigg, Ingrid. Contested Identities: Miroslav Krleža's Two Europes versus the Notion of Europe's Edge. In *Contesting Europe's Eastern Rim: Cultural Identities in Public Discourse*, Ljiljana Šarić, Karen Gammelgaard and Kjetil Rå Hauge (eds.), 173–187. Bristol: Multilingual Matters, 2010.

Stefan Scholl
Cooperation and conflict:

The case of the European Sports Conference
in the 1970s and 1980s

It will never be forgotten, that the European Sports Conference was for over 20 years one of the few bridges that reached over the whole of Europe, and where despite all the difficulties that persisted because of the complete governmental dependence of the European sports federations a lot of bridges were built between human beings.[1]

Introduction

These words of Walfried König, one of the West German protagonists of European sports cooperation in the 1990s, serve well to describe the role and, as we will see, especially the contemporary perception of the European Sports Conference (ESC) during the 1970s and 1980s. Of course, as indicated by König, the ESC was not the only European institution, where 'East' and 'West' met in sport during this period of the Cold War. Beside regular competitions and championships and the collaboration in the international and European federations such as UEFA,[2] there was a growing web of bilateral sport treaties between socialist and non-socialist countries spanning Europe which culminated in the 1970s.[3]

---

[1] König, Walfried. Der zukünftige europäische Binnenmarkt und die Konsequenzen für den Sport. In *Der Sport im zusammenwachsenden Europa. Sportpolitische und sportfachliche Aspekte*, Walter Tokarski, Ludger Triphaus and Karen Petry (eds.), 20. Köln: Sport und Buch Strauß, 1993 [All translations from German to English by me].
[2] Mittag, Jürgen. Europa und der Fußball. Die europäische Dimension des Vereinsfußballs vom Mitropa-Cup bis hin zur Champions League. In *Das Spiel mit dem Fußball. Interessen, Projektionen und Vereinnahmungen*, Jürgen Mittag and Jörg-Uwe Nieland (eds.), 155–176. Essen: Klartext Verlag, 2007; Mittag, Jürgen and Jörg-Uwe Nieland. Auf der Suche nach Gesamteuropa – UEFA und EBU als Impulsgeber der Europäisierung des Sports. In *Freunde oder Feinde? Sportberichterstattung in Ost und West während des Kalten Krieges*, Christoph Bertlin and Evelyn Mertin (eds.), 208–229. Gütersloh: Medienfabrik Gütersloh, 2013; Vonnard, Philippe, Grégory Quin and Nicolas Bancel (eds.). *Building Europe with the Ball: Turning Points in the Europeanization of Football, 1905–1995*. Oxford: Peter Lang, 2016.
[3] For example, in the 1970s the West German sports federation signed treaties with the responsible authorities from Yugoslavia (December 1973), the German Democratic Republic (May 1974),

The ESC was both a symbol of that growing cooperation as well as a motor for further contacts. Yet, this platform was exceptional, because it was the only forum of that kind where leading sports officials from the Western European non- (or semi-)governmental organizations (such as the West German Deutsche Sportbund, the Dutch Nederlandse Sport Federatie, the Österreichische Bundes-Sportorganisation (Austria), the French Comité National Olympique et Sportif, or the British Sports Council) conferred and discussed with top officials from the Eastern European sports departments (such as the Soviet Committee for Physical Culture and Sport, the East German DTSB, the Czechoslovakian ČSTV, or the Hungarian OTSH).

The example of the ESC shows that a history that focuses exclusively on conflict and confrontation in sport during the Cold War tends to miss an important facet: the numerous channels for communication, a web of bilateral sport relationships and even collective efforts in different sport-related domains that existed in that period. As David L. Andrews and Stephen Wagg put it:

> Although sport is more regularly mobilized as a means of nurturing positive relations with allied nations, during the Cold War sport brought enemies together, and provided opportunities for initiating and developing diplomatic ties that would otherwise have been harder to instigate.[4]

Of course, these opportunities were not independent of the outside world. Rather, as we will see, it was a characteristic of the ESC that the will to communicate was hindered and sometimes overshadowed by the hardened East-West division. By stressing the ambiguous character of the ESC, this article follows recent debates about the role of international organizations and transnational forms of communication and exchange during the Cold War. In general, this line of research points out that international organizations and platforms were important

---

Romania (April 1975), the Soviet Union (March 1977), Bulgaria (August 1977), Poland (March 1978), Hungary (April 1978), China (June 1979) and Czechoslovakia (December 1979).

4 Andrews, David L. and Stephen Wagg. Introduction: War Minus the Shooting? In *East Plays West. Sport and the Cold War*, David L. Andrews and Stephen Wagg (eds.), 1–10. London, New York: Routledge, 2007, here 4. For further case studies see also Dichter, Heather L. and Andrew L. Johns (eds.). *Diplomatic Games. Sport, Statecraft and International Relations since 1945*. Kentucky: University Press of Kentucky, 2014; Bertling, Christoph and Evelyn Mertin (eds.). *Freunde oder Feinde? Sportberichterstattung in Ost und West während des Kalten Krieges*. Gütersloh: Medienfabrik Gütersloh, 2013.

sites of bloc confrontation, while at the same time enabling identification and pursuit of common interests and initiatives.[5]

To add another analytical concept to these studies, this article proposes to interpret the ESC as a special case of 'Europeanization' that reached over and beyond the Iron Curtain. Within the tradition of political science, the concept of Europeanization has been used to describe processes whereby supranational European policies or laws gain influence on national policy or jurisdiction, as in sport for example in the case of the "Bosman ruling" from 1995.[6] In a certain shift of perspective, other scholars have argued that everyday forms and practices of social exchange should be integrated to a higher degree into the concept of Europeanization.[7] In sports sociology as well as in sports history, this "culturalist" notion of Europeanization has been absorbed and tested, especially for football.[8] Alexander Brand and Arne Niemann have pointed out that the role of "transboundary networks or actors, whose interests and perceptions are either aggregated or amalgamated within these networks and institutions" is crucial.[9]

---

[5] See for example Suri, Jeremi. Conflict and Co-operation in the Cold War: New Directions in Contemporary Historical Research. *Journal of Contemporary History* 46 (2011): 5–9; Kott, Sandrine. Par-delà la guerre froide. Les organisations internationales et les circulations Est-Ouest (1947–1973). *Vingtième Siècle. Revue d'histoire* 109 (2011): 142–154; Autio-Sarasmo, Sari and Katalin Miklóssy (eds.). *Reassessing Cold War Europe*. New York: Routledge, 2011. An important reference for the role of international organizations in the twentieth century in general is the work of Akira Iriye, for example Iriye, Akira. *Global Community. The Role of International Organizations in the Making of the Contemporary World*. Berkeley: University of California Press, 2002.
[6] See for example Featherstone, Kevin and Claudio M. Radaelli (eds.). *The Politics of Europeanization*. Oxford: Oxford University Press, 2003.
[7] See for example Delanty, Gerard and Chris Rutherford. *Rethinking Europe. Social Theory and the Implications of Europeanization*. London: Routledge, 2005; Bornemann, John and Nick Fowler. Europeanization. *Annual Review of Anthropology* 26 (2007): 487–514.
[8] Mittag, Jürgen and Benjamin Legrand. Towards a Europeanization of Football? Historical Phases in the Evolution of the UEFA European Football Championship. *Soccer and Society* 11 (2010): 709–722; Roche, Maurice. Cultural Europeanization and the "Cosmopolitan Condition": EU Regulation and European Sport. In *Cosmopolitanism and Europe*, Chris Rumford (ed.), 126–141. London: Liverpool University Press, 2007; Bancel, Nicolas, Grégory Quin and Philippe Vonnard. Introduction. Studying the Europeanization of Football in a Long Term Perspective. In *Building Europe with the Ball*, 1–18.
[9] Brand, Alexander and Arne Niemann. Europeanization in the Societal/Trans-national Realm: What European Integration Studies Can Get Out of Analysing Football. *Journal of Contemporary European Research* 3 (2007): 182–201, here 185. See also Levermore, Roger and Peter Milward. Official Policies and Informal Transversal Networks: Creating "Pan-European Identifications" Through Sport? *The Sociological Review* 55 (2007): 144–164; Ther, Philipp. Comparisons, Cultural Transfers, and the Study of Networks. Toward a Transnational History of Europe. In *Comparative*

A useful analytical definition of Europeanization has been proposed by the German historians Ulrike von Hirschhausen and Kiran Klaus Patel, stating that it comprehends "a variety of political, social, economic and cultural processes that promote (or modify) a sustainable strengthening of intra-European connections and similarities through acts of emulation, exchange and entanglement and that have been experienced and labelled as 'European' in the course of history". However, they stress that: Europeanization is not limited to integrative elements such as these, but also encompasses parallel processes of delimitation and 'othering', as well as fragmentation and conflict. It is the sum of these transnational processes that constitutes Europeanization.[10]

As expressed in this quotation, the concept of Europeanization does not refer to a "success story" of peaceful collaboration and steadily ongoing integration, but includes fractures, inconsistencies and resistance. In our special case of the ESC, conflict, failed attempts to reach a higher degree of institutionalization and the emphasis on being different (to the Eastern or Western counterpart) framed the specific form of Cold War Europeanization.

In this article, I will try to give both a first historical sketch of the ESC as well as an analytical interpretation, placing it more deeply within the conceptual framework of Europeanization in sport. In order to do so, I will first briefly retrieve some basic aspects of the ESC in the next section. This seems necessary as an introduction since there exists virtually no scholarship about the ESC. In the following, I will then describe the development of the ESC during the 1970s and give a short review of its further development in the 1980s.

As for sources, my historical assessment of the ESC relies on the published records of the conferences, unpublished archive material from the German Olympic Sports Federation (DOSB) and contemporary press coverage (mainly examples from West Germany).[11] Of course, this is an important, albeit necessary restriction, creating a predominantly West German perspective of the ESC. Further research in the future will have to complement and correct this evaluation by integrating source material from other participating countries.

---

and Transnational History. Central European Approaches and New Perspectives, Heinz-Gerhard Haupt and Jürgen Kocka (eds.), 204–225. New York: Berghahn Books, 2009.
10 Hirschhausen, Ulrike von and Kiran Klaus Patel. Europeanization in History: An Introduction. In *Europeanization in the Twentieth History. Historical Approaches*, Martin Conway and Kiran Klaus Patel (eds.), 1–18, here 2. Basingstoke, Hampshire: Palgrave MacMillan, 2010.
11 I have to thank Ulrich Schulze Forsthövel and his colleague Sigrid Jürgens from the DOSB for their help and the preparation of archive material.

The European Sports Conference in brief

Of course, cooperation, mutual exchange, but also conflicts in sport have a long history in Europe.[12] After 1945, this history cannot be written without taking into account the context of the Cold War. While in different sports, little by little, federations on a European level were formed, the situation on the top level of sports associations was marked by a sharp separation between East and West: the socialist countries collaborated closely on different levels under the lead of the USSR,[13] the sports representatives of the Western European countries from the 1960s met in the informal "NGO Club" and the Committee for Out-of-School Education of the Council of Europe.[14] First ideas to launch a series of sports conferences in which *all* European countries could participate evolved precisely during these meetings of the NGO Club of the Western European sports organizations under the aegis of the Council of Europe in Strasbourg during the second half of the 1960s.

In 1967, the Comité de liaison, which prepared the consultations between the sports NGOs and the Committee for Out-of-School Education of the Council of Europe, stated that the cooperation between Western NGOs and the Council of Europe should not lead to the constitution of a "bloc". According to its memorandum, sports organizations throughout the whole of Europe were confronted by similar questions and problems. Therefore, a conference for "*l'Europe géogra-*

---

12 For the first three decades of the twentieth century, see for example Tomlinson, Alan and Christopher Young. Sport in Modern European History: Trajectories, Constellations, Conjunctures. *Journal of Historical Sociology* 24 (2011): 409–427.
13 See Kobierecki, Michał Marcin. Sport as a Tool for Strengthening a Political Alliance: The Case of the Eastern Bloc during the Cold War. *The Polish Quarterly of International Affairs* 12 (2016): 7–24.
14 The "NGO Club" was formed in the 1960s by the sports associations of the Netherlands, Denmark, Switzerland, Norway, Iceland and the Federal Republic of Germany and was quickly enlarged to include other Western European countries. In the early 1990s, it would become the European Non-Governmental Sports Organization (ENGSO). The Council of Europe was created in 1949. Based on the European Cultural Convention (1954), it began to take sport into its field of activity as an inter-governmental organization in 1960. For the Council of Europe in general, see Wassenberg, Birte. *History of the Council of Europe*. Strasbourg: Council of Europe Publishing, 2013. For its activities in sport, see König, Walfried and Matthias Gütt. Der Europarat und sein Beitrag zur Sportentwicklung. In *Handbuch Sportpolitik*, Walter Tokarski and Karen Petry (eds.), 80–97. Schorndorf: Hofmann, 2010; Scholl, Stefan. Die Europäische Sport für Alle-Charta (1975/76) in ihrem historischen Entstehungskontext. *Themenportal Europäische Geschichte*, 2016. http://www.europa.clio-online.de/essay/id/artikel-3929; Scholl, Stefan. Sportwissen im Europarat: Überlegungen zur historischen Analyse (1960er–1990er Jahre). In *Europäische Sportpolitik. Zugänge – Akteure – Problemfelder*, Jürgen Mittag (ed.). Baden-Baden: Nomos, 2017: in press.

phique" should be prepared.¹⁵ Beside the influence of overall contemporary preferences to reach change through rapprochement, more sport-specific reasons played a role, for example the rapid development of European championships, broadly discussed plans to organize European Olympic Games as well as other commonly faced developments in sport, such as the problem of doping, the growing influence of economic interests and plans to develop Sport for All programmes. It was quickly agreed, though, that the Council of Europe should not be involved because of its exclusively "Western" scope. Rather, the United Nations Educational, Scientific and Cultural Organization (UNESCO) seemed the appropriate umbrella organization to host the event. A Swedish-Dutch working group under the lead of Bo Bengtson was entrusted with the task of contacting Eastern sports organizations in 1968.¹⁶

Although those organizations were interested in the idea, it took three more years to realize, because of a certain reluctance on the part of UNESCO and difficulties of finding a host country. Finally, Austria complied with the organization and proposed the project to representatives from the USSR, Yugoslavia and Hungary in early 1972.¹⁷ A preparation committee consisting of representatives from Sweden, France, West Germany, Austria, the Soviet Union and Hungary was set up and agreed in November 1972 to hold the first European Sports Conference in May 1973 in Vienna, chosen because of Austria's neutral position in the Cold War after the State Treaty of 1955.¹⁸ From then on, the ESC met on a regular two-year basis:

---

15 Council of Europe. CCC/EES (67) 23 rév. "Rapport de la réunion de l'Organe de liaison ayant eu lieu à Strasbourg, les 23 et 24 octobre 1967", 2.

16 Dritte Beratung des Europarates mit den freien Sportorganisationen der Mitgliedsländer am 25–26 April 1968. Archives of the DOSB, Folder "Liaison Committee, Castejon, 1972".

17 Solf, O. I. Bericht über die VII. Sport-NGO-Konsultation beim Europarat in Straßburg, 27–28 April 1972, Franfurt am Main, 4.5.1972, 5–6. Archives of the DOSB, Folder "Liaison Committee, Castejon, 1972".

18 For the role of Austria in the Cold War see: Suppan, Arnold and Wolfgang Mueller (eds.). *"Peaceful Coexistence" or "Iron Curtain". Austria, Neutrality, and Eastern Europe in the Cold War and Détente, 1955–1989*. Münster: LIT Verlag, 2009; Steininger, Rolf. *Austria, Germany and the Cold War. From the Anschluss to the State Treaty, 1938–1955*. New York: Berghahn Books, 2009.

Table 1. The meetings of the European Sports Conference in chronological order

Number	Year	City
I.	1973	Vienna (Austria)
II.	1975	Dresden (German Democratic Republic)
III.	1977	Copenhagen (Denmark)
IV.	1979	Berchtesgaden (Federal Republic of Germany)
V.	1981	Warsaw (Poland)
VI.	1983	Belgrade (Yugoslavia)
VII.	1985	Cardiff (Wales)
VIII.	1987	Athens (Greece)
IX.	1989	Sofia (Bulgaria)
X.	1991	Oslo (Norway)
XI.	1993	Bratislava (Slovakia)
XII.	1995	Vienna/Budapest (Austria/Hungary)
XIII.	1997	Amsterdam (Netherlands)
XIV.	1999	Malta
XV.	2001	Thalinn (Estonia)
XVI.	2003	Dubrovnik (Croatia)

Participation in the ESC started with groups of two to five delegates from 26 nations in 1973, plus representatives from UNESCO, the International Council of Sport Science and Physical Education (ICSSPE) and the IOC, then stayed relatively stable at around 30 countries and around 100 participants per conference. A non-exhaustive list of persons that attended at least at four conferences shows that the ESC really brought together some of the leading sports officials of that period, that is either ministers responsible for sport or presidents and heads of international relations of sports associations.[19] Countries such as Great Britain, Italy, France, Belgium, Spain or Greece, which are not listed here, had either small or frequently changing delegations; in some cases this shows their relative disinterest in the ESC, in other cases it was due to changes in the organizational structures of the sports federations.

---

[19] Among them were: Helmut Dembsher and Felix Nepotilek (Austria), Trendafil Martinksi (Bulgaria), Ernest Demtrovic and Antonín Himl (Czechoslovakia), Kurt Moeller and Emmanuel Rose (Denmark), Mauri Oksanen (Finland), Robert Pringarbe (France), Willi Weyer and Karl-Heinz Gieseler (Federal Republic of Germany), Manfred Ewald and Günther Heinze (German Democratic Republic), Tibor Gál (Hungary), Barry Holohan (Ireland), Hannes Sigurdsson (Iceland), Milan Ercegan (Yugoslavia), Nicolaas Vlot and Wim de Heer (Netherlands), O. J. Bangstad and Thor Hernes (Norway), Bolesław Kapitan and Zygmunt Szulc (Poland), Alfonso dos Santos (Portugal), Ion Siclovan and Lia Manoliu (Rumania), Bo Bengtson and Bengt Sevelius (Sweden), Ferdinand Imesch (Switzerland), Sergej Pawlow and Dimitri Prochorow (USSR).

The different sessions of the ESC were thematically planned by an international preparatory committee, consisting of seven to eight delegates meeting three to four times prior to the conference. Special attention was paid to a balanced East-West relationship in this committee. In Copenhagen in 1977 it was agreed that countries should leave the preparatory committee after three years in order to guarantee a rotation.

The final organization and funding lay in the hands of the hosting country. Usually, the conferences lasted three or four days and included thematic sessions and a social programme, often consisting of dinners, folkloristic elements and sports performances. This seemingly marginal activity was actually very important, because it created time and occasion for informal meeting and discussion outside of the plenum in a more relaxed atmosphere. Regarding funding, the hosting organization was responsible for financial resources. For example, the first conference in Vienna was financed by the Austrian Ministry of Education and Art and the City Council of Vienna itself.[20] For Berchtesgaden in 1979, the West German sports federation estimated a sum of 1 million Deutsche Marks. The federal government provided half of it, other parts came from the *Land* of Bavaria, the sports federation itself and the region of Berchtesgaden. The public relations organization Pro Sport Press Service in Munich received 45 per cent of this sum.[21] This was heavily criticized by the Social Democrats in the parliament.[22] The 1981 conference in Warsaw apparently received sponsoring from Coca-Cola and Adidas, because the organizers could not raise enough money for the expenses by themselves.[23] In both cases, the participants had to pay additional fees for hotel rooms and travel costs.

Journalists too were invited to the ESC. Very often, information and press material was distributed to them in advance in the form of official bulletins. In general, it seems that the bulk of journalists came from the country that organized the conference. For example, only nine out of the 27 participating countries sent journalists to Berchtesgaden in 1979.[24] In Dresden (1975) there was a dispropor-

---

20 Europäische Sportkonferenz 1973, 12–17 Mai 1973 in Wien, Record, 2. [The bibliographical data of the written records of the ESC are only fragmentary. Usually, no publisher, publishing house or year of publication is indicated. For this article, I used the exemplars deposited in the library of the *Deutsche Sporthochschule* in Cologne, Germany.
21 Gieseler, Karl-Heinz. Die Europäische Sportkonferenz. Fakten und Folgerungen. Archives of the DOSB, Folder 1.2.43 "IV. ESK 1979".
22 Günthner, Wolf. Mehr Schein als Sein. *Stuttgarter Zeitung*, 12 October 1979.
23 Deister, Günther. Wie auf einer Insel. Warschau als Konferenz des Zwiespalts. Archives of the DOSB, Folder "V. ESK Polen (Warschau) 1981 / VI. ESK Jugoslawien (Belgrad) 1983".
24 Letter from the *Berchtesgadener Anzeiger* to Karl-Heinz Gieseler, 13 November 1979. Archives of the DOSB, Folder 1.2.43 "IV. ESK 1979".

Figure 1. Official emblem of the European Sports Conference. It was slightly adapted to different backgrounds at the conferences.

tionately high number of journalists – more than two-thirds – from both parts of Germany.[25] Even if this might have been due to the exceptional situation of the East and West German political and sports relations in that period,[26] it seems as

---

25 Informationen der Sozialdemokratischen Partei im Bundestag, 2. Juni 1975. Archives of the DOSB, Folder 1.71 "II. Europäische Sportkonferenz 27–30 May 1975 Dresden".
26 See for example Bösch, Frank (ed.). *Geteilte Geschichte. Ost- und Westdeutschland, 1970–2000*. Göttingen: Vandenhoeck & Ruprecht, 2015; Apelt, Andreas H., Robert Grünbaum and Jens Schöne (eds.). *2 x Deutschland. Innerdeutsche Beziehungen 1972–1990*. Halle (Saale): Mitteldeutscher Verlag, 2013; Fink, Carole and Bernd Schaefer (eds.). *Ostpolitik, 1969–1974. European and Global Responses*. Cambridge: Cambridge University Press, 2009. Especially for sports rela-

if in general the ESCs had more coverage in the German media than in other participating countries. However, these assessments concerning the media coverage have to be checked by further historical media analysis.

In general, the ESC was quite a loose forum for meeting and discussion. As we will see in the next sections, the question of the degree and liability of institutionalization was one of the major contemporary points of conflict and critique. Therefore, I will try to go into more detail regarding the modes of cooperation and conflict in the history of the ESC in the 1970s and 1980s.

A difficult and disillusioning beginning: Vienna 1973, Dresden 1975, Copenhagen 1977

The early stage of the ESC was marked by a rather stiff atmosphere, distrust, sometimes mutual allegations and sharp conflicts about its institutional status as well as its meaning and relevance in political terms. It seems as if nobody was really sure about the purpose of this new forum which, at the same time, has been welcomed by nearly everybody involved.

Right from the start the ESC was explicitly situated by most of the participants within the context of the policy of détente, especially the Conference on Security and Cooperation in Europe (CSCE), which also took off in 1972 to 1973.[27] This can be grasped in the official communiqués of the conferences, but also in the speeches and interventions. As expressed in the final communiqué of the first conference in Vienna:

All of the participants agree, that especially in present times, where the peoples of Europe are striving for European cooperation and security, also in the realms of sport the need has grown in all European countries to realize the humanistic and social mission of sport and to achieve effective contributions for agreement and friendly cooperation without difference of race, religion or political convictions. [...] The participants of the first European Sports Conference are filled with satisfaction that just now a clear sign has been shown, that sport can

---

tions, see Balbier, Uta. *Kalter Krieg auf der Aschenbahn. Der deutsch-deutsche Sport 1950–1972. Eine politische Geschichte*. Paderborn: Ferdinand Schöningh, 2007; Blasius, Tobias. *Olympische Bewegung, Kalter Krieg und Deutschlandpolitik, 1949–1972*. Frankfurt/M.: Peter Lang, 2001.

27 For the context of the CSCE see Bange, Oliver and Gottfried Niedhard (eds.). *Helsinki 1975 and the Transformation of Europe*. New York: Berghahn Books, 2008.

be as relevant for relations between peoples as for the well-being of every single people.[28]

Variations of that theme can be found in every conference that followed. Willi Weyer, head of the West German sports federation seems to have been standing alone in criticizing overtly this political emphasis of the ESC, stating in Dresden (1975):

There is no reason to expand our dialogue politically into the field of responsibility of the Conference on Security and Cooperation in Europe. We meet here not as politicians who aim to combine politics with sport, but as sportsmen who try to do the best for sport given the political situation.[29]

Of course, this statement has to be judged as a classical rhetorical figure of an international sports leader, especially one representing the Federal Republic of Germany. Previous to the conference in Dresden a journalist of the renowned *Frankfurter Allgemeine Zeitung* had already warned that the conference would be "politically transformed" by the Eastern representatives in order to prepare for the heavily debated "third basket" of the final declaration of the CSCE.[30] Accordingly, Karl-Heinz Gieseler, the general secretary of the West German sports federation, wrote after the Dresden conference that it had been "synchronized" from "one particular side" with the CSCE. The inputs of the "socialist sports leaders" were directed more to the CSCE than to the ESC.[31] Indeed, during the conference, the delegations from Rumania and Czechoslovakia opted for an official declaration by the ESC that should be sent to the CSCE. Eventually, after the West German delegation suddenly changed its stance, a clear reference to the CSCE was made in the final declaration of the ESC in Berchtesgaden (1979) following a proposal from Eastern Germany, claiming that the ESC wanted "to contribute to the principles and measures laid down in the final declaration of the Conference on Security and Cooperation in Europe".[32]

---

28 Europäische Sportkonferenz 1973, 12–17 May 1973 in Wien, Record, 404–405.
29 II. Europäische Sportkonferenz 1975, 27–30 May 1975 in Dresden, Record, 25.
30 Haffner, Steffen. Nach Dresden nicht der Ausflüge werden: Europäische Sportkonferenz soll politisch umgemünzt werden. *Frankfurter Allgemeine Zeitung*, 28 May 1975. On the "third basket", see i.a. http://www.humanrights.ch/en/standards/europe/osce/helsinki/.
31 Gieseler, Karl-Heinz. Politische Nachhilfestunde. *Olympische Jugend* 20 (1975): 6.
32 IV. Europäische Sportkonferenz 1979, 9–13 October 1979, 206. See also Holzweißig, Gunter. Multilaterale Aktivitäten des Deutschen Sportbundes. In *Geschichte der Leibesübungen, Band 3/2*, Horst Ueberhorst (ed.), 806–807. Berlin: Bartels & Wernitz, 1982. The final declaration at Helsinki had stated: "In order to expand existing links and co-operation in the field of sport the participating States will encourage contacts and exchanges of this kind, including sports meetings and competitions of all sorts, on the basis of the established international rules, regulations and practice."

In fact, the ESC was built upon the will to communicate and exchange views on developments in sport commonly faced by all participating sports federations. As the international preparatory committee stated in 1973 before the first ESC in Vienna:

It is the purpose of the conference to analyse the function of sport in the societies of the European countries, examine its further development and initiate an exchange of experience in all domains of sport and physical education.[33]

In this regard, it seems interesting that the participants largely agreed in their perception and general diagnosis of current problems and prospects in sport. As the Danish representative Kurt Moeller expressed, certain facts had to be accepted: "We are organized in different ways and have to put up with this. Therefore, we have to concentrate upon problems that are common to all of us."[34] First of all, there can be identified a strong concern for Sport for All, which remained the main theme of the ESC throughout its existence. This is a very interesting aspect, because so far the development of Sport for All policies has been stressed mainly for Western European countries.[35]

At the different sessions of the ESC one can see that the aims of the Sport for All concept (to activate more people to do sport, whether competitive or non-competitive, and especially to reach those parts of the population that were thought of as being discriminated against in sports participation, namely women, children, old-aged and handicapped people) were shared by all of the countries, as well as the rationale behind them: for example, changes in the organization of modern societies, the challenging growth of leisure time, or the spread of "civilization diseases".[36] Apart from the Sport for All orientation, important themes of common perception included the construction of sports facilities and questions of urban development, the growing importance of the media, and the doping problem. Referring back to our analytical framework, we can see here an important element of Europeanization which consisted of the construction and identification of commonly perceived problems. The vice-president of the West German sports federation, Hans Gmelin, put it in a geographical frame, stating that "sport should be open for everyone from childhood to old age, and should be in effect under different names from Reykjavik to Moscow, from Oslo to Bukarest".[37]

---

33 Europäische Sportkonferenz 1973, 12–17 May 1973 in Wien, Record, 3.
34 Europäische Sportkonferenz 1973, 12–17 May 1973 in Wien, Record, 187.
35 For example, in 1975, the Council of Europe adopted the Sport for All Charter.
36 See for example the classical account of the Hungarian sport official Sándor Beckl in Europäische Sportkonferenz 1973, 12–17 May 1973 in Wien, Record, 128–129.
37 Beckl, Europäische Sportkonferenz 1973, 12–17 May 1973 in Wien, Record, 312.

However, the emphasis on shared perspectives could not overwrite the dissonances that frequently manifested themselves. One fundamental cause for conflict that accompanied the ESC from its beginning was the discussion about the role the state had to play in sport. Whereas in many speeches and contributions of representatives from the socialist countries a pivotal role was given to the state in providing and organizing sport activities, some of the Western delegations (especially those from the Federal Republic of Germany, the Netherlands, Austria and Norway) repeatedly criticized this view, claiming an autonomous and apolitical role for physical education and sport. In Copenhagen (1977), the president of the Soviet Committee for Physical Culture and Sport, Sergej Pawlow, defended himself vehemently against this kind of knee-jerk criticism, stating:

> It seems as if cooperation is from time to time hindered by artificial problems. Lots of comments have been made about the so-called "interference" in sport by institutions of the state. It is hard to say what prevails here – naivety, primitivism or demagogy.[38]

Even if this passage of his speech appeared only in the previously distributed written version, it evoked an intervention by the West German Willi Weyer, calling on Pawlow to explicitly name who he had in mind with this reproach.[39] Pawlow prevented an open dispute by claiming that no participant of the conference was meant. At the same conference a certain kind of fatigue was expressed, when Ole Jacob Bangstad, president of the Norwegian sports federation, remarked that in the future no more time should be wasted in discussing the role of the state, since these discussions would lead nowhere.[40] However, it is very telling that the discussions about the role of the state in sport were so prominent in the meetings of the ESC in the 1970s, because this was an era where government departments responsible for sport started to exchange views more regularly on an international level, for example at the Council of Europe's Conferences of European Ministers Responsible for Sport from 1975 or UNESCO sports conferences from 1976.

That the Eastern countries were accused of bringing too much state intervention into sport was in large part due to their preference for bilateral sports treaties. Those were championed as a way towards closer cooperation especially by

---

38 III. Europäische Sportkonferenz 11–15 May 1977, Protokoll, 71.
39 III. Europäische Sportkonferenz 11–15 May 1977, Protokoll, 187. See also: Pawlow bringt Weyer auf die Palme. Sind wir naiv, primitiv oder demagogisch? / Attacke des UdSSR-Sportministers. In *Süddeutsche Zeitung*, 15 May 1977.
40 III. Europäische Sportkonferenz 11–15 May 1977, Protokoll, 203 f.

the USSR and the German Democratic Republic. In fact, one concrete effect of the ESC was that it did contribute to the conclusion of numerous sports treaties between socialist and non-socialist countries.[41] However, the bilateral treaties were criticized by some of the representatives from the Western sports federations, because of their seemingly political character. As Nicolaas Vlot, representing the Dutch sports federation, deliberately pointed out, treaties signed by autonomous sports organizations were by no means political or state treaties.[42] Again, Willi Weyer warned that the system of bilateral treaties should not lead to the erosion of the authority of the international federations, and to the "shifting of the ingenious idea of a free world sports system to the level of state treaties", which would "cause much more political trouble than already [exists] in the present-day situation."[43]

Beside bilateral treaties, the majority of the socialist countries[44] tried to move the ESC to a closer cooperation with – or even merging into – UNESCO.[45] Already during the first conference, Konstantin Kulinkovic from the USSR and Manfred Ewald from the GDR introduced the idea of a qualified sports organization within UNESCO.[46] Symptomatically, a controversy arose at the end of the conference around the number of delegates UNESCO should send to the international preparatory committee of the next ESC. Mainly Karl-Heinz Gieseler from West Germany opposed a draft that allowed for two delegates – one from UNESCO itself, and one from the UNESCO-affiliated International Council of Sport and Physical Education (ICSPE). But the big offensive came in Dresden in 1975. Sergej Pawlow suggested that the ESC could become a "European Sports Council" under the umbrella of UNESCO,[47] and was immediately supported by

---

[41] Just to give an example, following the first conference the USSR signed sports treaties with Sweden, Austria and France, and Yugoslavia signed a treaty with Sweden. See II. Europäische Sportkonferenz lässt neue Impulse erwarten. Interessante Pressekonferenz nach Konstituierung des Vorbereitungskomitees. In *Deutsches Sportecho*, 29 April 1974, 1 and 4.
[42] III. Europäische Sportkonferenz 11–15 May 1977, Protokoll, 172.
[43] II. Europäische Sportkonferenz 1975, 27–30 May in Dresden, Record, 22.
[44] Yugoslavia, which was extremely critical about any type of institutionalization, was an important exception.
[45] The history of sport within UNESCO is almost as poorly known as the ESC. As an exception see: Desplechin-Lejeune, Blaise, Saint-Martin, Jean and Pierre-Alban Lebecq: L'UNESCO, l'éducation physique et le sport: Génèse et évolution d'une éducation corporelle internationaliste (1952–1978). *Stadion. Internationale Zeitschrift für Geschichte des Sports* 34 (2008): 119–142. For UNESCO in general, see Maurel, Chloé. *Histoire de l'UNESCO. Les trente premières années (1945–1974)*. Paris: L'Harmattan, 2010.
[46] Europäische Sportkonferenz 1973, 12–17 May 1973 in Wien, Record, 125 and 97.
[47] II. Europäische Sportkonferenz 1975, 27–30 May in Dresden, Record, 18.

delegates from the GDR, Poland and Bulgaria. Eventually, the approach did not have the consent of all the delegations. Yugoslavia was against any form of institutionalization, René Bazennerye from France pointed to the fact that the ICSPE already existed.[48] The West German press heavily criticized Pawlow's proposition. The commentators were unanimous in condemning his idea as an attempt to further politicize sport:

What is meant to be called European Sports Council and set up within UNESCO is no other than the continuation of previous Soviet efforts to institutionalize sport by creating an intergovernmental body, whose political effectiveness would necessarily further restrict the scope of traditional sports organizations – such as the IOC or the international federations.[49]

The Dresden conference in general was described in the press as a "private teaching in politics"[50] for the Western sports organizations. "Simple-hearted sports officials" from the West had been confronted with "professional politicians" from the East.[51]

In Copenhagen (1977) the institutional future of the ESC and its relationship to UNESCO was once again subject to discussion, although in this case, a higher level of institutionalization of the ESC was favoured by Nicolaas Vlot from the Netherlands in order to "counter the potentially dangerous endeavours of UNESCO".[52] Eventually, it was decided to mandate the international preparatory committee for the 1979 conference with the drafting of a proposition for the further institutionalization of proceedings.

In sum, it seems appropriate to say that the ESC had a difficult beginning in the 1970s. As Willi Weyer declared after the conference in Copenhagen in 1977, it was already a positive development that the different sports organizations got together at all.[53] Indeed, as pointed out, the atmosphere was determined on the one hand by a strong will to communicate – sometimes only in order to show

---

48 II. Europäische Sportkonferenz 1975, 27–30 May in Dresden, Record, 67.
49 Knecht, Willi. Alter Hut mit neuem Etikett. *Sport-Informations-Dienst* 31 (28 May 1975): 1. See also Haffner, Steffen. Pawlowsche Vorstellungen von Sport und Politik. *Frankfurter Allgemeine Zeitung*, 30 May 1975.
50 Gieseler, Karl-Heinz. Politische Nachhilfestunde. *Olympische Jugend* 20 (1975): 6. See also Kunkel, Ralf. Kein Ersatz für Fortschritt. *Die Zeit*, 6 June 1975.
51 Haffner, Steffen. Die Dresdner Sportkonferenz: Ein Lehrstück in Sachen Politik. *Frankfurter Allgemeine Zeitung*, 3 June 1975.
52 III. Europäische Sportkonferenz 11–15 May 1977, *Protokoll*, 173.
53 Für saubere Aufgabenteilung. Interview mit dem DSB-Präsidenten Willi Weyer nach der III. ESK, die vom 11.–15. Mai in Kopenhagen stattfand. *DSB-Information* 20 (1977): S. 1.

the achievements one's own country.[54] On the other hand, the tactical moves of the "other" were sceptically observed. Taking again a West German perspective, two aspects are worth mentioning. Firstly, the West German sports federation undertook attempts to coordinate its strategy with other Western sports organizations via the NGO Club. Apparently, this was not very successful.[55] According to the journalist Steffen Haffner who wrote for the *Frankfurter Allgemeine Zeitung*, most of the delegates from the Western countries judged the behaviour of Willi Weyer in 1975, when he opposed several formulations of the final communiqué, as a case of annoying "*querelles allemandes*".[56] Secondly, and linked to the first aspect, the delegates (and journalists) from the FRG were *indeed* obsessed with small details of formulation. As Haffner again wrote shortly before the ESC in Dresden, it would be about single terms like "coexistence", "liberty" or "international understanding".[57] In fact, the West German sports federation archive contains a general memorandum and linguistic analyses of the "Soviet theses" with clear references to positive and negative language use.[58] After the conference, Karl-Heinz Gieseler sent an explanatory letter concerning the final communiqué to the Department of Foreign Affairs, asserting that it was not possible to emphasize to a higher degree "free, unhindered sports relations in the sense of liberal, human encounters", nor to fully avoid the term "friendly coexistence".[59]

To conclude, after 1977 not only the West German sports officials but the bulk of the participants as well as most of the commentators agreed that the ESC had to change its character. Primarily, it was argued that more concrete action should follow the beautiful rhetoric displayed at the conferences.

---

54 In the West German press, of course, primarily the speeches of the Eastern delegates were described as mere propaganda shows and socialist agitations.
55 In 1975 Karl-Heinz Gieseler wrote a letter to the Chancellery of the FRG complaining about the non-homogenous performance of the Western NGOs, although there had been strategic meetings before the conferences in Vienna and Dresden. Also, he announced a forthcoming strategic meeting in Frankfurt. Letter from Karl-Heinz Gieseler to Min. Dir. Hermann Marx (Bundeskanzleramt), 11 November 1975. Archives of the DOSB, Folder "III. ESK Dänemark Kopenhagen".
56 Haffner, Steffen. Die Dresdner Sportkonferenz: Ein Lehrstück in Sachen Politik. *Frankfurter Allgemeine Zeitung*, 3 June 1975.
57 Haffner, Steffen. Nach Dresden nicht der Ausflüge werden: Europäische Sportkonferenz soll politisch umgemünzt werden. *Frankfurter Allgemeine Zeitung*, 28 May 1975.
58 See Für II. Europäische Sportkonferenz in Dresden im Mai 1975, and Bemerkungen zu den sowjetischen Thesen. Both in Archives of the DOSB, Folder 1.71 "II. Europäische Sportkonferenz 27–30 May 1975 Dresden".
59 Letter from Karl-Heinz Gieseler to I. K. Gracher (Auswärtiges Amt), 2 June 1975. Archives of the DOSB, Folder 1.71 "II. Europäische Sportkonferenz 27–30 May 1975 Dresden".

Berchtesgaden 1979: a turning point?

The international preparatory committee began to work on its task to set out a more concrete institutional framework for the ESC immediately after the conference in Copenhagen. In September 1977, it met for the first time in Frankfurt. It was agreed that the ESC should represent "a sort of umbrella organization of European sport" vis-à-vis UNESCO, the IOC and the newly formed General Association of International Sports Federations (GAISF). The West German sports federation was instructed to draft a detailed paper of principles and rules of procedure prior to the next meeting.[60] This draft, sent to the other members of the preparatory committee in March 1978 before its second meeting, went very far compared to the previous stance of the German delegates. It envisaged a "European Sports Committee", including an executive committee, which should among other things represent the organization between the conferences and should decide by majority vote, and further sub-committees.[61]

Already at the second meeting of the preparatory committee, the delegates from the Netherlands, the USSR, Great Britain and Yugoslavia reacted sceptically to the West German proposal and called for a revision, apparently because the draft went further than anything discussed earlier.[62] In addition, there were signs of distrust coming from the West German press and governmental sphere. One commentator at the end of 1978 expressed the fear that of all meetings the conference in Berchtesgaden could lead to the adjustment of European sport to the political strategy of the socialist countries. Since the West German sports federation failed to publicly explain its strategy, the preparations aroused a latent suspicion.[63] Indeed, Karl-Heinz Gieseler of the West German sports federation had already had to meet with sceptical officials of the Foreign Department in September 1977. From the report of the meeting, one can detect one side of the rationale behind this move. Gieseler explained that in the debate about the future organization of the ESC, it would be a strategic advantage to make the

---

60 Solf, Otto-Isao. Internationales Vorbereitungskomitee, 15 September 1977. Archives of the DOSB, Folder "Archives of the DOSB, Folder 1.2.43 "IV. ESK 1979".
61 "Statuten des Europäischen Sportkomitees" and "Geschäftsordnung für die Europäische Sportkonferenz". Archives of the DOSB, Folder "Archives of the DOSB, Folder 1.2.43 "IV. ESK 1979".
62 Solf, Otto-Isao. 2. Sitzung des Internationalen Vorbereitungs-Komitees (IVK) am 19 April 1978 in Herzogenaurach, 21 April 1978. Archives of the DOSB, Folder 1.2.43 "IV. ESK 1979".
63 Knecht, Willi. Der Sport auf den Spuren der KSZE. *Deutschland-Archiv* (December 1978): 1240–1243, here 1242.

first step. Since an integration into UNESCO was no longer an option,⁶⁴ and since in that forum, no one challenged the claim of the West German sports federation to also represent West Berlin – one of the contested points within East and West German/USSR sports relations – there was no argument against a further institutionalization, Gieseler argued.⁶⁵

Besides the strategic rationale, one can assume a certain demand for prestige on the side of the West German sports federation. Prior to the conference, its president Willi Weyer declared that Berchtesgaden could cause "a breakthrough" and "bring the European sports organizations closer together".⁶⁶ However, the initial draft of the statutes was already watered down by the international preparatory committee. The fourth meeting declared unambiguously that "an institutionalization of the ESC [was] not planned", that no international organization would replace the national ones, and that the only mode of decision making was by consensus.⁶⁷ This again clearly reveals that the ESC could only be institutionalized on the lowest common denominator.

During the conference in October 1979, Willi Weyer tried for the last time to convince the participants to support the final draft version, proposed by the preparatory committee. In a sudden change of argument – compared to his statements at previous conferences – he now associated the ESC voluntarily with the CSCE, claiming that sport was an integrative part of the "political process of rapprochement".⁶⁸ He once again argued in favour of a permanent committee that could represent the ESC internally and externally. In addition, he gave a list of suggestions for concrete cooperation ranging from the development of joint Sport for All programmes, organization of seminars and conferences as well as coordinated efforts to fight doping, to joint planning of development aid in

---

64 In 1976 UNESCO organized the first world conference of ministers responsible for sport and initiated the establishment of the Intergovernmental Committee for Physical Education and Sport in 1978.
65 Ergebnisvermerk über die Besprechung vom 6 September 1977 beim Auswärtigen Amt über Fragen der 1. Sitzung des Internationalen Vorbereitungs-Komitees vom 12–14 September 1977 in Frankfurt für die IV. Europäische Sportkonferenz 1979 in Berchtesgaden. Archives of the DOSB, Folder 1.2.43 "IV. ESK 1979".
66 Quoted in Gieseler, Karl-Heinz. Europäische Sportkonferenz 1979: Auf dem Weg zu neuen Strukturen. Es geht stärker um das sportliche Leben der Völker. *Frankfurter Allgemeine Zeitung*, 14 October 1978.
67 Solf, Otto-Isao. 4. Sitzung des Internationalen Vorbereitungs-Komitees (IVK) am 28. März 1979 in Dreieich-Sprendlingen bei Frankfurt/Main. Archives of the DOSB, Folder 1.2.43 "IV. ESK 1979".
68 IV. Europäische Sportkonferenz 1979, 9–13 October 1979, Berchtesgaden, 96.

sport.⁶⁹ He finished with the insistent appeal: "We can no longer release promising rhetorical balloons and produce documents for the archives. We should come back down to earth and ask how we will proceed with the ESC. Our highly praised principles will stay useless and empty, if we do not bring them to life."⁷⁰

Weyer's speech produced a heavy debate. Especially the delegations from Yugoslavia, Great Britain, the Netherlands and France opposed the idea of a permanent executive committee as well as any representative function of the ESC towards others. After Karl-Heinz Gieseler showed himself strongly disappointed due to the fact that even the countries who participated in the draft version now criticized it, the session had to pause for one hour.⁷¹ During that time the statutes were once again revised. In the final version, the claim to represent the ESC to other organizations was left out and the executive committee was renamed the Coordinative Committee. The German Democratic Republic was successful in bringing in the reference to the CSCE and a clause on the political and geographical balance of the Coordinative Committee and the working groups, formerly named subcommittees.⁷²

In the long run, the working groups would prove to be the most important innovation of the 1979 debate. In the final declaration, four seminars were announced: a seminar on the construction of sports facilities to be held in Austria, a seminar on Sport for All in Switzerland, a seminar on the evaluation of the 1980 Olympic Games in Moscow to be held in West Germany,⁷³ and a seminar on "the function of sport in the education of the youth".

In the immediate aftermath, however, the conference was seen as a failure: "Europe cannot speak with one voice in sport."⁷⁴ Above all, heavy criticism of Weyer's performance set the tone in the press coverage. One the one hand, he was blamed for not speaking out against allegations made by his East German counterpart Manfred Ewald, who polemicized in his speech against an "atmosphere of pogrom" and accused West Germany of helping GDR athletes to commit "*Republikflucht*" (desertion from the republic).⁷⁵ On the other hand, commentators expressed their lack of understanding for Weyer's insistence on stronger in-

---

69 IV. Europäische Sportkonferenz 1979, 9–13 October 1979, Berchtesgaden, 99.
70 IV. Europäische Sportkonferenz 1979, 9–13 October 1979, Berchtesgaden, 100.
71 IV. Europäische Sportkonferenz 1979, 9–13 October 1979, Berchtesgaden, 152–154.
72 IV. Europäische Sportkonferenz 1979, 9–13 October 1979, Berchtesgaden, 163–168.
73 IV. Europäische Sportkonferenz 1979, 9–13 October 1979, Berchtesgaden, 207. Since the FRG boycotted the 1980 Olympic Games, the seminar was cancelled.
74 Deister, Günter. Europa kann im Sport nicht mit einer Stimme reden. *Rheinische Post*, 13 October 1979.
75 IV. Europäische Sportkonferenz 1979, 9–13 October 1979, Berchtesgaden, 67.

stitutionalization. The danger existed, according to the newspaper *Die Welt*, that the ESC would become "a political sports organization".⁷⁶ The "political" character of the conference in Berchtesgaden was also expressed in a caricature in the *Süddeutsche Zeitung*:

SPORTKONFERENZ   SZ-Zeichnung: Gabor-Benedek

Figure 2. Caricature in the *Süddeutsche Zeitung*, 13–14 October 1979.

In the account of the journalist Günter Deister, the West German sports federation had made itself the puppet of Sergej Pawlow, acting as the "locomotive" with Pawlow and Manfred Ewald as firemen, and causing confusion "in their own camp and the Federal Ministry of the Interior".⁷⁷ Although still not fully enthusiastic, a more promising outlook was given by Harald Piper in the journal *Olympische Jugend*. After all, sports officials from both sides of the Iron Curtain *did* finally agree on common principles for future cooperation and a programme of subjects to treat. This could make "Berchtesgaden an important cornerstone on Europe's sports path".⁷⁸

---

76 Quednau, Frank. Am Ende fehlte nur noch der Bruderkuss. *Die Welt*, 13 October 1979.
77 Deister, Günter. Europa kann im Sport nicht mit einer Stimme reden. *Rheinische Post*, 13 October 1979.
78 Pieper, Harald. Europäische Initiativen. *Olympische Jugend* 23 (1979): 3.

New modes of action in a difficult environment: the ESC in the 1980s

In retrospect, it seems paradoxical that cooperation within the ESC was more conflict-ridden in the era of general détente during the 1970s and became more concrete in the 1980s when the Cold War intensified again, also in the realm of sport. This can be explained in part by the fact that by the 1980s the ESC was already a well-established network. The participants had known each other for years and did find a way to communicate despite all the differences. In addition, the view that sport could build bridges even in times of political conflict was well established and often endorsed by international sports leaders. However, the growing tensions in sports relations between the Eastern and the Western bloc also left their traces on the ESC, especially at the beginning of the 1980s. The conference in Warsaw in 1981, held only a couple of days before the declaration of martial law in Poland, stood under the shadows of the boycott of the Olympic Games in Moscow and the congress of the IOC in Baden-Baden earlier in 1981.[79] One of the key figures of the ESC, Willi Weyer, who had played an unfortunate role in the boycott, did not participate – officially because of an urgent commitment to the Federal government. Sergej Pawlow for his part declared in his speech at the conference that the Moscow Games had been a "victory over reactionary forces" who aimed at "dividing the Olympic family".[80]

The following conference in Belgrade in 1983 was also overshadowed by the looming Eastern boycott of the 1984 Olympic Games in Los Angeles. The USSR, Poland, Czechoslovakia, Bulgaria and Rumania sent only second-rank officials to the conference. Manfred Ewald from the GDR denounced American rearmament, Willi Weyer answered by criticizing the previous action of the Soviet Union. Eventually, the final communiqué, which was only made possible by informal background discussions between the delegations from Eastern and West-

---

[79] For the context of the boycott see Mertin, Evelyn. The Soviet Union and the Olympic Games of 1980 and 1984: Explaining the Boycotts to their Own People. In *East Plays West*, 235–252; Hulme, Derick L. *The Political Olympics. Moscow, Afghanistan, and the 1980 U.S. Boycott.* New York: Praeger, 1990; Sarantakes, Nicolas Evan. *Dropping the Torch. Jimmy Carter, the Olympic Boycott, and the Cold War.* Cambridge: Cambridge University Press, 2011.
[80] V. European Sport Conference, 8–12 December 1981, Warszawa: 143. For a summary of the ESC in Warsaw see: Fischer, Herbert. Nach Baden Baden hat man sich wenig zu sagen. Die fünfte Europäische Sportkonferenz in Warschau vom politischen Umfeld gelähmt. *Frankfurter Allgemeine Zeitung*, 14 December 1981.

ern Germany, appealed to both sides in the conflict and declared that "the ESC worried about the maintenance of peace". The participants urged those who were "politically responsible in all countries to reach an agreement, in order to help sport to enable open and humane contacts and create a more peaceful and better world".[81]

But in general, after the first two conferences in the 1980s, the danger of stagnation and loss of prestige was widely noticed. On the one hand, the project of some of the Western delegations to get the ESC to collaborate closely with the newly formed International Assembly of National Organizations of Sport (IANOS) was not successful. On the other hand, the working groups that were envisaged in Berchtesgaden in 1979 only slowly started to function properly. Although there were several meetings – in particular the working group "youth sport" was very active from 1981 on – their work was not very broadly discussed at the conferences. This changed, beginning with the conference in Cardiff in 1985. From then on, much more room was given to the reports and the discussion of the work and projects of the working groups, which met between the conferences. Usually, one country was entrusted by consensus with the organization and the thematic arrangement of the working groups. Sometimes, the working groups only stayed in place for two years, in other cases, they were accredited by the ESC for another term. During the 1980s, there existed working groups on "sports facilities" (organizing country: Austria), "Sport for All" (organizing country: Switzerland), "youth sport" (organizing country: GDR), "sport for women" (organizing country: Soviet Union/Sweden), "sport for the world" (organizing country: Norway), "doping" (organizing country: Great Britain), "European Sports Conference Charter" (organizing country: Denmark) and "sports science" (organizing country: Soviet Union).

Although the cooperation within the working groups did not always run smoothly and without conflicts, their work was much more concrete than the general discussions at the ESCs in the 1970s and the beginning of the 1980s. Their output was apparent primarily in the form of resolutions and recommendations concerning their respective subject fields, which were adopted at the conferences.[82] Other projects ensued. While the "sports science" working group failed to establish a scientific competition under the leadership of the ESC in the late 1980s, a European Youth Sport Camp was organized on the occa-

---

81 Gieseler, Karl-Heinz. Packen wir es an. *DSB-Pressedienst* 24 (10 October 1983): 1–4, here 1–2. See also: Fischer, Herbert. Gespräche geben Hoffnung auf ein Ende der deutsch-deutschen Eiszeit. *Frankfurter Allgemeine Zeitung*, 10 October 1983.
82 See for example European Sports Conference, Athens 1987, Minutes: 312–320.

sion of the conference in Athens in 1987 following a proposal from the Austrian and Dutch delegations in 1985.[83] A follow-up was planned for 1990. Finally, a working group installed in 1987 worked out the official charter of the ESC that can be read as a compressed version of the work done until then. The Charter was unanimously adopted in Sofia at the ninth conference in October 1989. It ends with the words:

The European Sports Conference, whilst being practical in both form and substance, must at all times look to the future. It must be prepared to review frequently the overall position of sport at European level and, as circumstances dictate consider ways and means of reinforcing this position. It must encourage the exchange of information, issue guidance on matters of common interest and produce programmes of action.[84]

Conclusion

After 1989 the ESC continued but slowly changed its character when the whole context of cooperation changed after the collapse of the socialist bloc. In the long run, the ESC lost its *raison d'être:* to serve as a multilateral forum of communication between Eastern and Western European sports organizations in the context of the Cold War. However, it is remarkable that it continued to hold biennial conferences until 2005.

It is quite clear that this article marks only a first attempt to approach the mostly neglected history of the ESC with a focus on the 1970s and a shorter overview of the 1980s. Much more research has to be done, more sources from different countries have to be included. A few relevant aspects, however, should be noted here. The ESC was an important platform of communication in sports between East and West during the 1970s and 1980s – if not for some time the only one of this kind. Due to sustained opposing views on the level of institutionalization that should and could be achieved, it maintained a rather loose structure throughout that period. Also and linked to this, its place within the rather overorganized world of international sports was not well defined, even if it claimed to represent an exclusive focus on Sport for All and the ethical questions of sport.

This might lead to the conclusion that its historical relevance is insignificant. However, this judgement would not be adequate to describe the contempo-

---

83 See the report European Sports Conference, Athens 1987: 271–275; Gesamteuropäische Initiative im Jugendsport. *Olympische Jugend* 10 (1987): 22.
84 The charter can be found in *IX. Evropejska sportna konferencija, Sofia 1989, Record,* 183–190.

rary ascriptions and perceptions of the ESC. For many participating countries and federations that regularly sent their highest officials to the conferences, the ESC *was* an important platform – and it was seen as one at least by the West German press analysed here. As discussed in the article, too, a lot of bilateral sports treaties that were signed during that period had their origins in the ESC. In the 1980s, more concrete projects were planned and realized, even if they did not receive a high degree of attention in public. From an analytical point of view, then, the ESC can be interpreted as a form of Europeanization, if one uses the concept in the culturalist and process-related manner proposed here. In analysing the ESC, one finds a continuing and commonly affirmed will to communicate and cooperate, although it sometimes was only to display one's own achievements. Furthermore, with regard to content, it is remarkable that the delegations, whether governmental or non-governmental, shared a common perception of the dominant contemporary problems and questions in sport, which explains the possibility and willingness to exchange experience and expert knowledge.

Nevertheless, the ESC also shows the limits and reservations that prevented a thorough agreement. Above all, this can be seen in the never-ending discussions about the way and the institutional form in which the ESC should be organized. Also, even if the participating countries of the ESC declared again and again that they tried to come together independent of political convictions, the East-West division framed the institutional working and also a good few discussions. Especially the controversial discussions about role of the state, together with the question of the "political" nature of sport, show how communication was sometimes obsessively overshadowed by bloc semantics. This, however, does not contradict an interpretation of the ESC as an example of Europeanization in sport, if one agrees that Europeanization can also include conflictual processes. Rather, it tells us about the specific discursive settings and institutional modalities in which communication and encounters in Cold War Europe were embedded.

Third Part. **Globalizing sport. Europe as a site of international sporting diplomacy**

François Doppler-Speranza
"Shooting Hoops with Foreign Teams":
Basketball Ambassadors on US Military Bases in France
(1916 – 1961)

Introduction

In the early years of twentieth-century military history, the status of physical activities in the armed forces moved from that of a necessary distraction to valuable operant conditioning. Athletic excellence brought not only fitness skills, much welcomed and serviceable on the battlefield but, as historian Steven W. Pope demonstrated, also conveyed moral or normative values, which contributed to the building of America as a nation.[1] In 1905, Lieutenant-Colonel William W. Wotherspoon of the US Army insisted that each soldier receive both "physical training, to develop his body so that it may meet the unusual and exceptional strains of warfare, and mental training that he may apply the lessons of experience and bring to bear upon the affairs of war every resource which science can give".[2] At that time, sport became increasingly popular with military leaders; they recognized its potential as a useful instrument of socialization in the armed forces, raising soldiers' awareness of the necessity to be fit to fight, both physically and mentally, for conflict resolution and global security.

As the Great War in Europe put increasing pressure on domestic issues, many civilians took upon themselves to organize the "Americanization" of the ever-growing number of "hyphenated-Americans", who had been arriving in the country since the 1870s.[3] As a result of the growing concerns with public health and patriotism, physical exercise entered military training camps in a major way: it was designed to train draftees and soldiers in both combat and ci-

---
[1] Pope, Steven W. *Patriotic Games: Sporting Traditions in the American Imagination, 1876 – 1926*. Knoxville, TN: University of Tennessee Press, 1997, 121 – 78.
[2] Wotherspoon, William W. The Training of the Efficient Soldier. *The Annals of the American Academy of Political and Social Science* 26 (1905): 151.
[3] The aim of "Americanization" was to allow for a better assimilation of the largely pauperized immigrant working-class population in the labour workforce, at a time when modernization was under way. Private organizations, such as the National Americanization Committee (NAC), or individuals, such as John Foster Carr, a long-time member of the American Library Association (ALA), took part in this process.

vilian skills. Military intelligence officers believed that physical activities were instrumental in keeping up army morale and maintaining fitness in the ranks, but also, as historian William J. Baker noted, promoting a strong level of patriotism.[4] In 1917, these civilian officers crossed the Atlantic alongside the American Expeditionary Forces (AEF), lending their expertize in domestic surveillance and psychological warfare abroad. As the US military was making more regular incursions beyond its own borders, Paul Hensler writes that civilian officers, on their part, observed "sport's commitment to the war effort and direct support of the troop[s] abroad".[5] On the same theme, the Young Men's Christian Association (YMCA) helped the army establish valuable contacts with foreign populations overseas through sporting events after the war. As Brett A. Berliner explained, baseball games were organized "under the direction of competent American athletic directors provided by the Department of Sports of *Les Foyers du Soldat*";[6] the same was true for basketball games. These initiatives intensified in peacetime, lending themselves to the promotion of American forces on French soil.

However, the development of a more durable US military presence in France after the Second World War revived the interest in the promotion of American sports overseas. Little by little, sport became a tool for the nascent Cold War public diplomacy network, serving both civilian and military purposes.[7] Public diplomacy, which historian Brian A. McKenzie defines as an expression of American interests abroad, aiming to showcase the national culture through any available medium, is a practice shaped by the aims and interests of the military and

---

[4] Baker, William J. *Playing with God: Religion and Modern Sport*. Cambridge, MA: Harvard University Press, 2007, 123–128.

[5] Hensler, Paul. 'Patriotic Industry': Baseball's Reluctant Sacrifice in World War I. *NINE: A Journal of Baseball History and Culture* 21 (2013): 98–106, here 100.

[6] Berliner, Brett A. 'Chasing the Elusive Pill': YMCA Men, the Paris Baseball League and Making Baseball French, 1919–1925. *International Journal of the History of Sport* 28 (2011): 1772–1787, here 1777.

[7] For US public diplomacy, see: Cull, Nicholas J. *The Cold War and the United States Information Agency: American Propaganda and Public Diplomacy, 1945–1989*. Cambridge: Cambridge University Press, 2008; Mor, Ben, D. Public Diplomacy in Grand Strategy. *Foreign Policy Analysis* 2 (2006): 157–176. For sport diplomacy, see: Gygax, Jérôme. Diplomatie culturelle et sportive américaine: Persuasion et propagande durant la Guerre froide. *Relations internationales* 123 (2005): 87–106; Verschuuren, Pim. Les multiples visages du 'sport power'. *Revue internationale et stratégique* 89 (2013): 131–136; Dichter, Heather L. and Andrew Johns (eds.). *Diplomatic Games: Sport, Statecraft and International Relations since 1945*. Lexington, KY: University Press of Kentucky, 2014.

political circles to protect US national security.[8] Indeed, historian Walter Lafeber states that US public diplomacy is entrusted with a prominent domestic function, pursuing "a strategy that is workable abroad and developing a political explanation that creates and maintains sufficient consensus at home".[9] During the Cold War, public diplomacy officers organized events promoting the US armed forces to the local population. On the other hand, the military took a more direct approach to public diplomacy in order to assist with national security issues and bolster transatlantic commitment, sending some of its best-rated basketball teams to play against local, European teams, and even rival teams from beyond the Iron Curtain. As this paper aims to demonstrate, based on oral interviews and US archival records from the State and Defense Departments, while the recurrent tensions between military and civilian offices drove public diplomacy practitioners to a dead end, a few army sportsmen willingly assumed the role of "basketball ambassadors" during the Cold War.

First, we will observe how sport – and especially basketball – participated in the necessary construction of a public diplomacy programme to promote the military in France. Then, we will see how such a programme contributed to the security of US armed forces, stationed in the most remote areas of France during the Cold War. Finally, we will explain how military and civilian public diplomacy officers jointly organized the work of "basketball ambassadors" in France during this time period, and how this process played an essential role in the safeguarding of the United State's national security from abroad.

Sport and the militarization of the US public diplomacy network in France

Sport played a pivotal role in the construction of the US public diplomacy programme, which was initially designed to counteract the increasing number of acts of espionage during the First World War. But in the interwar years and during the Second World War, foreign countries continued to spy on the US, target-

---

8 McKenzie, Brian. *Remaking France: Americanization, Public Diplomacy, and the Marshall Plan.* New York, NY: Berghahn Books, 2008, here 2–4.
9 Cited in: Johns, Andrew L. Hail to the Salesman in Chief: Domestic Politics, Foreign Policy, and the Presidency. In *Selling War in a Media Age: The Presidency and Public Opinion in the American Century,* Kenneth Osgood and Andrew K. Frank (eds.), 1–17, here 2. Gainesville, FL: University Press of Florida, 2010. Ricaud, Raphaël. La *'Public Diplomacy'* des Etats-Unis: Théories, pratiques, effets (1948–2008). PhD, Université de Paris Ouest Nanterre, 2012, here 281–305.

ing military facilities and collecting information, a trend which continued well into the Cold War. Public diplomacy programmes started during the First World War, as a project to inform the American people about US participation in the conflict, but gave rise to considerable distrust and a deep sense of alienation felt by many. In times of war, it seemed only natural to mobilize the powers and means necessary to form a unified front against the Central powers, whose positions were directly threatening the United States. Sport in general, and basketball in particular, played a crucial role in allaying the concerns raised by the launching of a full-scale propaganda machine, both at home and abroad. From the onset of Woodrow Wilson's internationalist doctrine,[10] questions about US public diplomacy have been inseparable from those of national security.[11] In the mid-1910s, the US Navy and War Departments struggled in their fight against recurrent acts of espionage on military premises in the United States. A few senators in the legislative branch worried that such leaks might put domestic security in jeopardy. In 1916 they supported a bill, which targeted employees "on contracts for the government", and punished "any one communicating to any foreign government any defense secret of the United States".[12] Any civilian or press agency that publicized pieces of information could be suspected of communicating intelligence to the enemy.

When the Espionage Bill was introduced a year later, press organizations and civil society groups voiced their concerns about the safeguarding of their freedom of speech. Indeed, Executive Order 2604 granted full control over the main means of communication to the military.[13] One week later, Wilson received "a communication recommending the creation of a Committee on Public Information (CPI), combining the two functions of censorship and publicity".[14] The CPI, well-known among historians of US public diplomacy, would be chaired by George E. Creel, a civilian. Although the protection of defence secrets is a necessary condition in times of war, manipulative opinion-making processes never played well with American audiences; the American democratic model, which demands citizens trust public judgment, is not fit for "grey areas", where infor-

---

10 Tournès, Ludovic. *Les Etats-Unis et la Société des Nations (1914–1946)*. Genève: Peter Lang, 2015, here 31–34.
11 Nau, Henry R. *Conservative Internationalism: Armed Diplomacy under Jefferson, Polk, Truman, and Reagan*. Princeton, NJ: Princeton University Press, 2015, here 48–50.
12 To Guard Defense Secrets: Senate Committee Acts Favorably on Bill Introduced by Tillmann. *The New York Times*, 3 May 1916.
13 Executive Order 2604: Censorship of Submarine Cables, Telegraph and Telephone Lines. 28 April 1917.
14 Censorship and Publicity. *The New York Times*, 3 May 1916.

mation can be subject to secrecy. But news and advertising corporations, which had first voiced concerns over censorship, cooperated nonetheless: they started to hammer home the message that the United States had to fight a battle against an enemy abroad, at the same time as it had to counteract the manipulations of an enemy within its own borders. Public diplomacy worked in the interest of national security.

From 1917 to 1919, the effectiveness of ongoing efforts to disseminate war information abroad rested on a formal but improvised network of diplomatic outposts called "United States Information Services" (USIS); this acronym would be used well into the Cold War.[15] But military intelligence officers, who were more comfortable with backroom negotiations, quickly identified the limits of public diplomacy.[16] Indeed, the American Forces in France (AFF) were "pulling out for home as fast as the nature of [their] duties allowed", while some Doughboys, as they were nicknamed, remained exposed to changing ideologies on French soil.[17] In order to counteract adverse effects of the military intervention in France, such as the import of bolshevism to the United States, the two main intelligence offices in the War Department – the Military Intelligence Division (MID) and the Office of Naval Intelligence (ONI) – assisted private organizations in the establishment of soldier-education programmes overseas.[18] Soldiers were also invited to practice sports, such as basketball, in operations placed under the auspices of the Young Men's Christian Association (YMCA). On the one hand, basketball games and tournaments served to keep up army morale after the Great War; on the other hand, they were instrumental in creating conditions for social interaction between soldiers and civilians of both countries. According to historian Fabien Archambault, political elites considered basketball was crucial for enhancing national prestige abroad.[19] In the small city of Chaumont, in the northeast corner of France, for example, soldiers could find both the US Army General Headquarters and the YMCA entertainment division.[20]

---

15 Arndt, Richard T. *The First Resort of Kings: American Cultural Diplomacy in the Twentieth Century.* Washington DC: Potomac Books, 2005, here 30–31.
16 At the end of the war, the military was faced with the duty to repatriate four million soldiers, not only to their homeland but also to civilian life, and more specifically to their jobs.
17 Marquis, James. The Last Squad Carries On: Remnant of America's Overseas Army is but a Shadow of the Greatest Expeditionary Force. *The American Legion Weekly* 19 (1919): 10.
18 The most notable achievement to date remains the Library War Service of the American Library Association (ALA), which launched the American Library in Paris in 1919.
19 Archambault, Fabien and Loïc Artiaga. Les soldats du stade: une armée de champions? *Revue de la Société des Amis du Musée de l'Armée* 145 (2014): 27–57.
20 Basketball exhibits resulted in the participation of a French and an American national team of soldiers in the Inter-Allied games in the summer of 1919. The American team won the compe-

On the other hand, intelligence officers were less open to publicity stunts organized by the few diplomats of the CPI. As a matter of fact, the army had shaped its own understanding of the nature and value of public diplomacy: as historian Peter Marquis explains, the Inter-Allied Games of 1919, which stood at the apex of military diplomacy after the First World War, served to enhance the physical superiority of US soldiers over their European counterparts.[21] But in the interwar period, civilian organizations kept the upper hand. Indeed, in June of 1920, Congress signed an update to the National Defense Act of 1916, allowing for the development of the National Guard and the Army Reserve, but limiting the growth of the Regular Army in – and of – the United States. The purpose was not merely to fulfil popular hopes for the signs of a long-lasting peace; it was rather to cut down expenses, at a time when the federal government did not yet have to provide an answer to a national economic crisis. The 1929 stock market crash would ultimately allow for less leverage than in any prior negotiations over the questions of appropriations and staff expansion. As a consequence, the interwar political paradigm undermined the competitiveness of sport as a core component of the army's public diplomacy and never fostered the development of what has been called an "army of athletes" after the First World War.[22] As historian Barbara Keys writes, "as the approach of war became ever more apparent, international sport competitions took on a distinctly militarist flavor and athletes became increasingly indistinguishable from soldiers".[23]

But in the United States, sport practices remained locked in the dormant power struggle between military and civilian offices. After a decade of decisions solely driven by domestic issues and national security interests, president Franklin D. Roosevelt started preparing America for war. In fact, the Second World War manifested the gap between "the Anglo-American brand of sport, as a form of culture steeped in an ethos of individualism, competition, and achievement that reflected its origins as an offshoot of capitalism" and the Soviet Union's attempt "to build an alternative international system based on a distinctly 'prole-

---

tition against Italy, while France finished third in the series. Needless to say that the French team received only little training: "The team was entered not for the purpose of winning laurels for the French but because of the desire to have competitors in as many events as possible and also in order to acquire a further knowledge of the new sport". Hanson, Joseph M. (ed.). *The Inter-Allied Games, 22nd June to 6th July 1919*. Published by the Inter-Allied Committee, 1919, here 90.

21 Marquis, Peter. La grenade, la batte et le modèle américain. Baseball et acculturation sportive dans la France de la Première Guerre mondiale. *Guerres mondiales et conflits contemporains* 251 (2013): 45–58, here 55.

22 How Uncle Sam Has Created an Army of Athletes. *Scientific American* 120 (1919): 114–115.

23 Keys, Barbara J. *Globalizing Sport: National Rivalry and International Community in the 1930s*. Cambridge, MA: Harvard University Press, 2006, here 186–187.

tarian' brand of sport and physical culture that eschewed individualism and record-seeking".[24] In March 1941, the War Department activated the Morale Branch of the army to conduct operations on military bases on US soil only.[25] Sport was instrumental in organizing the free time soldiers had on their hands: "In thirty-seven of the larger camps", wrote Major General Frederick H. Osborn in 1942, "there have been built large field houses, capable of seating four thousand men, ideal for basketball, mass athletics, boxing and even drill in bad weather".[26] Basketball became a wartime favourite among higher-ranked military officers, in spite of the predominance of baseball as the quintessential American sport.[27] The latter was seen as an essential means for domestic propaganda, while basketball was regarded as an efficient instrument for physical fitness and mental sharpness. It was the sport Lieutenant-Commander Frank H. Wickhorst favoured:

> Besides its use as a general body conditioner and a builder of physical stamina, basketball develops precise optical, muscular and mental coordination, body balance, deft touch and quick perceptions – factors which are of benefit to pilots. It improves the cadets' alertness and aids them in making instantaneous judgments and decisions.[28]

In times of war, service basketball fitted the traditional pattern of socialization in the armed forces: it helped maintain the soldiers' fitness and army morale.

The end of the Second World War shows that sport played an increasing role in international relations. The liberation of France was rich in sporting events, which took place mainly within US army camps. Indeed, due to the manipulation of sport by totalitarian states in Europe in the interwar years, and in order to not hurt French national pride, the US military took a stance against postwar policies enforced in other defeated European countries – such as Germany. The army

---

24 Keys. *Globalizing Sport*, 159.
25 The US Army Morale Branch was created on the order of Secretary of War Henry L. Stimson, on 8 March 1941. It was composed of six complementary services: The Exchange Service, the Motion Pictures Service, the Welfare and Recreation Division, the Services Division, the Information Division and the Morale Research Division.
26 Osborn, Frederick H. Recreation, Welfare, and Morale of the American Soldier. *The Annals of the American Academy of Political and Social Science* 220 (1942): 50–56, here 52.
27 In his famous "Green Light Letter" of January 1942, Roosevelt told Judge Kenesaw Mountain Landis, who sought advice on whether the professional baseball league should "continue to operate" in time of war, that he "honestly [felt] that it would be best for the country to keep baseball going".
28 Quoted in Stark, Douglas. *Wartime Basketball: The Emergence of a National Sport during World War II*. Lincoln, NE: University of Nebraska Press, 2016, here 132.

therefore did not stimulate the acculturation process as they had done after the First World War, and limited the use of sports – including basketball – in their effort to improve organized community relations after the Second World War in France.[29] Four factors can explain this anomaly. Firstly, the mandate of the Office of War Information (OWI), the wartime joint civilian and military propaganda bureau of the United States, was somewhat limited. OWI officers were mostly public diplomats in military outfits, and performed as such.

As civilians, they demonstrated their inability to understand the standards attached to basketball exhibits in post-conflict situations. They showed more interest in monitoring the army's public image – through large-scale exhibitions – than in developing contacts with the local populations. Secondly, the public diplomacy network moved into a new phase, and was almost inactive from 1945 to the end of 1947. With the advent of the Cold War, the ongoing threat against the US national interest could be sensed both within and outside the borders of the United States. The military took definite control over most of the public diplomacy network and activities, from the last days of the OWI in 1945 to the creation of the United States Information Agency (USIA) in 1953. Only the Smith-Mundt Act of 1948,[30] which forbade public disclosure of broadcast material on the domestic front, acted as a bulwark against propaganda. Meanwhile, in France, the higher-ranking military staff monitored part of the strategy of USIS outposts.[31]

A close look at the militarization process of the networks of information shows that basketball has played the role of a multifaceted instrument in US public diplomacy. The postwar period was marked by social unrest and demands to end racial segregation in the United States, which tarnished the reputation of America as a suitably democratic nation. And in 1951, State Department officials counted on the showmanship of the Harlem Globetrotters, an all-African-American team, to improve perceptions – however false – of equal opportunity in the

---

29 For a comparison with Germany, see: Bolz, Daphné. Sports Policy, the Press and the Origins of the Cold War in Occupied Germany, 1945–51. *Sport in History* 35 (2016): 195–216; Dichter, Heather L. Sporting Democracy: The Western Allies' Reconstruction of Germany through Sport, 1944–1952. PhD, University of Toronto, 2008.
30 US Information and Educational Exchange Act of 1948 (Pub. L. No. 95–352 § 204, 1948).
31 As Heather L. Dichter writes, the United States developed their public diplomacy programmes, especially in sport, because the US "came out of World War II with a renewed economy and, unlike its European Allies, did not have to rebuild its infrastructure resulting from the destructiveness of war". Postwar reconstruction in France "demanded a greater allocation of finances" on the latter's behalf, allowing civilian officers to carry out an all-out public diplomacy effort. Dichter. Sporting Democracy, 84.

United States.³² By the 1950s, basketball was already well known to the French, so much so that they had started appropriating what they had first encountered in several YMCA huts in the 1920s. In fact, the interwar years saw the birth of "a French sport by essence", known as *ripopo*.³³ Considered an improvised and more fluid type of basketball, with almost no dribbling, *ripopo* called for an opposition of Ancients against Moderns to be solved in future confrontations of French and American sport traditions in times of peace.

A small-scale sport model suitable for military and civilian purposes

The militarization process of the American public diplomacy network, which started in the mid-1910s, reached its zenith with the advent of the Cold War. For the several intelligence offices of the War Department – which was renamed Department of Defense in the late 1940s – it seemed clear that sports would play a role in the military strategy. The interest in sports grew with the installation of US military bases in France, under the auspices of the North Atlantic Treaty Organization (NATO).³⁴ In the early 1950s, thousands of young American soldiers settled in rural parts of the country. Military and civilian public information officers had an unusual balancing act to perform: to ensure the stability of Western Europe, to guarantee the security of the United States in return, and to press forward with the transition of the French economy to a free-market economy, with the Marshall Plan for example. In 1954, despite a staunch effort by the United States to further the cause of a continental defence system, the French voted against the creation of a European Defence Community (EDC). Despite a heightened sense of urgency, most US government officials felt that European disloca-

---

32 Thomas, Damion L. *Globetrotting: African American Athletes and Cold War Politics*. Chicago: University of Illinois Press, 2012, here 70 – 74. In France, the Globetrotters played several games over 33 days, sometimes on simple tennis courts; also, an eponymous film was screened in USIS outposts across the country.
33 Claverie, Eric. Le ripopo ou la naissance d'un style français. In Fabien Archambault, Artiaga Loïc and Gérard Bosc (eds.). *Double jeu: Histoire du basketball entre France et Amériques*, 155 – 166. Paris: Vuibert, 2007.
34 On April 4, 1949, Harry S. Truman signed the North Atlantic treaty, which led the way to the creation of a military alliance of Western countries. Following the Berlin blockade of 1948, and as the Soviet Union exploded its first atom bomb, NATO was designed to protect American interests in a developing and escalating Cold War, in countries such as France where the Communist Party was prominent.

tion could partly be countered by better planning of public information events organized on and outside the bases, especially regarding France's position toward the rearmament of Germany – the main reason for the failure of the EDC.[35] They were convinced of the necessity to disconnect wartime practices from public diplomacy procedures in peacetime, in order to convince the French, "after the start of the Cold War, [that] Germany was no longer an enemy to punish but a new ally in urgent need of help if it was to recover",[36] writes Victor Gavin. But only a proven record could persuade the military establishment to loosen – let alone relinquish – its grip on the public diplomacy programmes.

Indeed, General Alfred M. Gruenther, a high-ranking military official of the US Army in France, felt frustrated by the lack of efficiency of civilian public diplomacy practices. He believed military methods of psychological warfare were far more efficient than civilian ones. Give the French an afternoon with a few servicemen on a base, he once told NATO ministers in Paris, "and they will depart as crusaders".[37] New public diplomacy practices emerged from the debates, triggered by the anticipation of the failure of the EDC. At the request of the United States Information Agency (USIA) director Theodore C. Streibert, USIS-France created a bureau in charge of military affairs, which reported directly to Leslie S. Brady, the newly appointed Chief Public Affairs Officer (CPAO) in Paris.[38] Together, they offered a streamlined approach to public diplomacy, which eventually took the needs and concerns of the military into consideration.[39] A report forwarded by Brady to the USIA in Washington shows how civilian agencies designed a method to shape the image of the United States in France. The public image of the military fell under the theme of "European integration".[40] But Brady insisted that "approaches must be oblique or through indigenous groups". Furthermore, "because the European Army and the European Political Community are totally European concepts, the approach must in most cases be indirect".

---

35 See: Creswell, Michael. *A Question of Balance: How France and the United States Created Cold War Europe.* Cambridge, MA: Harvard University Press, 2006.
36 Gavin, Victor. Power through Europe? The Case of the European Defence Community in France (1950–1954). *French History* 23 (2009): 69–87, here 71.
37 NATO Conference on Information Policy: Statement by General Gruenther at NATO Ministerial Meeting, 17 December 1954, NATO Archives, AC/87-D/6, 14.
38 Establishment of USIA Area Offices. *Department of State Bulletin* 743, 21 September 1953, 390.
39 New Country Plan for USIS/F. 1 March 1954. US National Archives, RG 84 UD 2462, box 40.
40 This new approach revolved around four "cardinal points of US foreign policy in France": to forge a political alliance with countries defending Western civilization; to support a military structure to strengthen an integrated Europe; to push forward the idea that France and the United States share a common heritage; to promote a free-market economy. Country Action Plan for USIS/F (draft). 2 February 1954. US National Archives, RG 84 UD 2462, box 40: 1.

Most importantly, they considered that "top-level assertions from Washington" had to be excluded from this approach, therefore prioritizing military information officers over civilian ones when it came to local matters.⁴¹

Just as was the case after the First World War, sports were used to keep up army morale and allow soldiers to engage in social interactions with fellow servicemen or civilians. At this point, it seems important to underline the fact that the Selective Service Act of 1948, as well as the Executive Order 9981, establishing equality of treatment and opportunity in the Armed Services and signed the same year, had modified the social fabric of the armed forces. The army understood that, more than even before, the task to create social cohesion in its ranks was crucial, and was to be carried out by the military intelligence officers on site. As expected, the bulk of interpersonal exchanges was conducted within army bases. In the first years upon its return, the army was faced with issues regarding the soldiers' austere living conditions, for mud, ruts and isolation were part of day-to-day camp life. But to cope with the situation, the soldiers – who were also called GIs from 1941 – enjoyed inexpensive recreational activities. Baseball and basketball became the men's favourite sports, played cohesively around camp. But on certain bases, such as the Chambley-Bussières Air Force base (USAFE), located in the Meurthe-and-Moselle region in the northeastern part of France, GIs also formed teams to practice football, softball, golf, soccer and even skiing. Together, they formed a new army of athletes, and worked hard to defend the colours of the 21st Fighter Bomber Wing.

As Chambley veteran Charles R. Timms recalls in his account of his years on the air base in the 1950s, support for sport "was avid from top-down".⁴² The commanders of the base saw sport as a cohesion marker, or in other words a tool for voluntary subordination. This process, which stems from the progressive professionalization of the military during the Cold War, aimed ultimately to guarantee the national security of the United States. Organizing sport and physical activities became a matter of extreme urgency for all service branches, and each base soon had a dedicated team.⁴³ In Chambley, the base sports team

---

41 Country Action Plan for USIS/F (draft). 2 February 1954. US National Archives, RG 84 UD 2462, box 40: 1.
42 Timms, Charles M. *Chambley Air Base, France (1954–1967): The Best and the Worst Place We Ever Lived*. Assembled documents, 1993, here 100.
43 In 1948, the creation of the Inter-Service Sports Council (ISSC), rallying the Navy, the Army and the Air Force, allowed the military to consider a better organization of sports. In 1951, the United States joined the International Military Sports Council (IMSC), but it is only after 1954, when sport practices were regulated by the Department of Defense Instruction 1330.4 authorizing servicemen's "participation in armed forces, national and international sports activities",

was known as the Desert Rats, and was formed in the summer of 1955.⁴⁴ It was put together under the initiative of Colonel H. C. Hartwig, "an athlete of the first water himself [...] and an ex-pro with the New York Giants".⁴⁵ One has also to keep in mind the importance of sport to military elites, especially commanders, who saw in base teams an illustrious and noble way of demonstrating the prestige of the unit and the armed forces in general. For this reason, base commanders often pulled promising athletes off regular duties and made sure they dedicated enough of their time to athletic training or to completing adequate fitness workouts. In various fields of sporting competition, winning games was essential, almost as much as winning a war.

Needless to say, most of the time, the quest for prestige was none of the GIs' business: sport came mostly as a welcome initiative for a change of pace, once servicemen were off-duty. In Chambley, all servicemen trained and played ball in their free time in the 416th Fighter Bomber Squadron maintenance hangar, half of which had been transformed into a basketball court. The Desert Rats team was composed of players, some of whom had a good amount of experience in basketball and new ideas of the role of the United States in the world: fighter pilot Lief Carlson and First Lieutenant Jerry Kincheloe had played collegiately – for the Universities of Minnesota and California, respectively – while airman Jim Fields had been a shooting guard for the Harlem Globetrotters. All these men came to France with no prior experience of the war, but saw the Air Force as a way to be employed and avoid being sent to fight in Southeast Asia. Also, airmen Robert Sisk and Earl Redman had tried out for the University of Ohio in Cincinnati and the University of Texas respectively, but dropped out to enrol in the US armed forces. The players' profiles were versatile and the team's ambitions very modest. The opposing teams originated mostly from fellow NATO bases in the nearby area. As Sisk recalled, "we played the Canadians in Marville [...] and we always beat them in the first half; but they always had a case of Löwenbräu at half-time for us, and by the time we had that case of beer they beat us".⁴⁶ Such a rather unconventional method to improve army morale was bound to change with the creation of a European Air Force basketball league.

---

that army teams were allowed to travel across Europe to play against foreign military and civilian teams.

44 The Desert Rats were born at the initiative of Colonel Hartwig, former player for the NY Giants, then the only professional football team in New York. The team was named after the location of their base – George Air Force Base – located in the city of Victorville, California.
45 Colonel Hartwig to Coach All-Stars. *Chambley Sabre*, 9 December 1955, 4.
46 Interview with Robert E. Sisk, 21 April 2016.

In 1956, the Desert Rats entered the European Air Force basketball competition – a league steeped in the sporting tradition of the armed forces – with the clear objective of playing more than just surrounding army caserne teams and to fight the Cold War on a different ground. The army league was divided into four conferences – France, England, Germany and the Mediterranean, which included Spain, Italy, Morocco, Crete, Greece and Turkey – covering the entire NATO area. Eight teams competed in the French conference. But instead of fighting its war against the enemy – anyone sensitive to influence from Moscow – base teams fought a turf war, which tended to subvert the initial objectives of this initiative. For example, a game against Chateauroux-Déols USAFE air base, with whom the Desert Rats had a stormy competitive and sibling rivalry, was solved as follows:

> The Desert Rats traveled to Chateauroux AB, France, south of Paris, for a conference game. A fiercely fought contest and bad referee calls ignited a heated exchange of words between the Desert Rats Commander, Colonel Baker and the Chateauroux Commander. It was reported by team members on the bench that Colonel Baker asked the Chateauroux Commander what was his date-of-rank. Colonel Baker outranked the latter and the issue was settled – no blood shed.[47]

Military pride took over the competition, and commanders often used "their date of rank to silence the opposing commander". The development of a competitive spirit in inter-regiment sport resulted in affirming a base identity, ultimately conveyed through the base newspaper, an essential byproduct of military public diplomacy.

The base paper of Chambley, launched in 1955, was called the *Sabre*, in reference to the flagship jetfighter aircrafts used by the 416th and 531st bomber squadrons operating on site. Base papers were published under the authority of the Public Information Division (PID). The papers presented local events in a biweekly information platform composed of four to eight pages, while official news and instructions were disseminated by the Department of Defense in the famous *Stars and Stripes*. In the *Sabre*, information about sports were mostly relegated to the back pages, even if the base teams' good results in several competitions often promoted them to the front page. By 1956, the Desert Rats had become one of the most prominent basketball teams in the French conference, so much so that the American Forces Network (AFN) – the entertainment radio broadcasting to US military bases from Germany – "tape-recorded [several] games for re-broadcast at a later date".[48] Sport helped to project the image of

---

47 Interview with Robert E. Sisk, 21 April 2016.
48 AFN to Tape Game. *Chambley Sabre*, 13 January 1956, 4.

the military as a body of dynamic nationals, united in the core values of dedication and athleticism, and instilled a sense of pride in all servicemen and dependents. In January of the same year, after the Desert Rats had a run of twelve undefeated matches, the *Sabre* ran a headline that reinforced the sense of unity between players and spectators, using the motto of the United States seal, "E Pluribus Unum".[49] The public image of the Desert Rats, amplified by the circulation of the base newspaper, gave proof of the strength of the Atlantic Alliance. It also spread the message that Americans formed a vibrant and dynamic people, committed to supporting the creation of an integrated defence system in Europe. Ultimately, basketball played a pivotal role in forging links with the French population.

Public participation as the linchpin of the politicization of basketball

Since the 1920s, basketball had been one of the many sports that allowed for contacts between the French and the Americans, and the Cold War is no exception to this observation. As stated by historian Donna Alvah, US servicemen who were stationed overseas, sometimes with their families, were not entirely removed from their local host communities.[50] To the mind of military intelligence officers, bridging cultural gaps between the French and Americans seemed the safest way to carry out their duty to ensure both the security of the American people and the pursuit of the US national interest. At this early stage of the settlement of US armed forces in French provincial regions, when screening measures for foreign employees on a Department of Defense payroll were not always enforced consistently, informal contacts allowed foreign ideologies to permeate military camps and bases. Naturally, this raised security issues, but most importantly it circumvented the prerogatives of public information officers, who were prompt to react. As a 1955 information brochure issued by the public information office of the US European Command (EUCOM), published with the support of USIS-France recalls, informal contacts within the borders of the base allowed for cross-cultural negotiations over general sporting traditions. Indeed, "after the working day", we can read in the brochure, GIs took delight in "a small rec-

---

49 Desert Rats Winning Skein Broken at Twelve Straight as Chambley Splits at CAMA. *Chambley Sabre*, 27 January 1956, 4.
50 Alvah, Donna. *Unofficial Ambassadors: American Military Families Overseas and the Cold War.* New York: New York University Press, 2007, here 7.

reation: a football game in the field"; then, they "freshened up and had a drink at the mobile bar, while taking French lessons with the workers employed at the camp".[51] The proximity with French locals working for the Americans led the GIs to develop friendly cross-cultural relationships in the course of various sporting activities. The alleged apolitical nature of sports made them active agents of public diplomacy.

Yet, in spite of the thaw in international relations and before Sputnik "hit" America in 1957, US public diplomats encouraged Cold War confrontations, probably to overcome a gap in awareness about the US military presence in the field. The military seized some opportunities to engage citizens and servicemen directly in a cross-cultural experience. In the spring of 1956, Chambley-Bussières air base observed its first Armed Forces day; for safety purposes, the gathering took place inside the base. For the most part, it consisted of an open-base operation, allowing French locals to attend military parades and to take a closer look at the American way of life. It is, however, important to note that this operation had an ambivalent purpose. On the one hand, it helped attract Frenchmen and women into a "bastion of Americana" and increase their understanding of the US military presence in the French countryside. On the other hand, it proved instrumental in benchmarking the expectations and needs of both French locals and US servicemen. Base commander Robert R. Rowland struggled to get soldiers involved in the promotion of the American military presence in Meurthe-and-Moselle: the 18 May edition of the Chambley base newspaper features a message from president Dwight D. Eisenhower, which states that "in the present world situation, it is most important that our own people and others throughout the world who believe as we do should be cognizant of all aspects of our national strength – the spiritual and the moral, as well as the material and the military – and be reminded of our continuing efforts for peace".[52] And in the case of the Chambley-Bussières air base, only the Desert Rats basketball team would really manage to fulfil this mandate.

By 1956, the Desert Rats' acclaimed participation in the European Air Force basketball competitions granted them the authorization to compete with non-military teams. Indeed, military high command was supportive of any initiative to "create a deeper awareness of the general role of the military in American life".[53] The Desert Rats had an unofficial mandate to reach out to local populations and offer a hands-on taste of American culture. For instance, during the

---

51 *Un Américain en France*, 1955. US National Archives, RG 306 P 46, box 128: 19.
52 Armed Forces Day Messages. *Chambley Sabre*, 18 May 1956, 1 and 4.
53 An Important Reminder. *Chambley Sabre*, 17 May 1957, 4.

1956 open-base on the occasion of Armed Forces Day, after visiting a "static display of USAF aircrafts and equipment",[54] French locals were invited to attend a game between the Desert Rats and the defending French Cup champions, the Club Sportif Municipal (CSM) in Auboué. On paper, both teams had achieved significant sporting victories during the previous season, so the game was supposed to be balanced. However, the image conveyed by the *Sabre* offered a different perspective. Indeed, in a short article published in the French edition, which was intended to be distributed to and read by the visitors, the journalist introduces the two opposing teams. The reader learns that CSM Auboué "was formed in 1945 and owes its technique in large part to the contact with US teams stationed in our area after the Liberation". [55] On the other hand, "the composition of the Chambley team dates back to last fall only; it rose quite dramatically to the French base champion, having lost two games only".[56] In the end, the fact that the Desert Rats defeated Auboué didn't matter much: basketball helped provide French spectators with vivid images of modernity and offered a demonstration of strong friendship and cooperation.

However, public participation in basketball games also had a critical political significance. Indeed, as servicemen on duty were busy promoting American culture to the local population, base commander Rowland worked on developing relations with local elected officials and industrialists. The objective was not only to legitimize the presence of American servicemen in provincial Meurthe-and-Moselle – for which purpose the military needed to exert a larger influence on local, national and foreign investments – but also to ensure US global security interests. Moreover, two years after the French Assembly rejected the European Defence Community, the United States experienced some difficulty in containing the public debate over the military presence overseas in general. For this purpose, public diplomacy operations granted the military an opportunity to trigger supportive relationships with the French, pushing the army's social role beyond its traditional coercive function. On the other hand, the convergence of economic partners and their isolation from the local population sheds light on the social fabric of the military, and demonstrates how hierarchical relationships revolved around class interests and not individual profitability. The 1956 open-base operation in Chambley is a good example to illustrate this statement. Colonel Rowland carefully avoided establishing contact between the local population and

---

54 Seventh Armed Forces Day to be Observed Tomorrow with Open-House Program. *Chambley Sabre*, 18 May 18 1956, 1.
55 Le match des champions Auboué-Chambley. *Chambley Sabre*, 19 May 1956.
56 Le match des champions Auboué-Chambley. *Chambley Sabre*, 19 May 1956.

elected officials during the event. The prefect of the Meurthe-and-Moselle region, Jacques Samama, was invited, together with the representatives of French army generals René Cogny and Maurice Challe, to meet with the base commander as the game between the Desert Rats and the CSM Auboué was being played in the 416th maintenance hangar.[57] Despite the visitors being aware of these meetings – they were publicly announced in the French edition of the base newspaper – the two worlds never converged.

As a matter of fact, Chambley-Bussières air base provided the military high command with the proper conditions to operate a fragmented public diplomacy. Only a few days after the open-base exhibition game, the Desert Rats played against the Syracuse Nationals, a team that had won the 1955 NBA championship. According to the *Sabre*, "it was the Nats' final game of a State Department sponsored tour that had stretched 24,000 miles – from Iceland to Egypt".[58] Airman Robert Sisk recalls:

> We played against the Nationals with Dolph Schayes on our home court at Chambley, when they were on a United Service Organizations (USO) tour of military bases in Europe. Jim Fields, the Rats play-maker and hot shot scored 30 points to big Dolph Schayes 29. Yes, they beat us by 30 points. Just too big for the Rats to handle but a good game to watch. Again, our bleachers in the hangar were filled to capacity.[59]

Commander Rowland seized the opportunity given by the USO and the State Department to provide servicemen and their dependents with a unique entertainment experience.[60] And for him, there was much to rejoice about: the Nationals were closing a 26-exhibition round across Europe, and "Chambley was the only American team encountered during the tour".[61] In the end, despite the valiant resistance displayed by the Desert Rats, "Syracuse put a team on the floor that averaged 6'7" and Coach Hartwig's little guys didn't have a chance".[62] The Syracuse Nationals eventually defeated the Desert Rats by the wide margin of 112 to 72.

---

57 Edition Spéciale du *Chambley Sabre* pour les Français. *Chambley Sabre*, 19 May 1956.
58 Professional Height Stymies Desert Rats. *Chambley Sabre*, 8 June 1956.
59 Interview with Robert E. Sisk, 3 November 2014.
60 The USO is a non-profit, privately-owned organization that was created in 1941. It reunites several welfare entities, such as the Young Men's and Women's Christian Association, the Salvation Army, the National Catholic Community Services, the National Travelers Aid Association and the National Jewish Welfare Board. Source: uso.org/about (access date: 20 June 20, 2016).
61 Professional Height Stymies Desert Rats. *Chambley Sabre*, 8 June 1956.
62 Nats Dump Chambley, 112–72, in Exhibition Tilt. *Chambley Sabre*, 8 June 1956, 4.

Against all odds, the traditional distrust for civilian control over military activities was temporarily set aside, as all travel expenses for this exhibition game were covered by the USO. But that evening, despite the rising popularity of basketball in Europe, the gates of the Chambley air base remained closed to the French public. Rowland addressed the joint State Department and USO proposition with the firm intention of exploiting the game for political purposes. There were three different facets to his strategy. First, as mentioned above, civilian and military public information officers catered to specific target audiences. A photograph of the crowd cheering for the Desert Rats shows a few lieutenants and officers in military uniform, alongside their wives dressed in rich and festive clothing. One woman, wearing a white dress, stands out from the crowd: Marie-Thérèse Barre was the winner of the 1956 city of Metz beauty pageant, a contest sponsored annually by the local Chamber of Commerce. Second, AFN commentators travelled to Chambley with *Stars and Stripes* journalists. Together, they recorded the game live and wrote articles that would later be dispatched to other military or base newspapers. AFN eventually broadcast the game at a later date, after all commentaries had been edited and the message deemed suitable for public delivery. Third, this game served as an instrument for the military establishment to prove to both the spectators in the hangar and the listeners of the AFN network that sport was still an instrument for physical fitness and mental sharpness, proving the quality of the physical and military preparedness of the United States Army. Base commander Rowland used public participation in sports events to convince his fellow American citizens that the military was strong enough to guarantee the national security of the United States and safeguard its territorial integrity. Therefore, public participation was a decisive factor in the politicization of basketball. In this case, public diplomacy proves how active it had been on the home front, despite the boycott imposed by the Smith-Mundt Act on the active dissemination of information.

By the spring of 1957, the Desert Rats had eventually become "basketball ambassadors for Chambley",[63] said Sisk. This statement is certainly true, and first and foremost they were ambassadors on their home base. On March 9, Chambley hosted the first basketball All-Star Game of the 12th Air Force, the first of its kind in Europe. There, "twelve players from the US French conference [played] against twelve players from the US German conference; selectees from Chambley included Fields, Carlson, Redman, Kincheloe and Sisk",[64] Sisk recalls. But building on its experience, the Chambley public information office also called upon its net-

---

63 Interview with Robert E. Sisk, 21 April 2016.
64 Interview with Robert E. Sisk, 3 November 2014.

work to attend the event. The All-Star Game was indeed a matter of pride for the base commander: the sporting qualities of Chambley's players mattered less than the quality of entertainment and number of local officials and elites – such as the deputy prefect of Briey – as well as some of its representatives who had come to see the game. In its report, the *Sabre* reads:

> Halftime will be highlighted by the attendance of Monique Lambert, who won the Miss France title in 1955 and finished third in the Miss Europe contest of 1955. Also attending will be Marie-Thérèse Barre, Miss Metz and Queen of the Mirabelle of 1956. General Gerhart will crown Miss Lambert and her court during the half-time intermission. Miss Lambert will be crowned "All-Star Queen".[65]

Moreover, "the game will be broadcast by the Armed Forces Network, French National Radio and TV and also by Télévision Luxembourg; also attending will be representatives from French and American newspapers".[66] In the end, information broadcasts targeted both French and American citizens.

Ultimately, in the eyes of the military high command, the success of the 1957 All-Star Game gave enough credit to the Desert Rats to authorize a tour around Europe. They competed in international tournaments in Alfortville, Lyon, Dijon or Montbrison and, by the time the air base closed in 1961, had played multiple exhibition games. Sometimes, basketball even allowed for unexpected situations:

> Competition was against national, and to some extent, semi-pro talent. The Rats were the first Americans to play against an Eastern bloc country, Poland. The Cold War in the 1950s was a real concern. Air Force Command was concerned about the possibility of an international incident playing against Poland. After tournament play was concluded, and prior to the awards and banquet dinner, three American officers on the team were sent back to Chambley due to safety concerns, and the expendables (the airmen) and Coach (Colonel) Hartwig were left to enjoy the banquet festivities that followed. Everything went smoothly.[67]

Tracked by AFN radio and French and American newspapers, the Desert Rats had enough passion for basketball and enough motivation to break the monotony of army life to turn, more or less unknowingly, into agents of US public diplomacy. In Chambley, basketball was subject to a strategy of politicization by civilian and military offices. But for the 22-year-old players from the west of the United States, at a time when many American citizens were drafted and

---

65 All Star Game Here Tomorrow. *Chambley Sabre*, 8 March 1957.
66 All Star Game Here Tomorrow. *Chambley Sabre*, 8 March 1957.
67 Interview with Robert E. Sisk, 21 April 2016.

sent to Vietnam, it provided enough support to trust the military establishment and subsequently follow a military career. And for Sisk to conclude: "Chambley was not an American All Star team, just a group of talented players from all walks of life across America who just happened to be assigned to the 21st Fighter Bomber Wing stationed in France".[68]

Conclusion

This investigation questioned the practices of US public diplomacy throughout almost half of the twentieth century. In the American tradition, sports provided the US armed forces with a tool for civic, but also educational and physical well-being. During the Cold War, civilian officers such as Leslie S. Brady, Chief Public Affairs Officer of the US Information Services in Paris, jeopardized the possibility of using sports as a form of diplomacy, especially on the field, after the failure of the European Defence Community. If sports are hardly ever considered on equal terms with other forms of diplomacy – whether cultural, citizen or economic diplomacy – in promoting American democratic values to the French, this paper revealed the work of "basketball ambassadors" and demonstrated basketball's efficiency, both in achieving public diplomacy objectives and in complying with national security legislation. But it is most undoubtedly during the NATO era that basketball, unlike the cage players – ordinary men from all walks of life across America, who remain mostly apolitical today – became increasingly politicized.

However, the framework that provided for the implementation and the promotion of American sports abroad also brought its share of challenges, leaving both civilian and military offices somewhat helpless. Indeed, many observers and practitioners saw in the precepts of public diplomacy a set of tacit and unspoken understandings, which had become increasingly coercive. And yet, 31 years of casual acculturation through sports reveal, on two accounts, how unusual the trajectory of the Chambley Desert Rats was for a team of young American servicemen stationed in Cold War France. First, each base was functioning as a "little America", so their jurisdiction was entirely subject to the laws of the United States. Consequently, the players' morale depended on the legal status regimenting all US military premises established overseas. The enforcement of the Smith-Mundt Act of 1948 constituted therefore a domestic political boycott on sports practices. Second, caught between doctrinaire policymakers in Wash-

---

68 Interview with Robert E. Sisk, 21 April 2016.

ington, the Desert Rats overcame the pressure of the implicit military boycott abroad, induced by the Cold War foreign policy of the Western alliance. Allowing for a game against a team from the other side of the Iron Curtain must have been unheard of in the 1950s. But in both cases, while basketball bowed to political pressure, the Desert Rats enjoyed the publicity and continued "shooting hoops with foreign teams".[69]

---

[69] Interview with Robert E. Sisk, 21 April 2016.

Claire Nicolas
The Ghana Young Pioneers

Intertwining global connections to build a Pan-Africanist youth

> We went to let them know that we have something even superior in Ghana. [...] And to see us dressed smartly, long long people like us gents! They were so impressed about us! And these people were admiring so much![1]

Introduction

From the late 1950s, Cold War diplomacy went South. Indeed, the so-called "developing countries" or "Third World" became a key issue in the cultural fight between West and East. While both superpowers were rooted within an "all-encompassing effort involving such things as sporting events, cultural attractions, economic activities, education, trade, diplomacy, and scientific achievement",[2] they sought influence in the numerous countries becoming independent one by one during the 1950s and 1960s. British Prime Minister Harold MacMillan (alongside similar attempts by other declining colonial Empires) invited former colonies to choose the Western side of the Cold War in his 1960 "Wind of Change" speech. Meanwhile, the USSR had forged ties with independence fighters from the first half of the twentieth century. In order to attract African countries, both camps' strategies included implementing sport aid, exchange of expertise, equipment and personnel.[3]

However, this paper will not focus on the multiple ways Northern countries perceived African countries and their leaders as domino pieces in the Cold War diplomatic game. We choose here to take an an African-grounded perspective, in order to understand the mechanics allowing a newly independent Pan-Africanist nation such as Ghana to play along with the Cold War game, giving a special insight to the chosen envoys of this nation: Ghanaian youth. Scholars have recent-

---

[1] Interview with a former Young Pioneer. Accra, 6 June 2016.
[2] Cowan, Geoffrey and Nicholas J. Cull. Public Diplomacy in a Changing World. *The Annals of the American Academy of Political and Social Science* 616 (2008): 6–8.
[3] Parks, Jenifer. Welcoming the "Third World": Soviet Sport Diplomacy, Developing Nations, and the Olympic Games. In *Diplomatic Games: Sport, Statecraft, and International Relations Since 1945*, Heather Dichter and Andrew Johns (eds.), 85–114. Lexington: The University Press of Kentucky, 2014.

ly explored the agency of sport leaders from developing nations across the globe who challenged the Cold War framework, either by promoting transnational black solidarity[4] or their own national image,[5] and using the East/West rivalry for their own ends. The case of Ghana is of particular interest here, notably because of the radical political views and actions of its first elected president, the anticolonial fighter Kwame Nkrumah, famous leader of the Pan-Africanist movement.

The Ghana Youth Pioneer (hereafter GYP) movement had its roots within a vibrant Ghanaian sporting culture, and lasted until the final overthrow of Kwame Nkrumah by a military coup in 1966 (links between the CIA and the 1966 coup remain unclear). It was essential to the socialist, anti-imperialist and Pan-Africanist revolution promoted by Nkrumah,[6] since its young members (boys and girls under 20) were to become the future Pan-Africanist leaders of the new Ghanaian Nation. In this paper, we will try to clarify the international dimension of the GYP movement within the Cold War context and how this globalization process interacted with the Nkrumahist nation-building project. Indeed, the first and most prominent forebear of the GYP movement was British Scouting and Guiding, which were implemented in Ghana during the colonial era, giving the GYP a durable link with its former colonial master.[7] However, the GYP movement did not only interact with its former colonial masters, but – as underlined at the beginning of this introduction – was soon to become acquainted with ideologically closer friends, such as the Soviet Union's Komsomol,[8] China's Red Pioneers movement,[9] or – more surprisingly – Israel's Gadna (also transcribed as Ganda).

---

4 Booth, Douglas. *The Race Game: Sport and Politics in South Africa*. London; Portland: Frank Cass Publisher, 1998.
5 Parks. Welcoming the "Third World": Soviet Sport Diplomacy.
6 Ahlman, Jeffrey S. A New Type of Citizen: Youth, Gender, and Generation in the Ghanaian Builders Brigade. *The Journal of African History* 53 (2012): 87–105.
7 Block, Nelson R. and Tammy M. Proctor. *Scouting Frontiers: Youth and the Scout Movement's First Century*. Newcastle-upon-Tyne: Cambridge Scholars Publishing. 2009; Denis, Daniel, Le sport et le scoutisme, ruses de l'histoire. In *De l'Indochine à l'Algérie: la jeunesse en mouvements des deux côtés du miroir colonial, 1940–1962*. In Nicolas Bancel, Daniel Denis and Youssef Fatès (eds.), 195–209. Paris: La Découverte. 2003; Lamba, Isaac C. Moulding the Ideal Colonial Subject: The Scouting Movement in Colonial Malawi up to 1961. *Transafrican Journal of History* 14 (1985): 63–77.
8 Fainsod, Merle. The Komsomols – A Study of Youth under Dictatorship. *American Political Science Review* 45 (1951): 18–40; Neumann, Matthias. *The Communist Youth League and the Transformation of the Soviet Union, 1917–1932*. London: Routledge, 2012.
9 Shuman, Amanda. The Politics of Socialist Athletics in the People's Republic of China, 1949–1966, PhD, University of California, 2014; Woronov, Terry. Performing the Nation: China's Children as Little Red Pioneers. *Anthropological Quarterly* 80/3 (2007): 647–672.

The Ghana Young Pioneers stood at the intersection of multiple layers of inspirations, each of them intersecting, connecting and converging in Ghana, even when these influences would seem irredeemably opposed to Nkrumah's Pan-Africanist project. Through a diachronic approach, we may observe "circulations, borrowings and hybridizations that are socially situated within the historical time".[10] Indeed, even though the various movements crossing the Pioneers' path appear to stand for quite different countries and ideologies (communism, socialism, anti-imperialism, zionism, or colonialism) they also rely on similar sets of activities, symbols and values: uniforms and badges, military-like organization, open-air activities, outdoor games, self-government, resourcefulness, comradeship or loyalty, for example. Hence, the concept of "hybridization"[11] allows the understanding of the mechanisms through which the various cultural, political and social models are entangled and therefore converge, diverge and interact at large in Ghana, notably the marxist and imperial ones, though supposedly standing on opposite sides of the barrier drawn by the Cold War. The Young Pioneers appear to act as intermediaries, information smugglers and ambassadors for the newly independent Ghana. From the perspective of these actors, their logics and their circulations, we may grasp how Cold War dynamics did not necessarily drive their actions and aims nor those of the leaders of the movement, whatever the intentions of their friends and foes.

In order to craft this study from a Ghanaian perspective, we used archive material from the British National Archives and London University archives[12] but also from the Ghana National Archives.[13] Our aim being to understand the agency of the Young Pioneers themselves, we also conducted interviews in May to June 2016 in Accra with former Pioneers and draw on the memoirs written by two former prominent GYP leaders: Matthew Narh Tetteh and Ajimburu Syme.[14]

---

10 Minard, Philippe. Globale, connectée ou transnationale: les échelles de l'histoire. *Esprit* 12 (2013): 20–32, here 26. (This author's translation).
11 Subrahmanyam, Sanjay. *Explorations in Connected History: From the Tagus to the Ganges*. New Delhi: Oxford University Press. 2005.
12 Hereafter TNA and LU. We used files from the Foreign Office (FO), the Dominion Office (DO) and the Colonial Office (CO) and files from the London University archives related to the GYP. The British services papers show the Soviet activity in Ghana as well as the influence of Israel.
13 Hereafter PRAAD. We went through the Education files (RG/3/*), Sports files (RG/9/*), the *Daily Graphic* newspaper archives (NP/1/*) and Cabinet meetings (ADM). Notably, these records show the perception of foreign influences within Ghana and detailed relationships and connections between Ghanaians and foreigners.
14 The first memoir is located among the author's personal archives and the second is from the New York Public Library. Syme, Adjingboru A., *Salute to Israel: The Story of the Ghana Youth Delegation to Israel*, 1957. Accra, Guinea Press, 1958, here 38; Tetteh, Matthew Narh. *The Ghana*

To forward this analysis we will focus on the British imperial background of the GYP movement, notwithstanding the subversion of this very same imperial ideological framework. Then, we will deploy the usages of the young Ghanaians; the movement allowed them to become international, going either West or East, easily navigating among opposed ideologies and blocs. Finally we will see how, as far as Young Pioneers were concerned, the main aim of the GYP movement was to showcase Pan-Africanism and the greatness of the Ghanaian nation to the world, beyond the ideological and socioeconomic fight between East and West across the globe. However, in order to fully understand this, we will first present a quick historical overview of Ghana from the late 1940s to the mid-1960s.

Historical setting

The anticolonial movement became popular in the Gold Cast (as Ghana was known during the colonial era) after the Second World War. Due to the rapid inflation, Africans from Accra and its surrounding area saw their way of life worsening and boycotted European companies while the unemployed veterans started marching.[15] Kwame Nkrumah returned from England to be part of the mobilization in 1948, as a member of the United Gold Coast Convention (the middle-class based nationalist party) and joined the fight. Along with his followers, he directed the local anger toward a greater purpose: the fight against colonial and capitalist oppression over the whole African continent.[16] He quickly took the leadership of the independence struggle and formed the Convention People's Party [CPP].[17] Party members took part in strikes, boycotts and other activities[18] until the 1951 general election. Nkrumah became the first black prime minister of the Gold Coast (1952–1957), along with an all-African government. From that point, he stood as a symbol of the struggle against the "yoke of imperialism".

Young Pioneer Movement: A Youth Organisation in the Kwame Nkrumah Era. Accra, Institute of African Studies, University of Ghana, 1985, here 24.
15 Rathbone, Richard. The Government of the Gold Coast after the Second World War. *African Affairs* 67 (1968): 209–218.
16 We will discuss the Pan-Africanist struggle and the Non-Aligned Movement in more detail in our final section. Both were critical in making a truly modern Ghanaian youth.
17 Allman, Jean. The Disappearing of Hannah Kudjoe: Nationalism, Feminism, and the Tyrannies of History. *Journal of Women's History* 21 (2009): 13–35.
18 Nkrumah, Kwame. *What I Mean by Positive Action*, Accra: Unknown, 1950.

The CPP, nicknamed the "supreme party", became the sole party in 1964 as, for some prominent CPP members, political opposition was considered a legacy of colonial rule and a potential tool of neo-colonial influence. The CPP was built around a strong cult of Kwame Nkrumah's personality; he was known as Osagyefo [The Saviour]. Nkumah's eponym political theory, "Nkrumahism" [sic] was the leading mode of governance, and was strongly influenced by the socialist experiences of Eastern Europe. Its economic, social and political setting has been widely discussed since then.[19] To build a new independent nation, the CPP aimed at forming a new type of citizen through youth movements.[20] Therefore, the party created various national institutions placing youth at their core: the Builders Brigade, the Worker Brigade and the Ghana Young Pioneers. These movements were to help build the social and political revolution and "train the soul, body and mind of the youth of Ghana".[21] Officially born on 17 June 1960, the movement was meant to be an:

> [...] extensive school of citizenship, pioneering and social activity, to instil into the youth of Ghana, a high sense of patriotism, respect and love for Ghana as their fatherland, whilst providing them with the opportunities for healthy association; further education, discipline and training; and patriotic service to Ghana, during their leisure and recreative period.[22]

The GYP, through its sporting and outdoor activities, was embedded within a long-term (pre)colonial sporting culture in the British Gold Coast. The Asafo pre-colonial boxing institutions were progressively associated with the rising middle class in the 1920s and 1930s.[23] Associations directly originating from Brit-

---

19 Williams, Michael W. Nkrumahism as an Ideological Embodiment of Leftist Thought Within the African World. *Journal of Black Studies* 15/1 (1984): 11–134.
20 Ahlman, Jeffrey S. *Living with Nkrumahism: Nation, State, and Pan-Africanism in Ghana.* Athens: Ohio University Press, 2017; Pool, Jeremy. Now is the Time of Youth: Youth, Nationalism and Cultural Change in Ghana, 1940–1966. PhD, Emory University, 2009.
21 Shardow, Zacharie B. *Inspiration and Purpose of the Ghana Young Pioneers.* Accra: Research Department. Unknown: 1. LU: PG/GH/GYP.
22 "Legislation to provide for the Ghana Young Pioneer Authority" by the Minister of Social Welfare, 14 September 1960. PRAAD: 3/1/447.
23 Military associations of men were associated with Akan local governance from the eighteenth century. See Akyeampong, Emmanuel. Bukom and the Social History of Boxing in Accra: Warfare and Citizenship in Precolonial Ga Society. *The International Journal of African Historical Studies* 35 (2002): 39–60; Simensen, Jarle. The Asafo of Kwahu, Ghana: A Mass Movement for Local Reform Under Colonial Rule. *International Journal of African Historical Studies* 8 (1975): 383–406.

ish sport culture arose in Accra, the capital city (mainly football or boxing)[24] or within the British missionary schooling system (field hockey, cricket, athletics and so on). Sportsmanship became a symbol (among others) of acculturation to the British colonial system by the "Educated" (as the African civil servants, medical doctors and so on were designated then). Besides, the Gold Coast joined international sporting institutions long before gaining political independence: FIFA in 1948 or the IOC in 1951. At the same time, the scouting movement rose quickly in the country. Scouting was imperial at its root – Baden-Powell, its founder, was indeed a colonial officer. The movement was widely encouraged in the schooling system by both missionaries and colonial civil servants.

The foundational dual relationship between Ghana and Great Britain

The first layer allowing the invention of the GYP in 1960 was therefore this fertile ground of British associations from the late colonial era in the Gold Coast. These associations dedicated to youth gathered the exact population that the newly elected CPP aimed at targeting: young boys and girls attending school and willing to be part of a youth association. Even though, as the government pointed out, beyond that "worthy ideal [...] they [were] not Ghanaian or African in outlook or tradition",[25] meaning they were considered to be neo-colonialist movements.

Table 1. Youth associations inherited from the British Empire in 1960[26]

Associations	Membership
Young Men Christian Association	4,000
Young Women Christian Association	800
Boy Scout Association	7,000
Girls Guide Association	2,500
Methodist Youth Fellowship	1,400

---

24 Dunzendorfer, Jan. The Early Days of Boxing in Accra: A Sport is Taking Root (1920–1940). *The International Journal of the History of Sport* 28 (2011): 2142–2158.
25 "Legislation to provide for the Ghana Young Pioneer Authority" by the Minister of Social Welfare, 1960. PRAAD: 3/1/447.
26 "Legislation to provide for the Ghana Young Pioneer Authority" by the Minister of Social Welfare, 1960. PRAAD: 3/1/447.

Table 1. Youth associations inherited from the British Empire in 1960 *(Continued)*

Associations	Membership
Catholic Youth Organization	6,000
Presbyterian Young People's Guild	3,000
Young Farmers Club	12,000
Voluntary Workcamp Association	300
Boys Brigade	600
Advent Youth Society of Missionary Volunteers	1,500
Youth Hostel Association	500
Total	**39,600**

Most of these associations targeted boys and were mainly based in middle-sized or large cities (such as Accra, Kumasi or Tamale). Usually linked to Christian parishes, they relied on the proximity of school-educated children of whom there were fewer in the countryside, even though, from 1951, the new government implemented numerous social reforms – notably in education.[27]

These pre-existing colonial associations were essential to the formation of the GYP, especially the Boy Scout Association (the largest and the closest to GYP objectives). Founded by Robert Baden-Powell, Gold Coast Scouting (and Guiding) gathered children into age groups, placed under the authority of a slightly older peer, while adults stepped back. There was a whole apparatus of flags, uniforms and games. Children performed games, marches, sports, music and arts. Scouting and Pioneering both claimed the legitimacy of an education which brought the body into play in order to train children's moral- and civil-mindedness.[28] In this perspective, Scouting and Pioneering were very alike in the way they used physical activities (including games, sports, salutes and marches) and for the importance given to moral values.

The similarity of activities was reinforced by the involvement of Scouting executives within the GYP. The GYP recruited most of the Scout leaders and commissioners because of their valuable skills.[29] For instance, Mowbray Elliott (National Executive of the GYP) had been a Scout Chief in the past and according to

---

[27] Foster, Philip J. *Education and Social Change in Ghana*. London: Routledge and Kegan Paul, 1965.
[28] Bancel, Nicolas and Daniel Denis. Eduquer: comment devient-on *Homo Imperialis?* In *Culture impériale: les colonies au coeur de la République, 1931–1961*. Pascal Blanchard, Sandrine Lemaire and Nicolas Bancel (eds.). 93–106. Paris: Autrement. 2004.
[29] Interview with a former scout leader (May 2016), friend of the deceased Mowbray Elliott.

the British services, "he still [tried] to maintain some of the idealism acquired through his early youth training".[30]

Nevertheless, the GYP leaders also feared this British influence. Great Britain used sports (among other strategies) to maintain some sort of control over their former colonies when they sensed the strength of the nationalist political movements. Hence sports were part of the making of a "Commonwealth of Nations", notably through the Empire and Commonwealth Games launched in the 1950s. The Games were meant to preserve an imperial identity without the administrative weight of the Empire, given that the decolonization process appeared to be ineluctable.[31] Being well aware of this control process, the Ghanaian leaders wished to turn it upside down. They juggled between the "due provision [that] should be made for the effective control and direction, but also continued operation, of these youth organisations".[32] Indeed, these associations lacked "state control and co-ordination", so the multiplicity of youth organizations might have led to "serious overlapping and dangerous rivalries";[33] most of all, British-based movements carried the "colonial mentality Nkrumah [tried] to eradicate".[34] On the other hand, Scouting and other organizations were very popular among youngsters and Ghanaian Christians (the first religion of the country). The takeover of Christian movements (notably through mandatory leadership courses organized by the GYP[35]) was eventually to provoke some turmoil in Ghana and Great Britain. Lady Baden-Powell herself expressed her concerns at the downgrading of the Guiding movement. We even find the expression "Nkrumah Jugend" – in reference to the Hitler Jugend – to describe the GYP.[36] Moreover, the British government went further in its wish to control the GYP movement. They feared the GYP would become "a nazi-cum-Communist type of youth organisation"[37] and considered it had a duty to help to "recreate [the GYP] in a

---

30 Letter from F. S. Miles to the Civil Secretary's Office of Gambia, 26 February 1962 (TNA: DO 195/32).
31 Charitas, Pascal. L'Afrique au Mouvement Olympique: enjeux et stratégies de l'influence de la France dans l'internationalisation du sport africain (1944–1966). PhD, Université Paris Sud, Paris XI, 2010.
32 "Legislation to provide for the Ghana Young Pioneer Authority" by the Minister of Social Welfare, 1960, 6. PRAAD: 3/1/447.
33 "Legislation to provide for the Ghana Young Pioneer Authority" by the Minister of Social Welfare, 1960, 6. PRAAD: 3/1/447.
34 Interview with a former GYP member (in June 2016), who is still involved in the CPP.
35 "Confidential Ghana Dispatch n°14", 26 June 1963. TNA: DO 195/32.
36 Dorkenoo, Mary. The Nkrumah Jugend. *Sunday Times*, 19 August 1963.
37 Letter from Tom Keeble (Office of the High Commission for the United Kingdom) to John Chadwick, 10 June 1961. TNA: DO 195/32.

new image".³⁸ Consequently, they formed relationships with some of the less radicalized leaders, notably former scout chiefs like Mowbray Elliot, in order to influence the ideological orientation of the movement.

Because of this heated climate, the promoters of a full and uncompromised independence could not rely unquestioningly on former colonial movements: physical activities, education, moral values and the organizational system itself were to be modelled from elsewhere – ideally from Africa, but given the lack of an efficient model (as underlined by George Padmore, Pan-Africanist activist, journalist and adviser to Nkrumah himself)³⁹ the GYP was to be remodelled from more distant areas.

Information smugglers: young Ghanaians going back and forth

British Scouting had been implemented all over Europe and successfully influenced the birth of totalitarian and authoritarian "open air" youth movements, as a means of social control.⁴⁰ Youth movements, as training schools for bodies and minds, were essential tools in the Cold War fight between the Eastern and Western blocs in the 1960s and numerous youth organizations across the globe were set up following the 1948 East German Communist Party statement: "Who owns the youth, owns the future".⁴¹

The GYP was meant to frame youth political education, in order to train the leaders of tomorrow according to CPP ideals. Therefore, given the socialist and anti-imperialist orientation of the CPP, the assumed and explicit model was that of Ghana's main political ally, the USSR and its Komsomol.⁴² Indeed, Kwame Nkrumah's party's political orientation was supposedly neutral (being part of the Non-Aligned Movement, as we will develop further), but was in fact closely related to the USSR. Yes, Nkrumah dared talk of an African revolution instead of identifying himself with the international proletarian fight. But the Communist Party was closely interested in the development of anti-imperial struggle, not least since it was also an anti-occidental fight. Therefore, Nikita

---

38 Note from V. E. Davies (British Council), June 1961. TNA: DO 195/32.
39 Ahlman. *Living with Nkrumahism.*
40 Kater, Michael H. *Hitler Youth*, Cambridge: Harvard University Press. 2009.
41 Droit, Emmanuel. Jeunesse allemande et sortie de guerre dans la zone d'occupation soviétique (1945–1949). *Vingtième Siècle. Revue d'histoire* 108 (2010): 99–111.
42 Neumann, Matthias. *The Communist Youth League and the Transformation of the Soviet Union, 1917–1932*. London and New York: Routledge, 2011.

Krutchev offered increasing encouragement to African states through numerous aid policies, sending material and experts while welcoming envoys from the newly (or soon-to-be) independent nations.[43]

In the USSR, between the 1920s and 1940s,[44] sports of British origin were integrated into a plan for youth education, creating a modern and powerful image of the country in the face of the "imperialists" and reinforcing the idea of a national communion. Besides, the Soviet Pioneers[45] took up Baden Powell's scouting practices and techniques in order to place them at the service of the construction of socialism in Soviet Union and its satellite countries.[46] The Komsomol and Soviet Pioneers used physical activities (among other practices) to align children's morality to the marxist ideal and to form the recruiting base for future Communist Party leaders.

GYP structures appear to be a copycat of the USSR youth organization. Children were sorted by age, co-educated, and more and more connected to party activities as they grew up.

Table 2. Pioneers' activities according to their age group[47]

Groups	Ages	Activities
Young Party League	21–25	Political activities
Nkrumah Youth	17–20	Technical and ideological training, sports, marching
Young Pioneers	8–16	Arts and crafts, sports, drums, ideological training, marching
Children of African Personality	4–7	Singing and reciting poems to honour the Great Osagyefo

---

43 Parks. Welcoming the "Third World": Soviet Sport Diplomacy.
44 Keys, Barbara. Soviet Sport and Transnational Mass Culture in the 1930s. *Journal of Contemporary History* 38 (2003): 413–434; Gounot, André. De l'hygiène du corps à l'obsession des records. Les mutations politiques et idéologiques de la "fizkul'tura" en Russie 1921–1937. *Sciences sociales et sport* 1 (2013): 9–34.
45 The Vladimir Lenin All-Union Pioneer Organisation (also known as Soviet Pioneers) is meant for children from nine to 14 years old, followed by the Komsomol organization (the All-Union Leninist Young Communist League), for 15- to 18-year-olds.
46 Adler, André. Le mouvement des pionniers en URSS. Ses rapports avec l'école. *Enfance* 2 (1949): 266–270.
47 Shardow. *Inspiration and Purpose of the Ghana Young Pioneers.*

Hence, Ghanaians followed the Soviet youth organizational model by strictly aligning sports, youth activities and politics in one movement. For instance, in November 1965, the inaugural match of the new fancy hockey pitch in Accra, was to be played between Ghana and Nigeria. Therefore, Ms Theodosia Salome Okoh, chairwoman of the Ghana Hockey Federation asked her "comrade" Zachary Shardow the following:

In accordance with the wishes of Osagyefo Dr. Kwame Nkrumah, plans are in hand to develop the game of hockey alongside with other departments of Sport to world class. [...] In the circumstances, the first match is being planned to attract as many people as possible – and I would be grateful if you would arrange for about 30 Young Pioneers, in uniform, to assist on the pitch during the game. [And] let me know [...] the number of Young Pioneers who would like to watch the game.[48]

Theodosiah Salome Okoh, being a close relative of the CPP head, worked hand-in-hand with the GYP to promote the successes of Ghana and was part of this entanglement between politics, sports and youth.

Beyond an organizational and structural perspective, very specific sets of skills and knowledge were imported from the Soviet Union to Ghana. In 1960, Kwame Nkrumah implemented a cultural agreement with the USSR followed by similar agreements with Eastern European countries such as Rumania, Albania, East Germany, Yugoslavia, Czechoslovakia, Bulgaria or Hungary[49] during his 1961 "grand socialist tour".[50] He secured numerous exchanges between young Ghanaians and Soviets and between Ghanaians and Eastern Europeans on sports, ideological training, youth leadership, academic studies and military skills. The year 1962 showcased interesting examples related to these various fields of expertise.

As a priority, many Young Pioneers went to train in Soviet Union and its "satellite countries" to master military skills. This was obviously the activity most watched and feared by the British services and press. In 1962, five Pioneers – aged between 20 and 26 – went to the military flying centre of Chrudim in Czechoslovakia to train as parachutists and flight "mechanicians"[51] as part of the internationalization of Pioneers' expertise.

---

48 Letter from Theodosia Salome Okoh to Zacharie Shardow, 13 November 1965. PRAAD: RG 9/1/125.
49 Cultural Agreement with Eastern bloc countries. PRAAD: MFA/4/*.
50 Mazov, Sergey V. *A Distant Front in the Cold War: The USSR in West Africa and the Congo, 1956–1964*. Washington: Stanford University Press, 2010.
51 Progress reports by Mr Kohoutek, Chrudim, 25 May 1962. PRAAD: RG/1/540.

The very same year, 59 scholarships were granted to the best Pioneers to learn "youth work" within the Komsomol for a year. They took this opportunity to learn skills including physical education, seamanship, agricultural economics, geology, electrical engineering, linguistics, arts, medicine, dentistry, nursing, child care and home economics. The 59 Pioneers came from all over Ghana and included ten girls (taking the degrees related to "care" but also degrees in geology or linguistics).[52] These scholarships were explicitly meant to "sustain and further [Ghanaian] cultural and friendly relations with the Soviet Union [and] realise the great efforts and achievements of Osagyefo".[53] These scholarships are only a few examples among the multiplication of connections between the Soviet block and Ghana which included flying cadets training in Moscow, university students in Bulgaria, future sports trainers in Georgia and so on. Pioneers learned skills related to leadership and training, took general academic degrees, undertook military training (in seamanship and in flight schools) and sports (trainer courses, and training and schooling for athletes). These envoys were supposed to learn from their allies in order to become the nucleus for spreading knowledge within Ghana.

Hence, USSR sports being known worldwide[54] as a school for excellence, the best GYP members were selected to train according to Soviet standards. For instance, a batch of six boys and six girls were granted a scholarship in Moscow to learn "scientific gymnastics" from 1962 to 1967. They were selected from the Pioneers because of their "near perfect physique [...] with a view to forming the nucleus for teaching and coaching in the Ghana Youth Organisations".[55] This was in line with the official objectives of the Pioneer movement: to "prepare future Olympic champions for the Central Organisation of Sports".[56]

Hence, just as in the USSR, the national youth movement was responsible for both political and physical activities. In the USSR, sporting performance was conceived as a means to produce exceptional citizens, as a way to select

---

52 Letter from Zacharie B. Shardow to Mr Impraim, the Secretary to the Cabinet, 18 October 1962. PRAAD: RG/1/540.
53 Letter from Zacharie B. Shardow to Mr Impraim, Secretary to the Cabinet, 12 December 1962. PRAAD: RG/1/540.
54 The *Daily Graphic* newspaper often showcases Soviet successes at the Olympics, in football or elsewhere (see PRAAD: NP/1/*).
55 Letter from J. B. Elliott, Ambassador of Ghana in the USSR, addressed to Zacharie B. Shardow, 26 July 1962. PRAAD: 3/1/540.
56 Shardow. *Inspiration and Purpose of the Ghana Young Pioneers*, 9. Ghana was also a member of the International Olympic Committee from 1951.

and value some individuals who were to become national heroes.[57] In Ghana as well, the entanglement of sports, youth organization and politics led to training young people within the GYP both politically and physically, so they could become the heroes of tomorrow.

Even though this inspirational theme was originally strongly connected to British practices, Ghanaians going abroad to look for foreign expertise became a source of concern for the British foreign services. Because of the Cold War context, the British Foreign Office[58] led various investigations regarding their former colony's influences and connections. They were particularly concerned by Ghanaians coming back from the People's Republic of China (PRC) or the USSR "spouting ideology and hot air and bearing heavy tomes of Leninism, but hav[ing] learnt nothing about the practical organisation of youth movement[s]".[59] As emphasized by Jeremy Friedman, "Visitors to China were lectured on the Chinese revolutionary experience and experience of socialist construction".[60] Chinese who received these guests eagerly solicited comments upon the assumed successes of the PRC and the popularity of Mao Zedung. Meanwhile, Ghanaians were seeking actual techniques with which to apply the Chinese experiment to the developing world.

Therefore, the British countered this harmful influence by sending invitations to Ghana Pioneers in the name of the Commonwealth Relations Office for actual internships in Great Britain, among the scouts, the police, or in youth exchange programmes. As underlined earlier, this programme was part of a more global policy of control over the former colony. Indeed, the exchanges mentioned earlier were embedded within the global game of control over youth played by the USSR versus the USA and its British ally. Hence, the Pioneers were part of the socialist-oriented World Federation of Democratic Youth (WFDY), which gathered youth from all over the globe for festivals where together they took part in cultural, political and sporting activities, which the Young Pioneers attended enthusiastically. The British tried to lure them into counter organizations (not so efficiently, as far as recruiting was concerned) such as the World

---

[57] Dufraisse, Sylvain. "Les Héros du sport". La fabrique de l'élite sportive soviétique (1934–1980). PhD, Université Paris 1 Panthéon-Sorbonne, 2016.
[58] As emphasized by the numerous archives related to this subject in the FO files in the British National Archives.
[59] Letter from Tom Keeble (Office of the High Commission for the United Kingdom) to John Chadwick, 10 June 1961. TNA: DO 195/32.
[60] Daily reports on Cuban delegation to PRC led by Che Guevara in November 1960, quoted by Friedman, Jeremy Scott. *Shadow Cold War: The Sino-Soviet Competition for the Third World*. Chapel Hill, University of North Carolina Press, 2015.

Assembly of Youth, created in 1948, and to influence the political orientation of the WFDY and its member associations, with little success.[61] Given the relative failure of such a strategy, the Crown services chose a more localized approach: the movement's leaders themselves were to be invited to go to England for internships, to train themselves in leadership practices. Zacharie Shardow – who ran the Pioneers for six years –spent six months training in England. Similarly, Bennard Kuma (Headquarter Commandant for the Pioneers) went to Lancashire in 1963 in order to attend a two-month-long police training. Indeed, the British services considered quite cynically that "it is worth taking a gamble. We have nothing to lose but a comparatively small sum of money, but a great deal to gain if the Youth Pioneers can recreate themselves in a new image".[62]

Finally, beyond the political instrumentalization of youth, the British worried about the militarization at work within the GYP movement (being, in this perspective, quite different from the explicitly pacifist Scouting movement). Notably, they were particularly alarmed by the connections between the GYP and the Israeli militarized youth movement, Gadna. The Young Pioneers' connection with Israel had its roots in the ties between Nkrumah and Ben-Gurion between 1957 and 1961. Having been free from the British colonial yoke for about a decade, Israel had recently been facing similar changes, and were worth considering as an inspirational source, according to CPP leaders.

Gadna was an organization for boys and girls of 14 to 18, under the joint responsibility of the Ministry of Education and the Defence Force. "Training is provided along Scout lines with special attention to agriculture and pioneering. There are naval and air section[s and] the paramilitary Gadna [was] so much admired by visitors from Africa".[63] In the Gadna movement, the thin line between sport training and military training in state youth organizations became even more blurred, and the GYP followed this example. Indeed, various delegations of young Ghanaians were sent to Israel to learn from the Gadna movement. The young CPP member Adjimboru Syme visited Israel as early as 1957. He wrote that the aim of Gadna was "to instill the spirit of living together, working together and playing together".[64] Syme admired the paramilitary training, the ideological studies and the use of games and sports to gather youngsters as one. Also, by early 1962, around 80 Israeli technicians had come to Ghana

---

[61] Kotek, Joël. Youth Organizations as a Battlefield in the Cold War. *Intelligence and National Security* 18 (2003): 168–191.
[62] Letter from V. E. Davies (British Council) to Mr Chadwick, 16 June 1961. TNA: DO 195/32.
[63] British Embassy (Tel Aviv) dispatch number 64: 2. TNA: FO 371/164375.
[64] Syme, Adjimboru A. *Salute to Israel: The Story of the Ghana Youth Delegation to Israel, 1957.* Accra: Guinea Press, 1958, 18.

under the aid partnership between the two countries and had helped to frame the GYP.

However, the Gadna movement was primarily meant to "imbue [children] with civic values lest the country become[s] levantinized [i.e. made Arabic] and looses its unique qualities".[65] In the end, this discouraged the former anti-colonial fighters – who themselves fought against a white colonial power. But the very fact that they drew inspiration and ideas for their movement from Zionists showcases once more the ability of Pioneer agents to use organizations dedicated to very different purposes for their own agenda – as they did with the Scouting movement or the Komsomol. That said, the close friendship between Ghana and Israel quickly diminished, mainly because "Nkrumah's ambition was to mediate the Arab-Israeli conflict",[66] Ghana meanwhile becoming more and more anti-Zionist and pro-Arab.

Therefore the multiple layers of influences on the Ghana Young Pioneer organization allowed the building of a singular youth movement, at the core of global connections, way beyond the Cold War barriers. The numerous back-and-forth of the young Ghanaians (boys and girls) across the globe allowed a constant hybridization of the movement. The Pioneers navigated between ideologies (Maoist anti-imperialism, Soviet communism, British imperialism and Israeli nationalism) and used technical help (experts from all over the globe and training abroad) to help shape very concrete physical activities: scouting, military training, "scientific" sport and so on. In the end, the Young Pioneers seem to have travelled whatever the ideological framework was, and appear to have had their own agenda within the Cold War framework.

Showcasing Nkrumahist values within global interactions

In order to understand the particular agenda of the Pioneers within the Cold War context, we need to come back to the key role played by Nkrumah in relation to the Non-Aligned Movement (hereafter NAM).[67] Nkrumah took part in the 1955

---

[65] Address by David Ben-Gurion to the leader of his party, 17 May 1962, quoted by the "British Embassy (Tel Aviv) dispatch n°64" (TNA: FO 371/164375).
[66] Levey, Zach. The Rise and Decline of a Special Relationship: Israel and Ghana, 1957–1966. *African Studies Review* 46 (2003): 155–177, here 162.
[67] Westad, Odd Arne. *The Global Cold War: Third World Interventions and the Making of Our Times*. Cambridge: Cambridge University Press, 2005.

Bandung Conference, alongside Nehru (India), Nasser (Egypt), Tito (Yugoslavia) and Sukarno (Indonesia) – also known as the "Initiative Five". They advocated for a third option between Eastern and Western blocs, as an attempt to thwart the Cold War. The movement grew within the developing countries, recruiting all over the globe until the final breakdown of the USSR in the 1990s. The NAM aimed to stay outside either Western or Eastern military alliances and to bring together very different views and politic agendas. However, Ghana's position was not entirely neutral, Nkrumah notably proclaiming his solidarity with the People's Republic of China, the Soviet Union and its satellite countries during his 1961 socialist tour.[68] But, more central than Cold War issues, his main objective was to build political Pan-Africanism.

The Fifth Pan-African Conference held in Manchester in 1948 was the first stone in constructing his dense political theory[69] and his activism to promote African political unity. The congress's conclusions insisted upon the unity of black people – either American, African or Caribbean – each of them being part of the same struggle. Most of all, Nkrumah stressed that all African liberation struggles were connected and should be supported collectively, until the full independence of all colonial territories was achieved. Hence, even within the NAM, Nkrumah stood as a particular voice,[70] being a prominent leader of the Pan-Africanist political movement. He organized the All-African People's Conference in Accra in 1958, leading to his life-project: the making of the Pan-Africanist Organization of African Unity (OAU), established in Addis-Ababa in 1963. His voice was heard all over Africa (as indicated by the large number of African leaders who attended both conferences and the OAU). Therefore, he became a key player neither Russians nor Westerners could avoid. The presence of USSR delegates at various Pan-Africanist conferences is highly significant in this regard. According to Nkrumah's Pan-Africanist stances, the government of the First Republic of Ghana was crafted upon "Nkrumahism", his anti-imperialist and marxist political theory:

> The ideology for the new Africa, independent and absolutely free from imperialism, organised on a continental scale, founded upon the conception of one and united Africa, draw-

---

[68] Friedman. *Shadow Cold War.*
[69] Nkrumah, Kwame. *Ghana: Autobiography of Kwame Nkrumah.* New York: International Publishers, 1957; Nkrumah, Kwame. *African Personality.* Accra: Thomas Nelson & Sons, 1963; Nkrumah, Kwame. *Africa Must Unite.* Accra: Thomas Nelson & Sons, 1963; Nkrumah, Kwame. *Neo-Colonialism, The Last Stage of Imperialism.* Accra: Thomas Nelson & Sons, 1965.
[70] Alongside African heads of state (like the Kenyan Jomo Kenyatta) or intellectuals (like the Afro-Americans W. E. B. Du Bois or George Padmore).

ing its strength from modern science and technology and from the traditional African belief that the free development of each is the condition for the free development of all.⁷¹

Therefore, at the crossroads of the international influences summarized earlier, the challenge was to breed a truly Pan-Africanist youth. Indeed, if we relate to Nkrumahism and the wish to rely on traditional Africa, one might find this patchwork of global connections paradoxical. However, the overlapping intersections and convergences of influences on the Pioneers were essential to their very identity, as we saw previously, and the multiplication of global interactions⁷² allowed the making of an internationalized elite, able to showcase Ghana's identity. After all, Nkrumah himself had left the Gold Coast to study for ten years in the USA, which was essential to shaping his political identity, meeting Pan-Africanist and marxist militants such as C. L. R. James, George Padmore, Raya Dunayevskaya and Grace Lee Boggs.⁷³

Through the Pioneers, the new Ghana – as imagined by Nkrumah and his followers – articulated itself with numerous spaces: from African countries and the Soviet sphere to Great Britain and China. These articulations followed various temporal paths: from several years of training as a football coach to a few days of a discovery trip or reading a few lines in the *Daily Graphic* about friendly countries and their sporting successes. And these influences were not one way. Indeed, when going abroad, the Pioneers were supposed to showcase their worth as Ghanaians and influence the welcoming countries in return. They represented the nation and the ideal of Pan-Africanist citizens, valuing physical fitness, respect for manual work, self discipline, sense of duty and responsibility and love for and desire to serve their country, as emphasized by the GYP curriculum.⁷⁴ Alongside the sense of comradeship and pride in blackness and their African origins, these values and the pride of being part of the movement remained vivid for the Pioneers as shown by the interviews conducted 60 years later. For instance, a former Pioneer gave us his recollection of his trip to the rival Côte d'Ivoire:

> We went to see the boy scouts. And the girl guides. And so we went to let them know that we have something even superior in Ghana. And it was a change, because they didn't have.

---

71 Letter from Kwame Nkrumah to S. G. Ikoku, 2 March 1964. PRAAD: RG 17/1/380.
72 Subrahmanyam. *Explorations in Connected History*.
73 Clarke, John Henrik. Kwame Nkrumah: His Years in America. *The Black Scholar* 6 (1974): 9–16.
74 "Programme for senior officers' course of the Ghana Young Pioneers", date unknown. PRAAD: RG 3/5/2215.

> And to see us dressed smartly, long long people like us gents. They were so impressed about us! And no mean just course back. They would let us go and display. And particularly when there were parades. We went and we would parade like that. We came and we found that [...] And these people were admiring so much!⁷⁵

The trips of the Young Pioneers were indeed meant as an occasion to showcase African traditions. Sylvain Dufraisse showed that USSR athletes were ambassadors of the country's greatness because of their virtuosity and strength on the sporting field but also because of their attitude and appearance outside of the stadium.⁷⁶ The situation is similar here. The Pioneers were supposed to impress their African neighbours and they seemed to enjoy doing so. Therefore, when going abroad, they multiplied activities. They did not only go on parades and played games and sports with their new friends. Being Pan-African ambassadors, they had to be so during their entire trip, which meant going on cultural visits, having lunch and parties with their hosts and so on.

The recollection of Matthew Narth Tetteh's trip to the PRC for the occasion of the 14th anniversary of independence (1963) is of particular interest in this perspective. He and his fellow leaders went to Beijing to visit the Chinese youth facilities (training centres and so on) and met the Chinese Pioneers' leaders. This visit was embedded in a carefully crafted relationship between Ghana and the PRC. In 1961, even though Nkrumah had just signed various agreements with the PRC, the Chinese were quite disillusioned by his version of socialist revolution, considering him to be under the ongoing control of the British, as a representative of the "national bourgeoisie"; trapped within the battle over African leadership with Nasser (Egypt) and Touré (Guinea) and mistaken in his promotion of non-violence. However, given Ghana's key position within the diplomatic game, the Chinese chose to circumvent Nkrumah from the left by attracting the most "progressive" elements to China. Besides, alongside the rivalry with the Western bloc, the PRC feared that Ghana was to become the mouthpiece of the USSR's foreign policy positions in West Africa, being "the most important target and most convenient venue for current Soviet cultural and propaganda activities"⁷⁷ in 1962. Indeed, as we saw earlier, the Soviets had built a tight network between themselves and Ghana. The rivalry between the PRC and the USSR over the control of Africa become more open, and Chinese diplomats urged Ghana-

---

75 Interview with a former Pioneer (in May 2016). This man remains a member of the CPP.
76 Dufraisse, Sylvain. Démontrer la puissance et parfaire les esprits. *Les Cahiers Sirice* 16 (2016): 35–45.
77 People's Republic of China Embassy of Conakry to Ministry of Foreign Affairs, 9 July 1962, quoted in Friedman. *Shadow Cold War.*

ians to use their own forces, encouraging anti-imperialist policies, instead of truly marxist measures, which appealed considerably to the African Nationalist movements. In order to engage in this cultural and propaganda rivalry, the PRC implemented their now famous Third-World Ping-Pong diplomacy[78] in Ghana. Hence, six table-tennis players (three men and three women, including former world men's champion, Jung Kuo-Tuan) went to play friendly games against Ghanaian star players (all of whom were Pioneers) during April and May 1962[79] as part of an African tour including Guinea and the United Arab Republic. The Chinese coach stayed in Ghana for three months to prepare the national team for the 1962 Pan-African championships held in Cairo, leading to E. A. Quaye's victory. A few years later, the African champion underwent a table tennis coaching course at Beijing Institute of Physical Education (1965).

Hence, the 1963 official invitation of the GYP leaders for the 14th anniversary of independence was a sign among others of the active will of the PRC to attract Ghanaians. Wishing to counteract Nkrumah's softness, they invited the GYP leaders, in order to get the young Ghanaian executives to be part of the building of a broad anti-imperialist front under the Chinese leadership. But, when visiting Beijing in 1963, the leaders of the GYP movement did not simply accept the anti-imperialist socialist policies of the PRC. They indeed discussed with the Chinese Pioneers, visited the training and sporting facilities of the youth centres, observed games and sporting demonstrations. But they also behaved as true envoys of the first Pan-Africanist nation, as ambassadors of Ghana. Hence, at Tiananmen Square, Zacharie Shardow, Mowbray Elliott and Matthew Narth Tetteh posed for a photograph wearing fugu (or smocks – typical striped cotton clothes from the Northern Region of Ghana) with Chinese Pioneers wearing Mao collars. Indeed, as emphasized by a Pioneer during his interview: "So our clothes, make them look African, we should not depend on the White [...] And if you dress, you should not disregard your traditional dress".[80] When Chinese in Mao collars and Ghanaians in fugu pose together, they stand out from the traditional suit-and-tie of the imperialists, either Soviets or Westerners. The envoys also took the oppor-

---

[78] Hong, Fan and Xiong Xiaozheng. Communist China: Sport, Politics and Diplomacy. *The International Journal of the History of Sport* 19 (2002): 319–342.
[79] The games and the whereabouts of the Chinese players were widely publicized in the *Daily Graphic* (PRAAD: NP/1/61, NP/1/62 and NP/1/63).
[80] Interview with a former Pioneer (in May 2016). Originating from the Northern Region, he went to Italy for his training and refused to go training in the USSR because he was a Catholic, even though he was a dedicated Pioneer and Nkrumahist. This underlines the complexity of the relationship between the actual Pioneers and the friendly countries, when analysing them at the scale of the agents themselves.

tunity to entertain the Chinese Young Pioneers with some Highlife music[81] – a very popular music genre born in the early twentieth century, incorporating Akan music and jazz[82] – allowing the display of Ghana's dynamic cultural life[83] to demonstrate more of African culture to their allies.

Moreover, the aim of these visits was to showcase the ability of the fatherland to train Ghanaian youth both morally and individually. Indeed, GYP members going abroad were carefully selected according to their individual value. When they wished to go abroad for training, the young members went through a thorough selection process. They were often recommended by their group leader, sent application letters showcasing their sporting and intellectual skills and went through an interview in Accra with the movement's chiefs.[84] The selection criteria were tough and mainly based on political credit, morality, physical fitness and involvement within the movement. Since the young boys and girls were to represent Ghana abroad during visits lasting up to several years, their selection was a key challenge for the Nkrumahist organization.

Therefore, when going abroad after passing the selection process, the Young Pioneers were to show personal skills commensurate with these expectations. Hence, most of the Pioneers sent to Chrudim flight school impressed their instructor by their behaviour and sense of duty: "faultless, disciplined, decent, industrious",[85] for the great pride of the movement, taking this opportunity to display accounts of the internship in the *Daily Graphic*.

Conclusion

The numerous photographs of groups of six or ten smiling Young Pioneers in uniforms just after landing at Accra's airport, returning either from a ten-day visit to Addis-Ababa or a six-month training in Moscow were weekly displayed in the *Daily Graphic* between 1960 and 1966 and viewed by most of Ghana's citizens. Bringing back gifts for their families and histories to tell their friends, the travelling pioneers returned with more than a specific set of skills in military

---

81 Tetteh, Matthew Narth. *The Ghana Young Pioneer Movement: A Youth Organisation in the Kwame Nkrumah Era*. Accra: Institute of African Studies, University of Ghana, 1985, here 87–90.
82 Plageman, Nate. *Highlife Saturday Night: Popular Music and Social Change in Urban Ghana*. Bloomington: Indiana University Press, 2013.
83 Akyeampong, Emmanuel. *Drink, Power, and Cultural Change*. Oxford: Heinemann, 1996.
84 Application Sheets, 1961–1964. PRAAD: RG/1/540.
85 Progress reports by Mr Kohoutek, Chrudim, 25 May 1962. PRAAD: RG/1/540.

training, youth leadership, ping-pong coaching or gymnastics – or spouting hot air about Marxism-Leninism.

Indeed, whatever the game played over the control of Africa by China, the USSR and Great Britain, the Young Pioneers were primarily the envoys of a Pan-Africanist nation. They were sent to discover their political allies and to embody the modernism of Ghanaian Pan-Africanist youth, taking advantage of aid programmes and learning sporting techniques while still following their own Nkrumahist agenda. And through a final twist, the Pioneers themselves became globally connected citizens full of stories and memories of their life abroad, gathering Soviet, Maoist, imperial and Pan-Africanist influences through a global hybridization process.

This research could be further developed from an international perspective: How was the movement and its envoys perceived abroad (in China, Soviet Union or Eastern Europe) by the young boys and girls who were playing sports? Moreover, the links between African youth organizations (whatever their colonial background) are still understudied and are worth consideration, in order to follow the "Southerning" path of Cold War studies. Finally, following Romain Tiquet's most recent works, we may also focus on the way youth organizations from newly independent countries were closely linked to forced labour, reconsidering a somewhat utopian view that has long prevailed in the studies of youth movements regarding their so-called "leisure" activities.

Souvik Naha
"The Russian deadpan expert" vs "America's white hope":
The personal, the national, and the global in the "Cold War" of chess

Introduction

In April 1972, ahead of his much anticipated World Chess Championship match against the Soviet grandmaster Boris Spassky, the American grandmaster Bobby Fischer came up with a political statement in an interview with the BBC:

> It is really the free world against the lying, cheating, hypocritical Russians. [...] This little thing between me and Spassky. It's a microcosm of the whole world political situation. They always suggest that the world leaders should fight it out hand to hand. And this is the kind of thing that we are doing – not with bombs, but battling it out over the board.[1]

The comment indicates that Fischer considered the upcoming match of 24 games to decide the best chess player for the next three years, slated to take place in Reykjavik from July that year, to be his one-man crusade against the Russians as a whole, not just their empire of chess. It was indeed a solo effort as Fischer, described by many as a loner and a social misfit, preferred to practice alone, contrary to Soviet grandmasters who worked as a team, vigorously training and spending time together. For this very reason Fischer's self-identification with the American political agenda against the Soviet Union came as a surprise to many. Nevertheless, the press exploited the statement by linking chess players to the drive for international supremacy that underwrote the history of the Cold War. Commenting on his bitter attitude, an editorial in *The Times* called him a self-appointed soldier of the free world against the Soviet Union "in an atmosphere akin to the Berlin blockade of twenty years ago".[2] Responding to the championship match's setting at a critical moment of détente, and taking for

---

[1] Edmonds, David and John Eidinow. *Bobby Fischer Goes to War: The True Story of How the Soviets Lost the Most Extraordinary Chess Match of All Time.* London: Faber & Faber, 2004, here 369.
[2] An Opening Move from Bobby Fischer. *The Times*, 8 May 1972.

granted Fischer's complicity as a Cold War hero, many reports of the match and particularly later recollections evoked Cold War imagery in their description.

The cultural turn in Cold War studies that began in earnest in the 1990s highlighted how different societies responded to the tensions of identity and culture generated by ideological conflict. Studies of sport as one of the cultural fronts of the Cold War have usually focused on diplomatic intent, cultural exchange and the restructuring of the international sport community.[3] Research on the American boycott of the 1980 Olympics in Moscow and the Russian snub of the 1984 Olympics in Los Angeles have envisaged sport as a major foreign policy drive in the Cold War's final phase.[4] As new social meanings arising as side effects of the bipolar antagonism suffused international and domestic sports, not even indoor games like chess were left untouched. Replete with martial imageries, chess surrogated as an intellectual battlefield and an ideal conduit of propaganda and mediatization of proxy wars.[5] The Fischer-Spassky duel in 1972 was described by many contemporary writers as a cultural expression of the polarized world – an image that has been perpetuated in later reports. The match, attended by a large contingent of international press correspondents, famous chess players and intellectuals, generated an extensive range of perspectives: from conjuring up the title contenders as representatives of their national characters to outright rejection of such metaphors of national cultural difference. Analysis of these reports from a global history perspective raises questions about the constitutive role played by interpersonal and inter-institutional encounters in a major event.

This article argues that the dominant narrative of this match, loaded with Cold War metaphors, was no less fragmentary than the volatility of politics and cooperation in the period. Taking an actor-centric and global history approach, it examines the narrative tropes in the context of the perception of the intermingled personal, national and global character of the subjects of Cold War politics. The World Chess Championship does not qualify as a mega-event

---

[3] Wagg, Stephen and David L. Andrews (eds.). *East Plays West: Sport and the Cold War.* London and New York: Routledge, 2007; Montez De Oca, Jeffrey. *Discipline and Indulgence: College Football, Media, and the American Way of Life during the Cold War.* New Brunswick, New Jersey and London: Rutgers University Press, 2013.

[4] Sarantakes, Nicholas E. *Dropping the Torch: Jimmy Carter, the Olympic Boycott, and the Cold War.* Cambridge and New York: Cambridge University Press, 2011; D'Agati, Philip. *The Cold War and the 1984 Olympic Games: A Soviet-American Surrogate War.* Basingstoke: Palgrave Macmillan, 2013.

[5] Sprengeler, Matthew John. Playing by New Rules: Board Games and America's Cold War Culture, 1945–1965. Unpublished Master thesis, University of Northern Iowa, 2013.

on the scale of public mobility, cost, infrastructural investment and legacy, or even an international event since it might be contested between players from the same country in their homeland. Hence, the extent of globality of an event such as this, complicated further by a simulacrum of national entanglement, is contingent on the mediated account of its impact. With a view to understand better the implication of national and international politics for a theoretically post-national sport event, this chapter explores press reports published from America, Russia, England, Ireland, India and Japan, countries which were either deeply involved, neutral or non-aligned during the Cold War. It uses English-language sources for the sake of their accessibility, whereas the newspapers under study were selected to demonstrate the global dimension of sport and the variety of political agency in the different countries where the texts were published.

Chess and the Cold War

The Cold War, the rivalry for global dominance between the USA and the Soviet Union couched in the idiom of ideological conflict, significantly shaped global political constellations between the late 1940s and the late 1980s. Nevertheless, the historical conditions of the Cold War were far more complex and uneven than this one-line exposition suggests.[6] Just as many countries across continents were embroiled in it in political and economic capacities, some stayed unaffected and others set up counter-groups as a political statement of neutrality. Historians have pluralized the framing of the superpower antagonism because of its cascading effects across the worlds of economics, science, technology, culture, ideology, strategy and diplomacy, rendering it as more of a concept than a conflict.[7] Areas and institutions which were considered mere objects of superpower politics, such as Southeast Asia in the 1950s and Europe in the 1950s–60s, have been ascribed more importance as interdependent actors by revisionist historians.[8] The relationship between America and the Soviet Union fluctuated throughout the Cold War. They narrowly avoided nuclear conflict in the wake of the Cuban Missile Crisis in 1962, which led to a hiatus in mutual hostility.

---

6 Duara, Prasenjit. The Cold War as a Historical Period: An Interpretive Essay. *Journal of Global History* 6 (2011): 457–480.
7 Romero, Federico. Cold War Historiography at the Crossroads. *Cold War History* 14 (2014): 685–703.
8 Autio-Sarasmo, Sari. A New Historiography of the Cold War? *European History Quarterly* 41 (2011): 657–664.

America improved its relationship with the People's Republic of China towards the end of the 1960s. The Soviet incursion into the liberal communist state of Czechoslovakia in 1968 and the Sino-Soviet border conflict in 1969 made China consider allying with America as a countermeasure to any future Soviet offensive. After several conciliatory exchanges, the American president Richard Nixon visited China in 1972 and issued the Shanghai Communique along with the Chinese Premier Mao Zedong. This first step towards a regular diplomatic relationship has been described by one analyst as the removal of "a chess piece from the Soviet side of the board".[9] The first Strategic Arms Limitation Talks treaty, signed between America and the Soviet Union in May 1972, restricted weapon development. Except for the race to build cooperation with the global South, the relationship between the USA and the USSR at the time of the championship match was one of delicate truce. Hence, to operate from within the state apparatus and yet knock out the Soviet regime, one had to be a fictional spy or masquerade as Bobby Fischer who, despite being a non-state actor, was nationalized in media discourses as an emblem of the American capitalist agenda in the post-war years. The conflation of Fischer with the imagined American hero without his consent or proper attention paid to his personality was arguably a by-product of Cold War culture.

The Fischer-Spassky match sparked interest across the world largely due to the high quality of the title contenders, and within American and Soviet political circles as another crack at world domination. National governments usually play an important role in propagating athleticism through their school systems, providing training for sportspersons and organizing sports events at national and international levels.[10] Hence, they are in an advantageous position to promote their political agenda and positive nation-branding through organized sport. Chess was a part of the Soviet political system just as much as the newspaper *Pravda* was. A board game invented in ancient India, chess is about two players moving pieces termed king, queen, bishop, knight, rook and pawn across a chequered board to capture the opponent's king. It reached Europe in the Middle Ages via Persia, undergoing several modifications in the Early Modern period before assuming its current form in the fifteenth century. The modern conventions about moving the pieces and the outcome were delineated in the nineteenth century. The Soviet Union emerged as the game's major force after 1945, having instituted a highly systematic training programme for chess aspirants. The one

---

[9] Adams, Chris. *Ideologies in Conflict: A Cold War Docu-story.* New York: Writer's Showcase, 2001, here 251.
[10] Houlihan, Barrie. *The Government and Politics of Sport.* London: Frank Cass, 1991.

non-Soviet grandmaster to have won the World Championship, and that for only a brief interlude till the Union's dissolution in 1991, was Fischer.

As the Soviet grandmaster Anatoly Karpov said in the 1980s, there was hardly a boundary between chess and politics in the country.[11] The government paid monthly salaries to its grandmasters and sponsored their tournament play. Spassky, for his role as "the last line of defence of Soviet chess hegemony against Fischer", received a flat on the fifth floor of Moscow's newest and largest apartment building.[12] The communist governments in Yugoslavia and Cuba, interested as they were in promoting their regime as the thinking person's government, organized extravagant global tournaments in the 1960s. In 1992, when a rematch between Fischer and Spassky was announced, the organizer, a Serbian businessman named Jezdimir Vasiljevic, was asked if the event was meant to improve the image of Slobodan Milosevic's reviled government. Although Vasiljevic denied this, the question reveals how firmly anchored in public memory is the history of the political mobilization of sport. There are instances of the IOC having banned a country from participating in the Olympics as punishment for its national government's crimes against humanity, but also for excessive interference in sport administration. The criteria for inclusion and exclusion in global sport are just as ambiguous as the underpinnings of power are in the making of sport policy.

Additionally, in spite of being one of the most individualistic of sports ever conceived, chess has not been able to shed national overtones. Grandmasters represent their countries at world championships and candidates' tournaments even when they receive no aid from their government for preparation. The unbroken presence of a system of national identification for sportspersons even at events which do not require citizenship for eligibility, such as golf and tennis opens, pre-empts the idea of sport's post-nationality.[13] Thus, the nation remains as a scaffolding around global sport, providing it with symbolic capital through the media. The figurative conferring of global citizenship to iconic sportspersons recasts their identity from being citizens of sovereign states to that of citizen of an interconnected world. Nevertheless, evocation of national character, not simply nationality, of athletes is a long-established device that journalists deploy to explain a sportsperson's behaviour and achievement, sometimes going so far out of line that such descriptions read as caricatures. Personal traits and national characters are thus ineluctably enmeshed in the global imagining of sport. The

---

11 Soltis, Andrew. *Soviet Chess 1917–1991*. Jefferson, NC: McPherson, 2000, here 2.
12 Barden, Leonard. Endgames People Play, *The Guardian*, 1 July 1972.
13 Rowe, David. *Global Media Sport: Flows, Forms and Futures*. London and New York: Bloomsbury Academic, 2011.

Soviet nation's attachment to chess is legendary. The relevance of chess in American society is comparatively under-reported despite the public recognition of Cold War characteristics in the two-player game.

American-Soviet chess rivalry in the 1950s did not quite catch public imagination as in later decades, except in isolated instances. During a set of games in New York in 1954, *Life* magazine assumed the partisan patriot's role, reporting, "Communism's rigid visage relaxed long enough to show Russian officials grimacing, fidgeting on their chairs and chewing their nails, like anyone else under tension".[14] The Americans were no match for the Soviets, which American journalists acknowledged, till Fischer emerged in the late 1950s. His impetuousness, according to a historian, symbolized the independent American character and made him "the human face of the Cold War".[15] He won the candidates' tournament in 1971, which allowed him to challenge the reigning world champion Spassky in the next World Chess Championship in 1972. Reykjavik was selected as the venue from a list of interested cities including Belgrade, Sarajevo, Buenos Aires, Bled and Dortmund, after a protracted negotiation involving the World Chess Federation (FIDE – Fédération Internationale des Échecs) and the managers of the chess players, as the prize money it offered was the highest once Belgrade dropped out. The match has been widely acknowledged as a site where the ideological tension of détente was played out, popularly billed not so much as a contest between Fischer and Spassky, but between Fischer and the Russians and America and the Soviet Union, particularly since Fischer projected himself as the symbol of "the free world" in its struggle against communism.

Fischer's long history of spats with Soviet grandmasters began at the 1962 candidates' tournament in Curacao, where he accused them of playing out quick draws among themselves, thus preserving stamina and intensity so that they could play to full strength against non-Russian opponents.[16] Later in the same year, Fischer complained that the then world champion Mikhail Botvinnik took advice from the team captain during the USA-USSR match at the 15th Chess Olympiad, a biennial international tournament. Nobody took his allegation seriously, not even his own captain who refused to lodge a complaint against Botvin-

---

[14] Stress Over Chess: Risky Play against U.S. Alarms Soviet Boss. *Life* 37, 12 July 1954, quoted in Sprengeler, Playing by New Rules, 47.

[15] Sprengeler, Playing by New Rules, 52.

[16] According to recent statistical research, the draws substantially benefited the Soviet teams, as their winning potential under simulation tests increased from 25% if they did not collude to 60% if they colluded. Moul, Charles C. and John V.C. Nye. Did the Soviets Collude? A Statistical Analysis of Championship Chess 1940–1978, *Journal of Economic Behaviour and Organisation* 70 (2009): 10–21.

nik. It transpired later that Fischer had spoken only three words to Botvinnik in his life. He uttered "Fischer" when they were introduced, said 'sorry' as they nearly bumped heads while taking seats for their game in 1962, and finally "draw" at the end of the game. His distrust of "Russians", his umbrella term for all Soviet people including Estonians and Lithuanians, gradually reached so high a level that in 1971, he checked the envelope of the draw personally to ensure that his opponent Mark Taimanov had legitimately been awarded the white pieces in their first game.[17] Fischer was against the choice of Iceland as the venue, which he called "primitive", and refused to stay in the best hotel for fear of being easily spied on by the Russians.[18] His continuous criticism caused Spassky at one point to say that Fischer showed "signs of persecution mania" even though the Russians were not so hostile to him.[19] Incidentally, while Fischer's personality and statements gave journalists the chance to bring up Cold War metaphors, international public reception of the match proved to be very different, and is analysed in the next section.

The match of the century

Many newspapers promoted the match as a battle between an "American" and a "Russian", instead of simply two individuals who were citizens of the US and the USSR respectively, even though it was not an international tournament. In an article for *The Washington Post*, Jim Murray described the Soviet competitors in an earlier event held in Argentina as "Russian shock troops". The problem of considering Fischer as the American hero appeared in the piece where the journalist quoted Fischer as having accused the American government of colluding with the Soviet chess body since the chess federation agreed to the venue and playing rules without his approval.[20] Fischer threatened to pull out of the match unless his demands about increasing the prize money and the removal of television cameras were met. He disappeared days before the match was due to begin, putting a question mark on the possibility of the match taking place. Commenting on the uncertainty created by Fischer, Michael Lake from the *Guardian* wrote that

---

17 Fischer routed Taimanov 6–0, which humiliated the Communist Party so much that they had Taimanov interrogated, his salary stopped, public musical performances and foreign travel prohibited. Johnson, Daniel. *White King and Red Queen: How the Cold War Was Fought on the Chessboard.* London: Atlantic, 2007, here 166–167.
18 Barden. Endgames, 1.
19 *The Guardian*, 17 June 1972.
20 Murray, Jim. Russians Try Rooking Bobby Fischer. *The Washington Post*, 18 June 1972.

even a meeting between Richard Nixon and Leonid Brezhnev would have been easier to arrange than the chess match.[21] He called Spassky "the adventurous chess hero of the Soviet Union" whose tortuous play over the previous year surprised the "brooding army of Soviet chessmasters". According to him, Fischer approached the match as "an extension of the cold war". Roy Perrott wrote in the same newspaper that Nixon could think of flying Fischer into Iceland in his presidential jet so that America did not miss the best chance for 35 years to interrupt the Soviet's monopoly over the championship.[22]

It was later revealed that Nixon and Henry Kissinger discussed the implications of the championship match, probably thinking of chess as a new soft power that America could exercise in the global intellectual sphere alongside its universities. The Soviet state strategically developed sport as a foreign policy tool of scoring against ideological opponents.[23] Success in sport also served to deflect attention away from the shortcomings of socialist development policy and economic downturn.[24] It was an apt moment for the US to counter the Soviet soft power with the intense feeling of nationalism expected to flourish following a very likely win by Fischer. Kissinger made a phone call to Fischer prior to the match when the chess prodigy considered withdrawing as his insistence on Belgrade as the venue and a larger share of television revenue was overruled.[25] American newspapers were not so certain about any long-term cultural benefit coming out of this match as chess was not an obvious sport for many of their readers and Fischer's temper too volatile to have faith in. Incidentally, British tabloids exploited the ideological confrontation more advantageously than the American press. In the *Daily Mirror*, the match was introduced as the clash between "Broody Boris the Russian deadpan expert" and "America's white hope",[26] where "the prestige of the two most powerful nations on earth" was

---

21 Lake, Michael. Chess Title Remains on Ice. *The Guardian*, 1 July 1972.
22 Perrott, Roy. Fischer Non-move Baffles Icelandic Chessmen. *The Guardian*, 1 July 1972.
23 Martin, Evelyn. The Soviet Union and the Olympic Games of 1980 and 1984: Explaining the Boycotts to Their Own People. In *East Plays West: Sport and the Cold War*, Stephen Wagg and David L. Andrews (eds.), 235–252, here 236. London and Routledge, 2007.
24 Katzer, Nikolaus. Soviet Physical Culture and Sport: A European Legacy? In *Sport and the Transformation of Modern Europe: States, Media and Markets 1950–2010*, Alan Tomlinson, Christopher Young and Richard Holt (eds.), 18–34, here 26. London and New York: Routledge, 2011.
25 Horowitz, Israel Albert. *The World Chess Championship: A History*. New York: Macmillan, 1973, here 269.
26 Dunne, Colin. Chess Bored: or How Iceland is Waiting for a King Among the Pawns. *Daily Mirror*, 1 July 1972.

at stake.[27] British newspapers, except for *The Times*, displayed a striking tendency to show the Russians in an unflattering light while arguing in favour of making concessions for a genius like Fischer.

The *Irish Times*, published from a country that remained neutral throughout the Cold War, was anxious about Fischer's behaviour setting back the improving political understanding between the two superpowers.[28] The Soviet ambassador to Iceland, Sergei Astavin, reportedly hoped the match would strengthen cooperation in the bipolar world.[29] Donald Stone, a vice-president of the American Chess Federation, was apprehensive about the political outcome of Fischer's disappearance. He expressed misgivings about the turn of events being interpreted as a diplomatic insult.[30] The American embassy in Iceland was extremely embarrassed by the absence of Fischer, who was supposed to conduct himself as the nation's cultural ambassador. The American admiral at the NATO base at Keflavik offered his guest quarters as Fischer refused to stay in the hotel reserved for him, but received no response. The soft power potential of the match, building some momentum in the world press, faded quickly due to Fischer's unreliability.

The Russian team assisting Spassky, which had so far maintained impeccable public relations, was encouraged by a universal implication that, unlike them, the Americans lacked sporting behaviour.[31] In a press conference they organized, the FIDE president, Dr Max Euwe, admitted to violating rules to get the match going and signed a letter criticizing Fischer's erratic behaviour. Spassky, so far very gentle and silent, openly criticized Fischer for the first time after the latter missed the opening ceremony. While doing so, he appeared to some to be acting under duress, on orders from Moscow.[32] With this public statement, the *Guardian* claimed, the palliative potential of the match was gone. The whole event intensified "from a sport into a revival of the cold war".[33] The correspondent had apparently surrendered to a journalistic trend of imbuing any sporting encounter between America, the Soviet Union, and their diplomatic associates with Cold War metaphors. Similar opinions were expressed during the Canada-USSR ice hockey summit series and the America-USSR Olympic basket final in 1972.

---

27 Dunne, Colin. They're Off at Last. *Daily Mirror*, 12 July 1972.
28 Editorial. Gambit. *Irish Times*, 5 July 1972.
29 Jones, Tim. Bobby Fischer, Still Missing, is Given a Two-day Reprieve. *The Times*, 3 July 1972.
30 Dunne, Colin. Anyone for Chess? *Daily Mirror*, 3 July 1972.
31 Lake, Michael. On the Bother Board. *The Guardian*, 3 July 1972.
32 Morris, Joe Alex. Bobby Fischer as the Ugly American. *The Washington Post*, 6 July 1972.
33 Lake, Michael. Apology Brings Truce in the Chess Cold War. *The Guardian*, 6 July 1972.

Aside from referencing the players as Cold War volunteers, newspapers justified their way of ordering the combat narrative by ascribing generic characteristics to them. Fischer's pre-match blustering about taking on the Russians was visualized by many as a patriotic statement that made the nation proud. A *Guardian* correspondent thought that Spassky possessed the "Celtic moodiness and artistic volatility associated with the natives of the city (Leningrad)".[34] A *Sunday Times* reporter called Fischer "individualist, adventurous and occasionally reckless" much in the cast of fortune hunters, whereas Spassky was "the more benign type of Soviet bureaucrat, cautious, noncommittal, evasive". The *Daily Mirror* correspondent portrayed the competitors as perfect embodiments of their societies in a piece replete with regional stereotypes:

> Fischer, like the good capitalist he is, got the prize money doubled to £100,000 with 30 percent of everything bar the latest cod catch. Spassky, a cunning Russian propagandist, bowed around kissing babies and signing autographs like a Westminster-bound Tory, scoring brilliantly on international goodwill. One is the champion of five-year plans, a profitless society and lady street cleaners. The other is in there pitching for mom's apple pie, Old Glory and the hamburger.[35]

A report in the *Irish Times* highlighted the contrast between the two characters in terms such as the "disciplined Russian" and "the self-indulgent, unpredictable and completely undisciplined American", making clear its distaste for the "American way of life".[36] Even an Indian newspaper was caught up with the clash of categories witnessed worldwide. It observed in Fischer's behaviour marks of "the brash, over-confident, bragging American", as opposed to "the quiet, cultured and self-effacing European" in Spassky.[37] India was part of the Non-Aligned Movement, an international group of nations which associated themselves neither with America nor the Soviet Union, when the championship took place. The descriptions of the match in Indian newspapers largely contained game analysis, with occasional allusions to the national characteristics of the players written in critical terms, particularly for the American. The *Times of India*, considered centrist and hence somewhat anti-imperial, compared Fischer to a clown, and advised him to remember that a world series was not "a circus act nor can chess be reduced to amateur theatricals".[38] It later mentioned

---

34 Perrott. Fischer Non-move.
35 Dunne, Colin. The Chessboard Jungle. *Daily Mirror*, 13 July 1972.
36 Editorial. Gambit. *Irish Times*, 5 July 1972.
37 Aries. A Poor Mixed-up Kid. *Times of India*, 18 August 1972.
38 Editorial. Petty Master. *Times of India*, 6 July 1972.

that Fischer came under severe criticism by Americans too, one of them having written, "you are a disgrace to the American people [...] you are mentally disturbed and should be treated at once".[39] M. V. Kamath, the editor of the newspaper, quoted in his article the opinion of the *New York Times* that many in the US were disturbed by Fischer's "psychological warfare" and wanted Spassky to teach him a lesson. Conversely, many in the Soviet Union supported Fischer for his resolve and defiance of prohibitive rules.[40] The match received wide coverage in India, almost as extensive as a FIFA World Cup would have, since chess was already very popular in the country and the play was excellent.

Fischer's gamesmanship had become so unpalatable that an editorial from the *Guardian* replaced war metaphors with a balanced analysis of the build-up to the match, criticizing Fischer and praising the calm and measured response from Spassky to the confusion caused.[41] It speculated that Fischer's ploy to unsettle his opponent could begin a new age in chess history when the preceding mind game would become more decisive in the final outcome. Fischer's demand for increased prize money was variously interpreted as a capitalist American's unreserved craving for wealth and also as a chess player's mission to boost incentives for his sport. Before the match, Spassky was quoted as having said to a Soviet journalist that Fischer's demand reflected the American attitude which prioritized the prize purse ahead of one's sporting skill.[42] According to a report from the *Japan Times*, he added, "His talk about money may be his way of asserting his individuality in a country like the United States where there is a lot of money".[43] This idea must have been prevalent in the USSR, since even the news agency Tass alleged that Fischer showed a "disgusting spirit of gain", which the *Washington Post* regarded as a comment befitting "Russia's hostile attitude to the savagely aggressive young American grandmaster".[44]

However, sources close to him confirmed that Fischer was the last person to be concerned with monetary gain. He turned down millions of dollars in commercial endorsements after winning the World Championship, and donated a large part of the prize money to the Christian sect he belonged to. According to his manager Fred Cramer, Fischer would leave money everywhere – in his py-

---

39 When Fischer Blushed. *Times of India*, 9 August 1972.
40 Kamath, M. V. Fischer's Win has Given Chess New Image. *Times of India*, 4 September 1972.
41 Checkmate Before You Move. *Guardian*, 3 July 1972.
42 Chess Champion's Chide. *The Washington Post*, 17 June 1972.
43 Chess Champ says Persecution Mania Besetting Fischer. *Japan Times*, 20 June 1972.
44 Kernan, Michael. Waiting for Bobby: The Chess World Waits for Bobby. *Washington Post*, 1 July 1972.

jamas, under pillows, under the bed and so on. As his former mentor Arnold Denker recounted, he clamoured for a large winner's purse because:

> He accepted implicitly the capitalist principle that value is what buyers freely bid. The higher the bid, the greater the worth of one's calling [...] Once, when offered $5 million to play a match, he termed the proposal totally inadequate because Mohammad Ali received $10 million for a mere 60 minutes work.[45]

Understandably Fischer was against any rule of authority, and whoever he thought stood between him and his coveted victory was an enemy. Hence, the Russians were his primary target and Americans made the list when they stood between him and what he wanted. His displeasure with America, evident throughout the championship, was overlooked by many journalists who were in no small part invested in portraying players as products and representatives of national culture. In 1965, the US government stopped Fischer from attending a tournament in Havana. Not one to knuckle under, he played the games at the Capablanca table at the Marshall Chess Club in New York in front of an arbiter, with his and the opponent's moves being sent to and fro by telex.[46] In 1966, he bettered his record of political subversion by playing chess with Fidel Castro. His opinion of Americans was quite low as is evident from an interview given to the grandmaster Svetozar Gligoric:

> When I beat Spassky, then Americans will take a greater interest in chess. Americans like winners [...] The U.S. is not a cultural country. The people here want to be entertained. They don't want any mental strain, and chess is a high intellectual form. Americans want to plunk in front of a TV and not to have to open a book [...].[47]

Not the American Cold War hero or ambassador that the press would make their readers believe, Fischer became more antagonistic to America than he ever was anti-Soviet, proving that his statement about defeating communists on the chess board stemmed from personal ambition rather than national duty. The author Arthur Koestler's foreboding that "as a propagandist for the free world he is rather counter-productive", written prior to the 1972 match, turned out to be prophetic.[48] In 1992, after decades spent as a recluse, Fischer was lured into a $5 million

---

[45] Denker, Arnold S. *The Bobby Fischer I Knew & Other Stories.* San Francisco: Hypermodern, 1995, here 106.
[46] Soltis, Andrew. *Bobby Fischer Rediscovered.* London: Batsford, 2003, here 9.
[47] Gligoric, Svetozar. *Fischer vs Spassky: World Chess Championship Match, 1972.* London: Fontana, 1972, here 9.
[48] Koestler, Arthur. The Glorious and the Bloody Game. *Sunday Times,* 2 July 1972.

rematch against Spassky in Belgrade. His then-19-year-old girlfriend, the Hungarian junior chess star Zita Reichany, persuaded him to play. Serbia and Montenegro was at the time facing UN sanctions for its war crimes against other former Yugoslav countries. The US treasury department threatened to fine Fischer $250,000 and/or jail for ten years for "trading with the enemy". Yet, Fischer played, won and consequently had an arrest warrant issued and his passport revoked by the US government.

These counterclaims suggest that the neat Cold War categorization of Fischer as the liberal consumerist and Spassky as the socialist intellectual was indeed problematic, and nothing could be further from reality. The Cold War gave Fischer the platform to flourish and become famous.[49] Spassky, more aware of the categories cooked up by the press, said, probably in self-defence, "When I sit at the chess board, I am a chess player, not a politician".[50] Although he spoke of himself as a "lazy Russian bear", he had no sympathy for the communist government or Soviet ideology. He was vocal against the invasion of Czechoslovakia, and shook hands with Czechoslovak grandmasters at the Lugano Olympiad in 1968. The Soviet state banned him from playing abroad three times. They prevented him from personally meeting Fischer in Amsterdam in January 1972 to settle the details of the upcoming World Championship match.[51] A correspondent felt that not being a member of the Soviet Communist Party and driving a Swedish Volvo could have put Spassky in the crosshairs of the Soviet bureaucracy, which could take retributive measures should Spassky lose the match and thus forfeit Soviet superiority.[52] The prediction was not farfetched as the grandmaster was indeed heckled on his return. *The Times* reported that there were rumours of Spassky applying for political asylum, which he denied.[53] He was not permitted to participate in tournaments in San Antonio, Texas and Palma de Mallorca over the next months. The State Committee for Sport and Physical Culture and its mouthpiece, the newspaper *Sovietsky Sport*, criticized not only Spassky for poor preparation but other grandmasters, Petrosian and Taimanov, who had lost to Fischer in the lead-up to the championship match.[54] These contradictory accounts of Spassky come from the same newspapers which had once stereotyped him as the archetypal Russian.

---

49 Johnson, *White King and Red Queen*, 146.
50 Fischer Delays Going to Iceland. *The Times*, 27 June 1972.
51 Barden. Endgames, 1.
52 Morris. Bobby Fischer as the Ugly American.
53 Boris Spassky Shunned. *Times of India*, 18 January 1973.
54 Smith, Hendrick. Spassky's Defeat Brings Shake-up in Soviet Chess. *Times of India*, 6 April 1973.

In their analysis of the journalistic agenda underpinning the championship's lasting image as a Cold War battle, David Edmonds and John Eidinow mention several factors behind this reflection. Firstly, the contrast between the insularity and sceptical behaviour of the Soviet team, specifically their inability to leverage the opinion of the world press in their favour, and Fischer's belligerence gave the press enough fodder. Secondly, they found really striking the tendency of the Western and American officials to take decisions during the match often without consulting the Soviet team, and just informing them about the decision, expecting compliance. Thirdly, the Western media stereotyped the Soviet team in terms of what they believed to be the Soviets' nationalist responsibility.[55] Finally, emphasizing Fischer's anti-Russia attitude was essential for the match to have been seen as part of the Cold War; it would otherwise have been recorded as a symbol of détente for bringing the US and the USSR to a table where (chess) moves were negotiated and undertaken.[56] Most of this media politicking, however, happened before the match. Once the games started, particularly after Fischer's crushing win in the third game, chess analysis took over from ideological musings.

The Soviet press changed remarkably. It was known to have shielded its citizens from the global network society.[57] Tass reported Spassky's wins within minutes and delayed the news of his championship loss for two hours.[58] The newspaper *Sovietskaia Rossia* put the passing of the title from Russian hands in a black-bordered box as used for an obituary.[59] The Russian press took it upon itself to pick up the broken pieces of the chess machine and hide them away from the public. Interestingly, after Fischer had beaten Taimanov and Bent Larsen in 1971, *Sovietsky Sport* had hailed him as a miracle. In an interview with Boris Ivkov, former world champion Mikhail Tal called Fischer "the greatest genius to have descended from the chessic sky".[60] Another Russian grandmaster called him "the perfect harmony of position and material".[61] Far outside the world of chess, in eastern Siberia, a state farm named its most rewarding cow Bobby.[62] The admiration did not vanish altogether after Fischer's win in 1972, evident

---

[55] Edmonds and Eidinow. *Bobby Fischer Goes to War*.
[56] Edmonds and Eidinow. *Bobby Fischer Goes to War*.
[57] Rantanen, Terhi. *The Global and the National: Media and Communications in Post-Communist Russia*. Lanham: Rowman & Littlefield, 2002.
[58] Fischer Late for his Coronation. *Times of India*, 3 September 1972.
[59] Edmonds and Eidinow. *Bobby Fischer Goes to War*, 373.
[60] Denker. *The Bobby Fischer I knew & Other Stories*, 105–106.
[61] Soltis. *Bobby Fischer Rediscovered*, here 11.
[62] Steiner, George. *The Sporting Scene: The White Knights of Reykjavik*. London: Faber and Faber, 1973, here 37.

from the praise for Fischer by the Russian public. Nor did the trappings of politics and national pride prohibit Americans from recognizing Spassky as a very special player.

Conclusion

This chapter has shown that the rhetoric used in the representation of the behaviour of the players and the public were disproportionate to the conflict between "the *pax Americana* and the *pax Sovietica*".[63] The press lent itself to a sense of historicism by often being governed by precognition rather than recognition. The chess event unfolded in the press through the dialectical narrative of how the match helped the winner's country to establish its intellectual superiority over the other country and, by extension, the world. This chapter emphasized the different attitude of press outlets, tried to find patterns in their political stance, and analysed the popular disposition of forging symbols where there should have been none. The nation in this narrative was, inappropriately, a self-replicating entity mapped onto the players involved. The Soviet Union's practice of anointing chess players as knights of the realm was transferred to its opponents, but on a different scale as perception and policy were subjective.

The championship match reiterated the nation's relevance for individual sport of a global nature as a coherent blend of categories. It also evinced the boundaries of the interplay between states and non-state actors in a global setting. Both Fischer and Spassky inhabited the threshold between the state and the non-state owing to the political investment in their performance. Spassky was an unwilling participant, whereas Fischer was a false prophet. Both were appropriated by the institutional forms of international exchange, in this case the press and the foreign office, as exemplars of their respective national cultures. It was very much in accord with the Cold War culture of discovering quotidian values in exceptional individuals and publicizing them as the triumph of the nation. This misleading attribution soon collapsed as later biographies and press coverage suggest, but it surely made Reykjavik 1972 a global byword for Cold War sport.

---

[63] Caute, David. *The Dancer Defects: The Struggle for Cultural Supremacy during the Cold War.* Oxford: Oxford University Press, 2003, here 1.

Quentin Tonnerre and Grégory Quin
A forgotten "ping-pong diplomacy"?
About the Chinese ping-pong players' tour of Switzerland (1972)

Introduction[1]

In December 1972, a report from the *Télévision Suisse Romande*, entitled "l'amitié sino-suisse", recounted the tour of ten Chinese[2] ping-pong players (men and women) in Switzerland.[3] During their stay – that took them to several cities over the country – the Chinese gave some demonstrations and played against the best Swiss players.

It is interesting to notice that this tour was organized one year after the famous visit to China by the United States ping-pong (table tennis) team. Better known as the episode of "ping-pong diplomacy", these demonstration games helped to establish contact between two countries that previously had no diplomatic relationship. In fact this event was a preliminary step in order to create a political link, which led to the official visit from the president of the United States himself, Richard Nixon, one year later. Many researchers have already focused on this event,[4] and it was not the first time that China used ping-pong to established relationships with other countries. Amanda Schuman has recently shown that since 1963–1964, numerous Chinese ping-pong players had travelled

---

[1] We wish to thank Philippe Vonnard and James Barras for their assistance during the process of writing this contribution, especially for some historiographical inputs about the Cold War.
[2] For practical reasons, in the present article China refers to People's Republic of China (PRC) and Taiwan refers to Republic of China (ROC).
[3] "L'amitié sino-suisse", programme broadcasted on 8 December 1972. You can watch it here: http://www.rts.ch/archives/tv/sports/camera-sport/3442225-l-amitie-sino-suisse.html (consulted 2 November 2016).
[4] Much research has been published on this topic. From an American point of view see: Eckstein, Ruth. Ping-Pong Diplomacy: A View from behind the Scenes. *The Journal of American-East Asian Relations* 1 (1993): 327–342. From a more Chinese, or Asian, point of view see: Hong, Zhaohui and Yi Sun. The Butterfly Effect and the Making of 'Ping-Pong Diplomacy'. *Journal of Contemporary China* 9 (2000): 420–448; Itoh, Mayumi. *The Origin of Ping-Pong Diplomacy: The Forgotten Architect of Sino-U.S. Rapprochement*. Basingstoke: Palgrave MacMillan, 2011.

https://doi.org/10.1515/9783110529098-011

to Africa to play demonstration games in different countries and several tours were also organized in New Zealand and in other Asian countries. These games revealed the increase of interest by the Chinese government in the use of sport as tool of diplomacy and the particular place of ping-pong, a game in which the Chinese were one of the best nations in the world. In the meantime, the Swiss government also developed a more precise policy, starting to use sport as a diplomatic tool, to develop, strengthen or restart international relations.

Our intention in this chapter is to understand motives and resonances existing around the Chinese ping-pong tour in Switzerland, considering it in the context of the reorganization of Swiss sports policy and of the changing state of the relationship between Switzerland and China, as shown by Ariane Knüsel.[5] Firstly, there were some obvious sports reasons to organize such an event then, as it was a wonderful opportunity for the Swiss players to compete against some the best opponents in the world. Secondly, regarding the fact that sports had been used by governments since the interwar period as a tool of diplomacy, we could consider that political matters were also important, especially as the Cold War created some deep divisions but never real disconnections.[6] Moreover, we could also argue that there were economic motivations that explained the organization of the tour, which included some visits to several famous Swiss firms. Our main hypothesis is that regarding its international popular success and the apolitical discourse of its leaders since the end of the Second World War, sport in Switzerland began to be a new tool of trade diplomacy, also used as a kind of "make up" to hide some economic or political interests, allowing governments to cross some ideological borders more easily.

The paper is primarily based on documents from several Swiss sporting bodies' archives (Comité Olympique Suisse (COS), Association Nationale d'Education Physique (ANEP), Association Vaud-Valais-Fribourg de tennis de table (AVVF)) and from the Swiss federal archives, creating an original corpus never used by historians before. The research has been completed through a broad review of generalist newspapers (*La Gazette de Lausanne, 24 Heures, Journal de Genève, Berner Tagblatt, Neue Zurcher Zeitung, Basler Nachrichten, Bund*) and specialized sporting newspapers (*La Semaine sportive, Sport, Tip*).

Firstly, we will briefly review current research on the use of sport as a tool of diplomacy and will make some key points about the Chinese and Swiss cases.

---

[5] Knüsel, Ariane. "Armé de la pensée de Mao Tsé-toung", on peut résoudre tous les problémes: l'influence de la Révolution culturelle sur les relations entre la Suisse et la République populaire de Chine. *Relations internationales* 163 (2015): 29–46.
[6] Hochscherf, Tobias, Laucht, Christoph and Andrew Plowman (eds.). *Divided, but not Disconnected: German Experiences of the Cold War.* New York: Berghahn Books, 2010.

Secondly, we will explain the Swiss and the Chinese sports diplomacy policies around 1970. Thirdly, we will describe in detail the different resonances of the tour and its different stops all over the country.

1 Sport as a tool of diplomacy and Chinese-Swiss relations in the early 1970s

1.1 Sport as a tool of diplomacy during the Cold War

In 2006, Antoine Fleury and George-Henry Soutou coordinated a special issue of the French journal *Relations Internationales* concerning the new diplomatic tools experienced during the twentieth century.[7] In this special issue, possibilities were offered to researchers to work on financial, cultural or scientific diplomacy, but even in their introduction, the authors did not indicate the existence of one of the most important tools of diplomacy: sport. Taking an opposite view, we argue that the dimension of sport cannot be underestimated given the studies written during the last decade,[8] especially researches on epistemological considerations;[9] a shift well illustrated by an article on sport in books recently published in the field of the history of international relations[10] and, closer to our topic, some recent developments in research on the history of diplomacy.[11]

In fact, sports have been used as tool of diplomacy since the beginning of the last century. Patrick Clastres showed that even the first Olympic Games

---

7 The special issue is entitled "Les nouveaux outils de la diplomatie" and was published in 2006.
8 For recent literature of sport and international relations, see: Keys, Barbara. International Relations. In *Routledge Companion to the History of Sport*, Steven W. Pope and John Nauright (eds.). London: Routledge, 2010.
9 Beacom, Aaron. Sport in International Relations: A Case for Cross-disciplinary Investigation. *Sport in History* 20 (2000): 1–23; Murray, Stuart. The Two Halves of Sports-Diplomacy. *Diplomacy & Statecraft* 23 (2012): 575–592; Dichter, Heather. Diplomatic and International History: Athletes and Ambassadors. *International Journal of the History of Sport* 32 (2015): 1741–1744.
10 Frank, Robert. Internationalisation du sport et diplomatie sportive. In *Pour l'histoire des relations internationales*, Robert Frank (ed.), 387–405. Paris: Presses Universitaires de France, 2012.
11 Black, David and Byron Peacock. Sport and Diplomacy. In *The Oxford Handbook of Modern Diplomacy*, Andrew F. Cooper, Jorge Heine and Ramesh Thakur (eds.), 708–727. Oxford: Oxford University Press, 2013.

held in Athens in 1896 was politicized by the Greek state.¹² The first turning point happened during the interwar period when totalitarian regimes such as Nazism and Italian Fascism used sport to show their new power on the international stage.¹³ However, democracies also started to focus more on sport as Peter Beck has well explained in the case of football in England.¹⁴ Thus, the sporting field was becoming a battle between athletes from different countries. This situation explained why George Orwell indicated, in a famous text written in 1945, that sport is "war minus the shooting".¹⁵ Nevertheless, the place of sport on the international stage is a little bit more complex than the writer of *1984* described because athletes could also be considered as ambassadors of their countries.

After the Second World War, the changed context marked by the increase of globalization and the onset of the Cold War gave sport a new legitimacy as tool of diplomacy. For instance, Sylvain Dufraisse showed how sport was used during the 1950s by the Soviet government to maintain or create relationships with the other blocs and demonstrates increasing sport exchanges between the Soviet Union and other countries.¹⁶ For the same period, Philippe Vonnard has also indicated that the European Union of Football Associations (UEFA), created in 1954, was probably the sole European organization that crossed the Iron Curtain.¹⁷ Thus, sport once again gave a wonderful opportunity to create original

---

12 Clastres, Patrick. La refondation des Jeux Olympiques au Congrès de Paris (1894): initiative privée, transnationalisme sportif, diplomatie des Etats. *Relations internationales* 111 (2002): 327–345.
13 See notably: Gonzalez Aja, Teresa (ed.). *Sport y autoritarismos. La utilización del deporte por el comunismo y el fascism*. Madrid: Alianza Editorial, 2002. Macon, Benoit. The Politization of Football: The European Game and the Approach to the Second World War. *Soccer and Society* 9 (2007): 532–55; Bolz, Daphné. *Les arènes totalitaires: fascisme, nazisme et propagande sportive* [Hitler, Mussolini et les jeux du stade]. Paris: CNRS, 2009; Bensoussan, Georges, Dietschy, Dietschy, François, Caroline and Hubert Strouk (eds.). *Sport, corps et sociétés de masse. Le projet d'un homme nouveau*. Paris: Armand Colin, 2011.
14 Beck, Peter. *Scoring for Britain: International Football and International Politics, 1900–1939*. London: F. Cass, 1999.
15 Quoted in: Beck, Peter. Confronting George Orwell: Philip Noel-Baker on International Sport, Particularly the Olympic Movement as Peacemaker. *The European Sports History Review* 5 (2003): 187–207.
16 Dufraisse, Sylvain. Démontrer la puissance et parfaire les esprits. Pratiques et objectifs des délégations sportives soviétiques à l'étranger, 1952 – fin des années 1960. *Les Cahiers Sirice* 16 (2016): 35–46.
17 Vonnard, Philippe. How did UEFA Govern the European Turning Point in Football? UEFA, the European Champion Clubs' Cup and the Inter-Cities Fairs Cup Projects (1954–1959). In *Building Europe with the Ball. Turning Points in the Europeanization of Football (1914–1989)*, Philippe Vonnard, Grégory Quin and Nicolas Bancel (eds.), 165–185. Oxford: Peter Lang, 2016.

and regular exchanges between Eastern and Western countries. This particularity of sport during the Cold War has already been noticed by some authors[18] but given recent reassessments of the Cold War – particularly the fact that the "two blocs were divided but not disconnected"[19] – it appears as a very interesting area for future research.

It is even more interesting in particular to consider smaller countries or connexions that did not directly include the two superpowers, not least the case of Switzerland and China and their sporting relations, especially in the context of new reorganization of the bilateral relations between China and Switzerland since the Second World War.

1.2 Swiss-Chinese relationships since the Second World War

In October 1949, Mao's victory over Chiang Kai-shek's (1887–1975) nationalist army on mainland China brought Cold War to the Far East.[20] Three months before that, Mao had announced he would support the Soviet Union in international affairs. The president of the United States, Truman, had reacted by launching a huge non-recognition campaign and publicly reaffirmed his support for the Republic of China that had withdrawn to a Taiwanese bastion which she would never leave. Since the Second World War, Switzerland was also confronted by diplomatic pressure. It had avoided destruction of its territory during the war, but its international image suffered considerably, because it had not fully supported the Allies in their battle against Germany. Opposed to multilateral relations because it could harm its neutrality, Switzerland tried to find bilateral alternatives. Regarding this, the very early recognition of the newly founded People's Republic of China on the 17 January 1950 was thus intended to reinforce

---

18 See notably some papers in: Wagg, Stephen and David L. Andrews (eds.). *East plays West: Sport and the Cold War.* London: Routledge, 2007; Bertling, Christoph and Evelyn Mertin (eds.). *Freunde oder Feinde? Sportberichterstattung in Ost und West während des Kalten Kriegs.* Gütersloh: Medienfabrik, 2013.
19 Hochscherf, Laucht and Plowman. *Divided, but not Disconnected.* On the same topic see also: Mitter, Rana and Patrick Major (eds.). *Across the Blocs: Cold War Cultural and Social History.* London: Frank Cass, 2004; Fleury, Antoine and Lubor Jilek (eds.). *Une Europe malgré tout, 1945–1990.* Bruxelles: P.I.E. Peter Lang, 2008; Romijn, Peter, Giles Scott-Smith and Joes Segal (eds.). *Divided Dreamworlds? The Cultural Cold War in East and West.* Amsterdam: Amsterdam University Press, 2012; Bott, Hanhimäki, Jussi, Schaufelbuehl and Wyss. *Neutrality and Neutralism in the Global Cold War: Between or Within the Blocs?*
20 Xia, Yafeng. The Cold War and Chinese Foreign Policy, *E-International Relations*, 16 July 2008, http://www.e-ir.info/2008/07/16/the-cold-war-and-china/

the credibility of Switzerland's neutrality. As Michele Coduri noted in his seminal thesis on Sino-Swiss relations, by establishing diplomatic relations, both governments attempted to maintain contact, but Switzerland wanted more.[21] It saw this contact as a continuation of pre-1949 Sino-Swiss relations, despite the difference of ideology. Thus, because of this difference, communist China could not accept such continuity in several domains. The Communist party nationalized Swiss companies and drove missionaries out of its territory. As a result, Swiss presence in mainland China decreased so much that by 1955 the colony had almost vanished. Thus, Sino-Swiss relations before 1971 were mainly determined by tensions that can be explored through two cases.

First, the Great Proletarian Cultural Revolution had bad consequences for Swiss officials of the delegation in Beijing. In a report written in 1966, Hans Keller, the Swiss ambassador, stated he was horrified by the daily scenes of public humiliation and torture he witnessed. He saw the Red Guards as the "scum" responsible for this chaos and considered the mass movement as a purge equivalent to Kristallnacht (Berlin, 1938); he compared the Swiss Embassy at this period to a concentration camp. Nonetheless, the Swiss Embassy was not damaged as were the embassies of some other western countries, probably because the decision-makers in China regarded Switzerland as a country that had to be treated relatively better. Switzerland was a capitalist country and had an especially acute anti-communist tradition, but Bern was not one of Beijing's most dangerous enemies. It was neutral and the Chinese Embassy in Switzerland was the backbone of Chinese communist presence in Western Europe.[22]

Second, since 1959, Tibet started to become a problem in Sino-Swiss relations. That was the year that Switzerland helped or tolerated anti-Chinese movements in several ways. Le Croix-rouge (The Red Cross) facilitated refugees' escape to Nepal. The Federal Council agreed to receive 1,000 refugees seeking refuge on its territory. Beijing protested against what it considered as an anti-Chinese campaign and intervention in a domestic issue. The Swiss Department of Foreign Affairs of that time, the Federal Political Department, justified its stand by the Swiss tradition of neutrality and solidarity to refugees. From then on Tibet and human rights remained a problem between the two countries.[23]

---

21 Coduri, Michele. *La Suisse face à la Chine: Une Continuité Impossible ? 1946–1955*. Louvain-la-Neuve: Bruylant-Academia, 2004.
22 Keller, Hans. Les relations entre la Chine et la Suisse. *Bulletin de Sinologie* 35 (1987): 22–28.
23 Knüsel, Ariane. 'Armé de la pensée de Mao Tsé-toung'.

Later on, in the seventies, China's bad reputation started to change, also its rupture with the Soviet Union made it interesting to some communist supporters in Switzerland, for whom China offered an alternative in the communist world.[24] Those groups were marginal though, promoting a third path, neither capitalism nor communism, but anti-imperialism. Deeply divided, China and Switzerland were not disconnected before the 1970s, but as mentioned in the *Berner Tagblatt*, "ping-pong was one of the first bridges that broke the Chinese isolation",[25] and the 1972 tour participated in a dynamic where Swiss-Chinese relations could slowly reach some new balance, at a time when the two countries started to implement more structured international sport policies.

2 Swiss and Chinese sport diplomacies around 1970: a contrast

2.1 Sport and the Foreign Office in Switzerland: "business as usual"

Thanks to the Chinese tour, we can see the new overall shape of Swiss sport diplomacy in the 1970s. Several points confirmed this hypothesis. Firstly, after 1964 and the Swiss "debacle" at the Innsbruck Olympic Games,[26] deputies of the Swiss parliament reacted:

> Given the very wide advertising which was made for the Winter Games which have just ended in Innsbruck, the failures recorded by the Swiss athletes damage the reputation of our country, considered formerly as a landmark of winter sports. [...] The more the victories in big sports events become national matters and the more states give importance to the number of medals won by their athletes, the more it is important that we encourage strongly in Switzerland sport practised with the aim of performance, because these performances are the symbol of the good physical condition of our young people.[27]

---

24 Koller, Frédéric. *Les Editions en langues étrangères de Pékin et leur diffusion à Genève (de 1949 à nos jours)*. Geneva: n. c., 1990, 24.
25 *Berner Tagblatt*, 4 December 1972, 27.
26 Loudcher, Jean-François and Monica Aceti. La 'débâcle' suisse aux Jeux olympiques d'hiver à Innsbruck en 1964 et ses conséquences sur l'organisation sportive nationale. *Stadion* 38 (2013): 183–205; Quin, Grégory. De la cure d'air à l'or blanc, une Interassociation Suisse pour le Ski face aux enjeux de l'essor du ski en Suisse (années 1920–années 1960). *Histoire des Alpes* 22 (2017): 135–155.
27 *Motions et postulats*, "Encouragement du sport pratique en vue de performances", 18 February, postulat Meyer, in *Rapport du Conseil fédéral à l'Assemblée fédérale sur sa gestion en 1964*, 9

In Switzerland, the mid-1960s was a period of deep reconsideration of the role of sport on the international stage and of its capacity to become a tool of soft power. Even though the first questioning on this topic begin in the 1920s, when the National Olympic Committee received its first grant after the success of several Swiss athletes during the first Olympic Games organized after the First World War, many debates still took place in the 1960s and generated the implementation of a National Elite Sport Committee in 1966 and the introduction of three weekly and mandatory lessons of physical education at school, by the "law encouraging sport and gymnastics" passed in 1972. Secondly, in the 1960s and the early 1970s, Swiss diplomacy was very active around the timekeeping question, especially to maintain the monopoly of Swiss industry in this market, formally supported by diplomats, federal councillors, and economic and sport circles. Thus, beyond the observation of the significance of sport in Swiss diplomacy, the period of the tour in Switzerland in the early 1970s was a moment of awareness about sport as a useful tool to foster Swiss trade relations. Finally, it may be necessary to recall that the commission for Swiss foreign presence which would become the nation branding body *Présence Suisse* thirty years later, was interested in sport since its establishment in the early 1970s. According to the commission, Switzerland should send abroad "only good athletes chosen carefully".[28] However, Swiss participation in international sports competitions abroad was not a priority at this time in comparison with other cultural events.

Beyond this last point, in the 1970s Swiss diplomacy did not any longer ignore the potential of sport as a matter of concern on the international stage and Swiss sport leaders were aware of the significance of the contacts they had with the Federal Political Department (DPF). However, despite these arguments, the links between the relevant bodies were still weak. The only case of a regular link between the DPF and the sport movement in the 1960s was the issue of sports relations with states from the East, which was regularly discussed in the Assembly of Delegates of the Association Nationale d'Education Physique. In the background, timekeeping was still a constant matter of concern, implying a permanent control of international sports competition by the Swiss state but which can also be considered as "business as usual".[29]

April 1965, quoted in Loudcher and Aceti. La 'débâcle' suisse aux Jeux olympiques d'hiver, here 190.

28 *Arbeitsausschuss der Koordinationskommission für die Präsenz der Schweiz im Ausland*, Zusammenfassendes Protokoll, session of 13 December 1972, dodis.ch/40556.

29 Bentele, Ursina and Sacha Zala. Neutrality as a Business Strategy: Switzerland and Latin America in the Cold War. In *Neutrality and Neutralism in the Global Cold War*. 178–195, here 189.

2.2 Chinese sport diplomacy: "Friendship first, Competition second"

Contrary to the case of Switzerland, the use of sport by the Chinese government on the international stage is better documented,[30] in particular by Fan Hong's work on the links between sport and diplomacy during the Cultural Revolution[31] or in 1963 around the organization of the GANEFO games.[32] Nevertheless, the topic that has interested scholars and the general public[33] the most on this theme is indisputably Chinese ping-pong diplomacy and its use for the reconciliation between China and USA in the early 1970s. Furthermore, about the same period, scholars noted that sport was also used by China to re-establish relationships with third world countries which had been suspended during the first year of the Cultural Revolution. To achieve this, the Chinese delegations of ping-pong players travelled mainly in Asia and Africa with the principle "Friendship first, Competition second" that the Chinese Sport Minister explained: "Friendship means politics. Friendship first means politics first. We use competition to project our socialist country's new image, and to make friends in the world".[34]

The journal of the Swiss Communist Marxist-Leninist Party *Octobre* described it in its September 1972 edition: "a lot of Chinese sport delegations (ping-

---

[30] Guanhua, Wang. 'Friendship First': China's Sports Diplomacy during the Cold War. *The Journal of American-East Asian Relations* 12 (2003): 133–153; Hong, Fan and Lu Zhouxiang (eds.). *Communists and Champions: The Politicisation of Sport in Modern China*. London, Routledge, 2012.
[31] Hong, Fan and Xiong Xiaozheng. Communist China: Sport, Politics and Diplomacy. *The International Journal of the History of Sport* 19 (2002): 319–342; Hong, Fan. Not All Bad! Communism, Society and Sport in the Great Proletarian Cultural Revolution: A Revisionist Perspective. *The International Journal of the History of Sport* 16 (1999): 47–71; Hong, Fan and Lu Zhouxiang. Sport in the Great Proletarian Cultural Revolution (1966–1976). *The International Journal of the History of Sport* 29 (2012): 53–73; Hong, Fan and Lu Zhouxiang. Politics First, Competition Second: Sport and China's Foreign Diplomacy in the 1960s and 1970s. In *Diplomatic Games. Sport, Statecraft, and International Relations since 1945*, Heather Dichter and Andrew L. Johns (eds.), 385–407. Lexington: University Press of Kentucky, 2014.
[32] Lutan, Rusli and Fan Hong. The Politicization of Sport: GANEFO – A Case Study. *Sport in Society* 8 (2005): 425–439; Connolly, Chris A. The Politics of the Games of the New Emerging Forces (GANEFO). *The International Journal of the History of Sport* 29 (2012): 1311–1324; Field, Russell. Re-Entering the Sporting World: China's Sponsorship of the 1963 Games of the New Emerging Forces (GANEFO). *The International Journal of the History of Sport* 31 (2014): 1852–1867.
[33] Ping-pong diplomacy was studied by the American journalist Nicholas Griffin: Griffin, Nicholas. *Ping-Pong Diplomacy. The Secret History Behind the Game that Changed the World*. New York: Skyhorse Publishing, 2015.
[34] Quoted in Fan and Xiaozheng. Communist China: Sport, Politics and Diplomacy: 336.

pong, soccer, ice hockey, track and field) participated these last years in friendly competitions in many countries".[35] Indeed, some Chinese students played ice-hockey games in Switzerland a while before their ping-pong compatriots. However, the ice-hockey players had not the same visibility as the ping-pong players. The magazine *L'Illustré*, from the French part of Switzerland, notes that the Chinese "have quickly used [ping-pong] as an export product" and the ping-pong players as "public relations". The journalist concludes: "In Sweden, in Austria, Chinese ping-pong players are, like in Switzerland, brilliant ping-pong delegates and skilful ambassadors of their country".[36] Beyond the rhetoric of friendship between peoples conveyed by Chinese propaganda and reused by Swiss authorities during the tour of 1972, the coming of Chinese ping-pong players to Switzerland is obviously an opportunity for discussing various important political and economic issues concerning the relations between China and Switzerland.

3 A Chinese tour in Switzerland

3.1 The stakes around the organization of the tour

The Chinese tour in Switzerland was part of a bigger European tour, which included other fixtures in Malta, Austria and Sweden.[37] From there the Chinese arrived at Kloten airport in Zurich on 29 November 1972. The first project was to organize the tour "as a prologue for the famous 'Six Days [Cycling] Race' in Zurich"[38] but this could never be done properly. Therefore the Swiss Federation (Fédération Suisse de Tennis de Table, FSTT) had to change its plan. Finally, the Chinese delegation stayed ten days in Switzerland, including eight days of an "official tour", passing through different cities. Regarding the selection of the different cities, some documents from the eastern part of Switzerland explained that there were no games organized in Saint-Gallen because officials from this region did not want to pay for them.[39] Officially, the tour was organized by the

---

35 *Octobre*, September 1972, 11.
36 Vuillemier, Jean-François. Les pongistes chinois en Suisse: des "public relations". *L'Illustré*, 7 December 1972, 71.
37 Concerning those national cases, one should read the relevant chapters in: Bott, Hanhimäki, Schaufelbuehl and Wyss. *Neutrality and Neutralism in the Global Cold War*.
38 *Basler Nachrichten*, 2 December 1972, 34.
39 Interview with Claude Diethelm, former president of the Swiss Table Tennis Association, 3 November 2016.

FSTT, and more specifically under the responsibility of Marcel Schaller,[40] General Secretary of the national body. He was a famous promoter of table tennis in the canton of Fribourg, soon involved in the organization of tours by foreign teams,[41] like the game against Belgium in 1956.[42] It was also interesting to highlight that the whole FSTT committee was involved in the different steps of the tour, including the central FSTT president – Hugo Urchetti – in Bern or the technical director – Werner Schnyder – in Basel.

After landing in Zurich, the Chinese delegation travelled through the entire country, staying in La Chaux-de-Fonds on 29 and 30 November, in Bern on 1 and 2 December, in Basel on 3rd and 4th, in Vevey on 5th, in Geneva on 6th and finally again in Bern for some unofficial days from 7 to 9 December, before leaving for Malta. Table tennis games were organized in each city, generally on the second evening, so on 30 November in La Chaux-de-Fonds, on 2 December in Bern, on 4th in Basel and on 6th in Geneva, leaving more than one day for social activities. Even a fifth game was organized in Vevey on 5 December, to celebrate the fortieth anniversary of the inter-cantonal body – the AVVF – grouping clubs from Waadt, Wallis and Fribourg.[43]

But along the way, the programme also included other activities, including some training sessions of course, but also visits to several Swiss companies, dinners with officials from different political levels and cocktails with both economic and political representatives. If there was some repetition during the different stages, it is interesting to note how precise were the visits they made along the way, pointing out the technical and economic traditions in each city and giving the opportunity for a large number of officials to meet the delegation.[44] In La Chaux-de-Fonds, the Chinese delegation was invited to visit the Technicum and the watchmaking museum. In Bern, they visited both a department store – Loeb – and some farms in Riedern (in the countryside west of the city). During the stay in Bern, they also moved to Magglingen, in order to discover the Ecole Nationale de Gymnastique et de Sport de Macolin, and meet the director, M. Kaspar Wolf. They found out about the facilities proposed for Swiss athletes. In Bern, the delegation was also welcomed at the Chinese Embassy, for an official

---

40 AVVF Archives, Documents about the 1972 Tour, Final Programme, 27 November 1972.
41 Some documents consulted in the AVVF archives show that there were other international games organized in the early 1970s in Switzerland, such as against Scotland in March 1972.
42 Fribourg Table Tennis Club's website, http://www.cttfribourg.ch/index.php/113-pages-fixes?limitstart=0 (consulted 2 November 2016).
43 AVVF Archives, Documents about the 1972 Tour, Final Programme, 27 November 1972.
44 AVVF Archives, Documents about the 1972 Tour, Final Programme, 27 November 1972. All the elements presented in the paragraph, come from the final version of the programme.

dinner, gathering Chinese and Swiss officials. In Basel, the delegation visited the Hoffmann-La Roche pharmaceutical firm. On their way to Vevey, they passed by the Nestlé Fabric in Broc – with some representatives from the Chinese Embassy – before being welcomed by the mayor of Vevey. In Geneva, they visited the Chinese Consulate and the United Nations (UN) building, also showing their sporting abilities "under the eyes of both the European director of the UN and that of the Red Cross International Committee (RCIC)".[45] Finally, going back to Bern on 7 December, there was a final dinner at the Chinese Embassy, which again included all the delegations, the organizers, the players and some journalists. Of course, the presence of several media was important throughout the tour, to cover both the sporting and political issues. For instance, the part of the tour which took place in the French-speaking region was presented in three different TV shows, as mentioned in a letter by a producer from the Télévision Suisse Romande (TSR).[46]

3.2 The multiple resonances of a "Celulloid Ball"

"Celluloid Ball Diplomacy",[47] "Chinese Table Tennis Diplomacy, in Switzerland too"[48] or "A Very Diplomatic Ping-Pong",[49] those titles are quite explicit on the "diplomatic" resonances of the tour. For the press it was very clear that in the aftermath of the "Ping-Pong Diplomacy" episode from 1971, the Swiss tour was a matter of diplomacy, but it also had other resonances in the sporting sphere, not only for national and local political authorities but also for several other actors such as big firms.

Within the sporting sphere, as the tour was organized and desired by the Swiss Federation, it was quite obvious that there were some sporting interests in having Chinese players in Switzerland in the early 1970s. Of course, the point was not to win victories, which was never a target, neither for the press, nor for the officials from the Federation. Thus, having the "best" in some some cities was a great occasion to organize good propaganda, even if Switzerland was clearly not an important nation within the international sphere of table tennis. It came only nineteenth and seventeenth (respectively for men's and

---

45 *Journal de Genève*, 8 December 1972, 15.
46 AVVF Archives, Documents about the 1972 Tour, Letter from Antoine Bordier to Maurice Abetel, 30 November 1972.
47 *Sport*, 29 November 1972, 9.
48 *Neue Zurcher Zeitung*, 30 November 1972, 41.
49 *Journal de Genève*, 8 December 1972, 15.

women's team competitions) in the last European Championship of 1971.[50] For instance, in Geneva, the defeat was presented as "cruel but normal [...] and was taken with a smile".[51] A bit earlier, while loosing 5 to 1, *24 Heures* celebrated the "only point taken from the Chinese by the Swiss athletes".[52] Given the difference between China and Switzerland, the development of table tennis was systematically presented in a comparative way contrasting the four million Chinese players – training on a daily basis since school – or the "300,000 participants competition"[53] to the 4,500 Swiss players.[54] After the tour, and beyond the difficulty of binding all the elements together, table tennis seemed to get a greater recognition in Switzerland. At ANEP's General Assembly in 1973, officials from the FSTT made a statement, alerting the executive committee from the institution, about the difficulties encountered by several clubs with halls too small for them to play.[55]

During the tour, some games were quite popular, often with over 1,000 spectators;[56] officials, such as Raymond Gafner[57] – president of the COS – attended some of them. The tour was also an occasion for political representatives to show their interest in sport, which was further rooted in public policy in Switzerland since the implementation of the "law encouraging sport and gymnastics" in March 1972.[58] This included the president from the Grand Conseil and the president from the Conseil d'Etat from Neuchâtel and La Chaux-de-Fonds, members of the government in Basel or several mayors or members of communal bodies. The only problem seemed to be the late organization of the whole tour, which implied that several authorities already had some scheduled appointment and were obliged to miss the games. Thus, besides official involvement from federal, cantonal and municipal officials, we do also have to mention the role played by several sections of an organization called Connaissance de la Chine, especially in La Chaux-de-Fonds and in Lausanne. As mentioned in the programme from

---

50 AVVF Archives, Documents about the 1972 Tour, Programme of the Games in La Chaux-de-Fonds, 30 November 1972.
51 *Journal de Genève*, 8 December 1972, 5.
52 *24 heures*, 1 December 1972, 47.
53 *Tribune de Lausanne*, 7 December 1972, 34.
54 AVVF Archives, Documents about the 1972 Tour, Programme of the Games in Vevey, 5 December 1972.
55 Swiss Olympic Archives, ANEP General Assembly Minutes, 1974, 3 November 1974, Bern, 17.
56 *Tribune de Lausanne*, 6 December 1972, sport supplement.
57 AVVF Archives, Documents about the 1972 Tour, Letter from Raymond Gafner to AVVF's committee, 27 November 1972.
58 Swiss Federal Archives, Official documents, law encouraging sport and gymnastics, 17 March 1972.

the stage in La Chaux-de-Fonds, this organization had an "essential aim to allow the discovery of the multiple aspects of Chinese culture".[59] It was linked with the Swiss Communist party and originated in the French-speaking part of Switzerland in the 1960s for economic purposes, especially around the watchmaking industry.

The tour was also clearly oriented to satisfy the interest of important Swiss companies, clearly even some of the "top" firms in all the crucial economic areas: pharmaceuticals (Hofmann-La Roche, Basel), watchmaking (La Chaux-de-Fonds),[60] and food (Nestlé, Vevey and Broc). The documents gathered never mentioned contracts signed during the tour. However, it seems obvious that it was an occasion to create links, especially between Chinese authorities and the leaders of those companies.[61] For the games in Vevey, a letter found in the AVVF's archives made clear that Nestlé participated directly in the organization of the game, probably giving some money to the Federation to "guarantee the great success of the event, both regarding its general and sporting aspects".[62] Another letter showed that Nestlé gave its commitment to cover a potential deficit, which was finally around 2,800 Swiss francs.[63] Thus, in a document sent by the FSTT to the Chinese Embassy on 18 November, it is also obvious that economic influences directly concerned table tennis. Indeed, the letter made clear that "all the games will have to be played with Urchetti Balls",[64] those manufactured by the company owned by the president of the FSTT – Hugo Urchetti – also a former successful player.

During the visit to the Technicum and the watchmaking museum in La Chaux-de-Fonds, the director of the museum explained: "I am glad that you are interested in our museum. We know that Switzerland had very close watch-

---

59 AVVF Archives, Documents about the 1972 Tour, Programme of the Games in La Chaux-de-Fonds, 30 November 1972.

60 It is interesting to note that the programme from the stage in La Chaux-de-Fonds included advertisements for almost all the watchmaking companies based in the region (Enicar, Favre-Leuba, Longines, etc.). AVVF Archives, Documents about the 1972 Tour, Programme of the Game in La Chaux-de-Fonds, 30 November 1972.

61 The Chinese ambassador attended the first dinner in La Chaux-de-Fonds and then the last one in Bern, organized inside the Embassy, when the Chinese delegation was on its way home. Thus members from the Embassy followed the delegation during its whole stay.

62 AVVF Archives, Documents about the 1972 Tour, Letter from the AVVF committee to the director of Nestlé, 21 November 1972.

63 AVVF Archives, Documents about the 1972 Tour, Letter from the AVVF committee to the director of Nestlé, 26 February 1973.

64 AVVF Archives, Documents about the 1972 Tour, Letter from Marcel Schaller to the Chinese Embassy in Bern, 18 November 1972.

making trade relations with China. Many of our factories are regular supplies of the Chinese State. I think that these relationships will be better, stronger, and China is for us an excellent client".[65] One of the organizers of the tour also said, "I guess that many traders hope for a better presence in the Chinese market after these meetings". Thus, it is interesting to analyse this event in the context of Swiss watchmaking industry policy around 1970. As shown by Pierre-Yves Donzé, China had been a rather problematic market since the establishment of a communist government in 1949.[66] Swiss watchmakers tried to continue their business through interpersonal relations. Furthermore, Chinese authorities wanted to set up a watchmaking industry on their own territory, which happened in the 1960s and alarmed the Swiss industry. In response, Swiss firms supported this development, which gave them access to a big market. Thus, Swiss watch exports to China grew in this period[67] and several events between Swiss and Chinese industries were organized in the late 1960s and early 1970s.

At the same time, some important relations between the Swiss pharmaceutical industry and China were implemented, as shown by the visits to China of delegations of the firms Hoffmann-La Roche and Ciba-Geigy in 1971 and 1972.[68] Moreover, communist China replaced Taiwan in the United Nations in 1971, and the presence of the director of the European Office of the UN and of the director of the ICRC during the competition in Geneva[69] illustrated the diplomatic significance of the event. Thus, in the same vein as the establishment of friendship associations with China in the French part of Switzerland in the 1960s, one of the main purposes of the Chinese tour in Switzerland in 1972 was to change the Swiss people's perception of the Chinese-Tibetan conflict.

---

65 "L'amitié sino-suisse", programme.
66 Donzé, Pierre-Yves. Les horlogers suisses et la Chine (II). Au temps de Mao. *Watch Around* 104 (2012–2013) http://www.watch-around.com/index.php?id=12&tx_ttnews%5Btt_news%5D=1887&cHash=0fc8b9010a750f5bc43bb6a20a771d57.
67 Reports read in *La Suisse Horlogère*, the official publication from the *Chambre suisse de l'horlogerie*, which published some export accounts before its General Assembly, shows us that there was an increase in watch exports to China (four times more between 1972 and 1973, both regarding the number of watches and their global value).
68 Letter from Albert Natural, Swiss ambassador in Beijing, to the Trade Division of Department of Public Economic Affairs, 15 August 1972, Archives fédérales, E7110#1983/13#1865*, dodis.ch/35905.
69 *Journal de Genève*, 8 December 1972, 15.

Conclusion

In the context of Cultural Revolution in China and of a reconfiguration of Swiss sports diplomacy, creating some good conditions for reconciliation around the sports field, contacts between China and Switzerland started to become more frequent on the eve of the 1970s. The two countries were soon to become closer partners, forging some new economic and political "alliances" evident during the nine days of the tour. Involving major firms like Nestlé and Hoffmann-La Roche, political representatives and also some sports officials (the director of Maggligen or the president of the COS), the event put a small country clearly in the centre of the pitch. Just a couple of months after the well-known episode between USA and China – creating the myth of "ping-pong diplomacy" – the American president made a first official visit in China in early 1972. The Swiss episode of this ping-pong diplomacy remained less well known than the USA-China one, still it was one of many steps in the rise of new diplomatic connections between the People's Republic of China and the Swiss Confederation and furthermore, between China and Europe.

Involved in a broader game, those new connections could be seen through their influences on other relations, such as with Taiwan. In 1974, Taiwan participated in the Shooting World Championship organized in Thoune, in Switzerland, though this created tensions with China. The Swiss organizers had to negotiate with the Chinese Embassy in Switzerland and decided not to show the Taiwanese flag in case of victory. Two years later, Switzerland welcomed a Chinese delegation of badminton players.[70] Before the competition, the Chinese Embassy in Switzerland openly contested the presence of a delegation from Taiwan at the same time, launching new discussions with the DPF.[71] If those events had apparently not the same diplomatic echo as the 1972 tour, they were some concrete manifestations of a turning point in the relations between China and Switzerland. In the same period, other sporting issues between the two countries confirm this analysis, such as Alpinists' mobility between them or a visit of Swiss gymnasts to China in 1975.

Moreover, one of our results, which have to be extended by further research made in other archive sites, like those from the FSTT, the Fédération horlogère or from several cantonal bodies, showed that sport was involved involved in a kind

---

70 *Tribune-Le Matin*, 22 April 1976, 14.
71 Swiss Federal Archives, Chinesische Vorsprache wegen interntionaler "Bada-ma-ton" – Wettkämpfen in Lausanne, from Kaufmann, Politische Direktion, 15 March 1976, E2200.174#1988/78#192*.

of trade diplomacy which includes economic firms promotion, trade negotiations and new diplomatic bridges with China in the early 1970s.

Martin Polley
Afterword

In July 2017, I had the pleasure of visiting the 1936 Olympic Stadium in Berlin as a tourist. The track at the heart of this icon of Nazi architecture and propaganda was being set up for the finish of a charity race. Tourists and citizens swam in the outdoor pool built for the Olympics. Around the site's perimeter, sport-themed fibreglass Buddy Bears, marking some of Berlin's recent sporting events, shared space with idealised super athletes form the Third Reich. Tents for the charity runners dotted the Maifeld, once the site of Nazi rallies and, in the final days of the Second World War, a training ground for Volkssturm soldiers being sent into the frontline against the Red Army. The walls around the Marathon Gate still hold the honours boards of the 1936, celebrating Jesse Owens and the other heroes and heroines of the Games, while the Olympic bell, cracked from the British army's demolition of the bell tower in 1947 and with its swastikas crudely disguised, sits outside, no longer able to call the youth of the world, but still a testament to the site's history.[1]

This iconic venue, with its imperial origins, its development under the Weimar Republic, its most famous days coming under the Nazis, its use by the British army during the occupation, and its re-invention after German reunification as a site for club football and contemporary mega-events, tells a clear story of continuity and change in the political history of sport. It offers lessons for all of us who want to understand how sport can serve as both an index for political history, and as a location for political dialogue. It is in this spirit that Berlin's Olympic Stadium came to my mind as I reflected on the themes contained in this book, with Berlin's role as one of the crucibles of the Cold War making the reflections even more pertinent. The history of international sport during the Cold War, as explored through these chapters that Quin, Sbetti, and Vonnard have brought together, can tell us so much about the ways in which sport reflects the political mood, while also serving as a site in which political tensions and reconciliations can be played out. I would like to thank the editors and contributors for giving me the opportunity to offer some personal reflections on the work they have done to advance our knowledge and understanding of these trends.

---

[1] Rother, Rainer (ed.). *Historic Site. The Olympic Grounds 1909–1936–2006*. Berlin: jovis Verlag, 2006.

This book is part of a welcome trend in the historiography of sport and international relations. It complements such recent collections as Alan Bairner and Gyozo Molnar's *The Politics of the Olympics* (2010)[2] and Heather Dichter and Andrew Johns' *Diplomatic Games* (2014),[3] as well as the companion piece to this book, the special issue of *Sport in History* (2017).[4] Taken together, works such as these, and the networks and conferences out of which they have emerged, have helped to both deepen and broaden our understanding of the ways in which sport and international relations meet. Historiographically, this is a fascinating trend, as it is symptomatic of the ways in which the end of the Cold War, and the new opportunities and tensions that have emerged in the world since then, have informed the historical conversation.

A personal reflection might help here. When I started my doctoral research on sport and diplomacy in 1987, the English language literature was strongly influenced by the sporting conflicts of the period, most obviously the Cold War Olympic boycotts of 1980 and 1984, and the struggles over apartheid in sport that were impacting on cricket, rugby union, and the Olympic and Commonwealth Games. With some notable exceptions, such as James Riordon's work on sport and communism,[5] and John Hoberman's exploration of the role of ideology in different political systems' approaches to sport,[6] the keynote for this literature was very much George Orwell's famous words on sport inspired by Moscow Dynamo's November 1945 tour of Great Britain: "Serious sport has nothing to do with fair play. It is bound up with hatred, jealousy, boastfulness, disregard if all rules and sadistic pleasure in witnessing violence: in other words it is war minus the shooting."[7]

---

[2] Bairner, Alan and Molnar, Gyozo (eds.). *The Politics of the Olympics. A Survey.* London: Routledge, 2010.

[3] Dichter, Heather and Johns, Andrew L. (eds.). *Diplomatic Games. Sport, Statecraft, and International Relations since 1945.* Lexington: University Press of Kentucky, 2014.

[4] Quin, Grégory and Vonnard, Philippe (eds.). Special issue «Negotiating the Cold War. The Case of International sport bodies during the First Period of the Cold War (1946–1971)». *Sport in history* 37 (2017).

[5] Riordan, James (ed.). *Sport under Communism. The USSR, Czechoslovakia, the GDR, China, Cuba.* London: Hurst, 1981; Riordan, James. *Sport in Soviet Society. Development of Sport and Physical Education in Russia and the USSR.* Cambridge: Cambridge University Press, 1977.

[6] Hoberman, John M. *Sport and Political Ideology.* Austin: University of Texas Press, 1984.

[7] Orwell, George. The Sporting Spirit. *Tribune,* 14 December 1945. Reprinted in Orwell, Sonia and Angus, Ian (eds.). *The Collected Essays, Journalism and Letters of George Orwell. Volume IV, In Front of Your Nose 1945–1950.* Harmondsworth: Penguin, 1968, p.63.

This theme, often backed up by Orwell's own words, could be found underpinning such key works as those by Espy and Kanin.[8] The end of the Cold War and the end of apartheid helped to shift the focus. The Cold War as a phase in international relations, and apartheid as a system of racial segregation, had both had a massive impact negative on sport, and with their demise came new ways of thinking about sport's role as a sphere of cultural international politics. Increasingly international collections, such as those edited by Riordan and Krüger[9] and Arnaud and Riordan[10] delved deeper into the varieties of historical diplomacy, and more was done on the ideological basis of sport in different countries and different political systems. They also helped to bring the wider politics of race, ethnicity, gender, and ethics into the story alongside the politics of state power. Since then, historians have increasingly looked beyond the superpower struggles best exemplified by the Moscow and Los Angeles boycotts, and moved in deeper on non-Olympic sports, on smaller struggles, on case studies of individual events, and on moments when sport helped to keep channels of communication between opposing sides open. These developments have been helped by access to archives that were more restricted during the Cold War, by the increasing opportunities for international scholarly travel, research, and networking that various state, EU, and educational agencies have promoted, and by the welcome presence of a generation of young scholars who have grown up with the Cold War as their history rather than as their present.

This collection is an excellent example of this trend. It has been edited by an international group of scholars, who work comfortably across borders and languages, and whose dynamism at facilitating international academic dialogue is impressive. They have developed the project, and the related special issue of *Sport in History*, out of a series of international academic conferences and network meetings. The authors represented here come from many countries, both in terms of their nationality and their professional academic affiliations. They come to the question of sport and the Cold War with post-Berlin Wall sensibilities and transnational approaches. They have, accordingly, delivered on the editors' aims for the book.

---

8 Espy, Richard. *The Politics of the Olympic Games*. 2nd edition. Berkeley: University of California Press, 1981; Kanin, D.B. *A Political History of the Olympic Games*. Boulder, CA: Westview Press, 1981.
9 Riordan, Jim and Krüger, Arnd (eds.). *The International Politics of Sport in the Twentieth Century*. London: Routledge, 1999.
10 Arnaud, Pierre and Riordan, Jim (eds.). *Sport and International Politics: the impact of Fascism and Communism on Sport*. London: Spon, 1998.

First, they have worked hard to avoid the Olympic Games, as requested by the editors. In some ways, this may seem like a perverse request, as the Cold War's most obvious sporting flashpoints were held around the Olympic Games. The US-led Moscow boycott of 1980, the retaliatory Soviet-led boycott of Los Angeles in 1984, and some key iconic moments of the Cold War, like Ervin Zador's bloodied face on the edge of the water polo pool at Melbourne in 1956, or Taiwan marching 'Under Protest' as Formosa in the opening ceremony of the Rome Olympics in 1960, remain central to our understanding of how sport and international politics were entwined throughout the Cold War. However, the editors have been justified in this decision, based precisely on how familiar the Olympics are in this story, and in the historiography. This is not to say that new work is not always needed on the Olympics – there are many aspects of the political history of the Games (both Winter and Summer, and the wider history of the governance of the Olympic movement and the IOC's relationship with states, non-state actors, and supranational bodies) that still require academic attention. However, by shining a light on less famous stories, this book is helping to move the predominant narrative 'beyond boycotts'.

Similarly, the emphasis on Europe has worked well, as it reminds us that while the Cold War was a global phenomenon, which underpinned proxy hot wars away from Europe, Europe remained its heart in the decades after the Second World War. The Iron Curtain, the Berlin Wall, the placing of troops and missiles by both superpowers throughout the continent, and the promotion of political systems that were favourable to each respective superpower ensured this. In this collection, the authors have grasped this European agenda. They have taken us into the sporting politics of some individual countries that are not always central to the grand narratives of the Cold War, such as Simon's work on Spain and Svensson and Åberg's piece on Sweden, into some of the key sites of the Cold War, as in Sbetti's essay on Trieste, and into the ways in which international sporting organisations tried to work within the constraints that the Cold War presented, as in Vonnard and Marston's piece on UEFA and Scholl's piece in the European Sports Conference. However, the influence of the wider world is not ignored, and the essays here by Doppler, Nicholas, Naha, and Tonnere and Quin explore many ways in which events in Europe were related to the dramas being played out at the global level in the USA, the USSR, China, and Africa. Taken together, these essays deliver on the editors' aims of looking at the myriad ways in which sport inter-related with national agendas, political systems, educational networks, sporting federations.

The authors have also delivered on the editors' key aim of emphasising the role of different agencies in the sporting relations of the Cold War. This theme, present in many of the chapters, takes us away from the headline sporting events of the track, pitch, pool, or slopes, and into the boardrooms and committees of state and sport bodies. Here, we can see the thinking behind key decisions, and how the individual politicians, diplomats, soldiers, and administrators applied their agendas to try – on the whole – to improve sporting relations. The stories that emerge from these chapters are thus predominantly about cooperation, collaboration, and facilitation, which is a far cry from so many of the conflict-based assumptions about sport in the Cold War. In this collection, we can see how decisions made at all levels, from city to state and from individual clubs to supranational federations, helped the key stages that sport had to go through to survive and thrive in a problematic international environment. How did clubs and federations re-form after the war? How were old enmities negotiated in a time of armed peace? How did governing bodies in newly-constituted states convince international federations to let them play? The essays in this book provide fascinating case studies of processes such as these at work, and of how they served to maintain old networks, and build new ones, that served as cultural meeting places throughout the Cold War.

This book and its companion issue of *Sport in History* are thus helping us to understand more about how international sport actually functioned during the Cold War. The case study approach that the authors have taken allows us to see details, and to explore relationships at a granular level, without losing sight of the larger political, cultural, military, and economic contexts. They have also set a challenge for new case studies to take us even further into these relationships, and I look forward to a further blossoming of this historiography. There are four areas that would significantly add both detail and nuance to our understanding of sport in the Cold War. First, we need more studies on the growing number of sporting events that developed around different communities, such as the Paralympics, the Special Olympics, the Gay Games, the Maccabi Games, and the World Transplant Games. How did the groups for whom these events emerged, whether defined in terms of religion, sexuality, disability, or medical condition, interact across the fault lines of the Cold War? In what ways did different ideological and cultural attitudes towards these communities and their identity politics affect the development of the events? Second, there is scope for more biographical work on the athletes, officials, administrators, and coaches who worked across those Cold War fault lines. Good work has already been carried out on this, but more could be done to fit the Cold War experiences into the wider sporting lives. This would be particularly interesting in the case of athletes who defected during the Cold War, and those whose nationalities changed due to the redefinition of nations in the wake of the Soviet bloc's decline. Third, additional local case studies of the sporting histories of individual cities and towns could add so much more to our appreciation of what Cold War sport felt like on the ground. How did clubs work within and outside their communities? How did cities experience Cold War sporting confrontations, such as the 1955 London v Moscow athletics event at the White City? In what ways did the post-Second World War trend of twinning towns and cities impact on local sporting cultures, and did this help in the processes of negotiation and communication that the authors in this book have identified? Finally, a grassroots approach that explores fans' experiences of Cold War sport would be edifying. How did travelling supporters who crossed the Iron Curtain experience the sport and communities they visited? How were their movements managed, and what did they see of local life and rival enthusiasts? Case studies on travelling football fans in Europe's burgeoning inter-club and international competitions during the Cold War would be particularly interesting.

This book will help us understand how sport worked during the Cold War, below the level of the Olympic Games, and 'beyond boycotts'. It tells a series of stories of progress, frustrations, reconciliation, ideas, opportunities, and constraints, and how steps taken by administrators, educationalists, politicians, diplomats, soldiers, and athletes helped to keep sport alive as a truly international meeting place in a difficult climate. It is probably naïve to end by trying to draw lessons from this for our own difficult times, but these essays show that sport can help to keep conversations and exchanges alive in the face of political and ideological enmity. Sport is inextricably linked with the politics of human rights, the identity politics of gender, sexuality, and ethnicity, modern slavery and labour conditions, environmentalism, and new nationalisms, and the popular forum that it offers for those who wish to unite rather than divide is precious. I close by hoping that we can all learn from this aspect of international sport in the Cold War.

Bibliography

This selected bibliography gathers all the scientific contributions from the chapters of this book concerning studies about sport during Cold War and texts about sport in international relations more broadly.

Aja Gonzalez, Teresa (eds.). *Sport y autoritarismos. La utilización del deporte por el comunismo y el fascismo*. Madrid: Alianza Editorial, 2002.
Andrews, David L. and Stephen Wagg. Introduction: War Minus the Shooting? In *East Plays West. Sport and the Cold War*, David L. Andrews and Stephen Wagg (eds.), 1–10. London, New York: Routledge, 2007.
Archambault, Fabien. Le football à Trieste de 1945 à 1954. Un affaire d'État. *Vingtième Siècle* 111 (2011): 49–58.
Archambault, Fabien and Loïc Artiaga. Les soldats du stade: une armée de champions? *Revue de la Société des Amis du Musée de l'Armée* 145 (2014): 27–57.
Archambault, Fabien. Trois secondes de Guerre froide. La finale olympique de Munich en 1972. In *Le Continent basket. L'Europe et le basket-ball au XXe siècle*, Fabien Archambault, Loïc Artiaga and Gérard Bosc (eds.), 159–190, Peter Lang: Bruxelles, 2015.
Ariffin, Yohan. Sport and Global Politics: Still an Unchartered Territory? In *Playing to Build Europe. Turning Points in the Europeanization of Football (1914–1989)*, Philippe Vonnard, Grégory Quin and Nicolas Bancel (eds.), 223–229. Oxford: Peter Lang, 2016.
Arnaud, Pierre and James Riordan (eds.). *Sport et relations internationales (1900–1941): les démocraties face au fascisme et au nazisme*. Paris: L'Harmattan, 1998.
Bahamonde, Ángel. *El Real Madrid en la historia de España*. Madrid: Taurus, 2002.
Balbier, Uta. *Kalter Krieg auf der Aschenbahn. Der deutsch-deutsche Sport 1950–1972. Eine politische Geschichte*. Paderborn: Schöningh, 2007.
Balbier, Uta. A Game, a Competition, an Instrument? High Performance, Cultural Diplomacy and German Sport from 1950 to 1972. *The International Journal of the History of sport* 26 (2009): 539–555.
Bancel, Nicolas, Quin, Grégory and Philippe Vonnard. Introduction. Studying the Europeanization of Football in a Long Term Perspective. In *Building Europe with the Ball: Turning Points in the Europeanization of Football, 1905–1995*, Vonnard, Philippe, Grégory Quin and Nicolas Bancel (eds.), 1–18. Oxford: Peter Lang, 2016.
Barcelo, Laurent. L'Europe des 52: L'Union Européenne de Football Association (UEFA). *Guerres mndiales et conflits contemporains* 228 (2007): 119–133.
Beacom, Aaron. Sport in International Relations: a Case for Cross-disciplinary Investigation. *Sport in History* 20 (2000): 1–23.
Beacom, Aaron, *International Diplomacy and the Olympic Movement: the New Mediators*, Basingstoke: Palgrave Macmillan, 2012.
Beck, Peter. *Scoring for Britain: International Football and International Politics, 1900–1939*. London: F. Cass, 1999.

Beck, Peter. Confronting George Orwell: Philip Noel-Baker on International Sport, Particularly the Olympic Movement as Peacemaker. *The European Sports History Review* 5 (2003): 187–207.

Bensoussan, Georges; Dietschy, Paul, François, Caroline and Hubert Strouk (eds.). *Sport, corps et sociétés de masse. Le projet d'un homme nouveau*. Paris: Armand Colin, 2011.

Bernasconi, Gabriel. De l'Universalisme au transnational: le Comité international olympique, acteur atypique des relations internationales. *Bulletin de l'Institut Pierre Renouvin* 31 (2010): 151–159.

Bertling, Christoph and Evelyne Mertin (eds.). *Freunde oder Feinde? Sportberichterstattung in Ost und West während des Kalten Kriegs*. Gütersloh: Medienfabrik, 2013.

Black, David and Byron Peacock. Sport and Diplomacy. In *The Oxford Hanbook of Modern Diplomacy*, Andrew F. Cooper, Jorge Heine and Ramesh Thakur (eds.), 708–727. Oxford: Oxford University Press, 2013.

Boivin-Chouinard, Mathieu. Chaïbou! *Histoire du hockey russe. 1. Des origines à la série du siècle*. Longueil: Kéruss, 2011.

Bolz, Daphné. *Les arènes totalitaires: fascisme, nazisme et propagande sportive. Hitler, Mussolini et les jeux du stade*. Paris: CNRS Ed, 2009.

Bolz, Daphné. Sports Policy, the Press and the Origins of the Cold War in Occupied Germany, 1945–51. *Sport in History* 35 (2016): 195–216.

Booth, Douglas. *The Race Game: Sport and Politics in South Africa*. London; Portland: Frank Cass Publisher, 1998.

Brand, Alexander and Arne Niemann. Europeanization in the Societal/Trans-national Realm: What European Integration Studies Can Get Out of Analysing Football. *Journal of Contemporary European Research* 3 (2007): 182–201.

Cary, Noel. Olympics in divided Berlin? Popular culture and political imagination at the Cold War frontier, *Cold War History* 11 (2011): 291–316.

Chatziefstathiou, Dikaia and Ian P. Henry, *Discourses of Olympism: from the Sorbonne 1894 to London 2012*. Basingstoke: Palgrave Macmillan, 2012.

Charitas, Pascal. La Commission d'Aide Internationale Olympique (CAIO): Un instrument de propagande soviétique? (1951–1962). *Sport History Review* 40 (2008): 143–166.

Charitas, Pascal. L'Afrique au mouvement olympique: enjeux et stratégies de l'influence de la France dans l'internationalisation du sport africain (1944–1966). PhD, University Paris Sud, 2010.

Clastres, Patrick. La refondation des Jeux Olympiques au Congrès de Paris (1894): initiative privée, transnationalisme sportif, diplomatie des Etats. *Relations internationales* 111 (2002): 327–345.

Clastres, Patrick. Paix par le sport et guerre froide : le neutralisme pro-occidental du Comité international olympique. In *Culture et Guerre froide*, Sirinelli, Jean-François and Georges-Henri Soutou (eds.). Paris: PUPS, 2008: 121–137.

Connolly, Chris A. The Politics of the Games of the New Emerging Forces (GANEFO). *The International Journal of the History of Sport* 29 (2012): 1311–1324.

Defrance, Jacques. La politique de l'apolitisme. Sur l'autonomisation du champ sportif. *Politix* 50 (2000): 13–27.

Dennis, Michael and Jonathan Grix. *Sport under communism: behind the East German 'Miracle'*. Basingstoke: Palgrave Macmillan, 2012.

Desplechin-Lejeune, Blaise, Saint-Martin, Jean and Pierre-Alban Lebecq. L'UNESCO, l'éducation physique et le sport: Génèse et évolution d'une éducation corporelle internationaliste (1952–1978). *Stadion. Internationale Zeitschrift für Geschichte des Sports* 34 (2008): 119–142.

Dichter, Heather L. Sporting Democracy: The Western Allies' Reconstruction of Germany through Sport, 1944–1952. PhD, University of Toronto, 2008.

Dichter, Heather and Andrew Johns (eds.). *Diplomatic Games. Sport starecraft and international relations since 1945*. Lexington Kentucky: University Press of Kentucky, 2014.

Dichter, Heather. 'A Game of Political Ice Hockey'. NATO Restrictions on East German Sport Travel in the Aftermath of the Berlin Wall. In *Diplomatic Games. Sport, Statecraft, and International Relations since 1945*, Heather Dichter and Andrew John (eds.), 19–51. Lexington: University Press of Kentucky, 2014.

Dichter, Heather. Sport history and diplomatic history. *H-Diplo* 122 (2014), http://h-diplo.org/essays/PDF/E122.pdf

Dichter, Heather. Diplomatic and International History: Athletes and Ambassadors. *International Journal of the History of Sport* 32 (2015): 1741–1744.

Diestchy, Paul. *Histoire du football*. Paris: Perrin, 2010.

Dufraisse, Sylvain. Les venues de Jules Ladoumègue, Marcel Thill, Henri Cochet: des séjours de spécialistes? In *Les Français dans la vie intellectuelle et scientifique en URSS au XXe siècle*, Alexandre Tchoubarian, Francine-Dominique Liechtenhan, Sophie Coeuré and Olga Okouneva (eds.), 48–61. Moscow: IRI-RAN, 2013.

Dufraisse, Sylvain, Momzikoff, Sophie, and Rafael Pedemonte. Les soviétiques hors d'URSS : quels voyages pour quelles expériences ? ". *Les Cahiers Sirice* 16 (2016) : 35–46.

Dufraisse, Sylvain. Les 'Héros du Sport'. La fabrique de l'elite sportive Soviétique (1934–1980). *Bulletin de l'Institut Pierre Renouvin* 44 (2016): 143–151,

Dufraisse, Sylvain. Les 'Héros du sport'. La fabrique de l'élite sportive soviétique (1934–1980). PhD, University Paris 1 Panthéon-Sorbonne, 2016.

Dufraisse, Sylvain. Démontrer la puissance et parfaire les esprits. Pratiques et objectifs des délégations sportives soviétiques à l'étranger, 1952-fin des années 1960. *Les Cahiers Sirice* 16 (2016): 35–46.

Edelman, Robert. *Serious Fun: A History of Spectator Sport in the USSR*. New York: Oxford University Press, 1993.

Edelman, Robert. The Russians are Not Coming! The Soviet Withdrawal from the Games of the XXIII Olympiad. *The International Journal of the History of Sport* 32 (2015): 9–36.

Eckstein. Ruth. Ping-Pong Diplomacy: a View from behind the Scenes. *The Journal of American-East Asian Relations* 1(1993): 327–342.

Field, Russel. Re-Entering the Sporting World: China's Sponsorship of the 1963 Games of the New Emerging Forces (GANEFO). *The International Journal of the History of Sport* 31 (2014): 1852–1867.

Fortune, Yohann. Emil Zatopek dans la guerre froide : de la soumission à la rébellion (1948–1968). *Sciences Sociales et Sport* 5 (2012): 53–86.

Frank, Robert. Internationalisation du sport et diplomatie sportive. In *Pour l'histoire des relations internationales*, Robert Frank (ed.), 387–405, Paris : Presses Universitaires de France, 2012.

Frank, William D. *Everyone to Skis!: Skiing in Russia and the Rise of Soviet Biathlon*. DeKalb, Ill.: Northen Illinois University Press, 2015.

Giuntini, Sergio. Lo sport italiano ai Festival mondiali della gioventù. *Il Calendario del Popolo* 673 (2003): 20–24.

Giuntini, Sergio. *L'Olimpiade dimezzata. Storia e politica del boicottaggio nello sport*, Milano: Sedizioni, 2009.

Goksøyr, Matti. *Sivilisering, modernisering, sportifisering: fruktbare begreper i idrettshistorisk forskning?* Oslo: Oslo Universitet, 1988.

Gounot, André. Entre exigences révolutionnaires et nécessités diplomatiques: les rapports du sport soviétique avec le sport ouvrier et le sport bourgeois en Europe, 1920–1937. In *Sport et relations internationales (1900–1941): Les démocraties face au fascisme et au nazisme*, Pierre Arnaud and James Riordan (eds.), 241–276. Paris: L'Harmattan, 1998.

Gounot, André. Sport or Political Organization? Structures and Characteristics of the Red Sport International, 1921–1937. *Journal of Sport History* 1 (2001): 23–39.

Graf, Maximilian, Meisinger, Agnes and Wolfgang Weber. Sport im Kalten Krieg, *Zeitgeschichte* 4 (2015).

Grant, Susan. *Physical Culture and Sport in Soviet Society: Propaganda, Acculturation, and Transformation in the 1920s and 1930s*. New York: Routledge, 2013.

Griffin, Nicholas. *Ping-Pong Diplomacy. The Secret History Behind the Game that Changed the World*. New York: Skyhorse Publishing, 2015.

Groll, Michael. UEFA Football Competition as European Site of Memory – Cups of Identity. In *European Football and Collective Memory*, Wolfram Pyta and Nils Havemann (eds.), 63–84. Basingstoke: Palgrave Macmillan, 2015.

Guanhua, Wang. 'Friendship First': China's Sports Diplomacy during the Cold War. *The Journal of American-East Asian Relations* 12 (2003): 133–153.

Gygax, Jérôme. Le retrait soviétique des Jeux de Los Angeles : Enjeux idéologiques et diplomatie publique américaine (1983–1984). In *Le Pouvoir des anneaux : les Jeux olympiques à la lumière de la politique 1896–2004*, Pierre Milza, Philippe Tétart and François Jequier (eds), 299–325, Paris : Vuibert, 2004.

Gygax, Jérôme. Diplomatie culturelle et sportive américaine: Persuasion et propagande durant la Guerre froide. *Relations internationales* 123 (2005): 87–106.

Gygax, Jérôme. *Olympisme et guerre froide culturelle: le prix de la victoire américaine*. Paris: l'Harmattan, 2012.

Hensler, Paul. 'Patriotic Industry': Baseball's Reluctant Sacrifice in World War I. *NINE: A Journal of Baseball History and Culture* 21 (2013): 98–106.

Hong, Fan. Not all bad! Communism, society and sport in the great proletarian cultural revolution: a revisionist perspective. *The International Journal of the History of Sport* 16 (1999): 47–71.

Hong, Zhaohui and Yi Sun. The Butterfly Effect and the Making of 'Ping-Pong Diplomacy'. *Journal of Contemporary China*, 9 (2000): 420–448.

Hong, Fan and Xiong Xiaozheng. Communist China: Sport, Politics and Diplomacy. *The International Journal of the History of Sport* 19 (2002): 319–342.

Hong, Fan and Lu Zhouxiang (eds.). *Communists and Champions: the Politicisation of Sport in Modern China*. London, Routledge, 2012.

Hong, Fan and Lu Zhouxiang. Sport in the Great Proletarian Cultural Revolution (1966–1976). *The International Journal of the History of Sport* 29 (2012): 53–73.

Hong, Fan and Lu Zhouxiang. Politic First, Competition Second: Sport and China's Foreign Diplomacy in the 1960s and 1970s. In *Diplomatic Games. Sport, Statecraft, and International Relations since 1945*, Heather Dichter and Andrew L. Johns (eds.), 385–407. Lexington: The University Press of Kentucky, 2014.

Houlihan, Barrie. *The Government and Politics of Sport*. London: Frank Cass, 1991.

Hulme, Derick L. *The Political Olympics. Moscow, Afghanistan, and the 1980 U.S. Boycott*. New York: Praeger, 1990.

Hughes, Gerald and Rachel Owen. 'The Continuation of Politics by Other Means': Britain, the Two Germanys and the Olympic Games, 1949–1972. *Contemporary European History* 18 (2009) ; 443–474.

Impiglia, Marco. Goliardi in gara. I Giochi mondiali universitari prima delle Universiadi. *Lancillotto e Nausica* 1 (1997): 8–39.

Itoh, Mayumi. *The origin of Ping-Pong diplomacy: the forgotten architect of Sino-U.S. rapprochement*. Palgrave MacMillan: Basingstoke, 2011.

Jackson, Steven and Stephen Haigh. Between and beyond politics: Sport and foreign policy in a globalizing world. *Sport in society* 11 (2008): 349–358.

Johnson, Daniel. *White King and Red Queen: How the Cold War Was Fought on the Chessboard*. London: Atlantic, 2007.

Katzer, Nikolaus. Soviet Physical Culture and Sport: A European Legacy? In *Sport and the Transformation of Modern Europe: States, Media and Markets 1950–2010*, Alan Tomlinson, Christopher Young and Richard Holt (eds.), 18–34, London and New York: Routledge, 2011.

Keys, Barbara. Soviet Sport and Transnational Mass Culture in the 1930s. *Journal of Contemporary History* 38 (2003): 413–434.

Keys, Barbara. *Globalizing Sport. National Rivalry and International Community in the 1930s*. London: Harvard University Press, 2006.

Keys, Barbara. International relation. In *Routledge Companion to Sports History*, Steven Pope and John Nauright (eds.), 248–267. London & New York: Routlege, 2010.

Keys, Barbara. The International Olympic Committee and Global Culture during the Cold War. In *Les relations culturelles internationales au XXe siècle. De la diplomatie culturelle à l'acculturation*, Dulphy, Anne, Frank, Robert, Matard-Bonucci, Marie-Anne and Pascal Ory (eds.), 291–298. Bruxelles: P.I.E Peter Lang, 2010.

Kobierecki, Michał Marcin. Sport as a Tool for Strengthening a Political Alliance: The Case of the Eastern Bloc during the Cold War. *The Polish Quarterly of International Affairs* 12 (2016): 7–24.

Kowalski, Ronald and Dilwyn Porter. Political Football: Moscow Dynamo in Britain, 1945. *The International Journal of the History of Sport* 14 (1997): 100–121;

Kowalski, Ronald and Dilwyn Porter. Cold War Football: British-European Encounters in the 1940s and the 1950s. In *East Plays West. Essays on Sport and the Cold War*, David L. Andrews and Stephen Wagg (eds.), 64–81. London: Routledge, 2006.

Levermore, Roger and Peter Milward. Official Policies and Informal Transversal Networks: Creating 'Pan-European Identifications' Through Sport? *The Sociological Review* 55 (2007): 144–164.

Loudcher, Jean-François and Monica Aceti. La 'débâcle' suisse aux Jeux olympiques d'hiver à Innsbruck en 1964 et ses conséquences sur l'organisation sportive nationale. *Stadion* 38 (2013): 183–205.

Lutan, Rusli and Fan Hong. The Politicization of sport: GANEFO – A case study. *Sport in Society* 8 (2005): 425–439.

Macon, Benoit. The Politization of football: the European Game and the Approach to the Second World War. *Soccer and Society*, 9 (2007): 532–55.

Malz, Arié, Rohdewald, Stefan and Stefan Wiederkehr (eds.). Sport zwischen Ost und Est. Beiträge zur Sportgeschichte Osteuropas im 19. Und 20. Jahrhundert. Osnabruck: Fibre, 2007.

Mertin, Evelyn. The Soviet Union and the Olympic Games of 1980 and 1984: Explaining the Boycotts to Their Own People. In *East Plays West: Sport and the Cold War*, Stephen Wagg and David L. Andrews (eds.), 235–252, London and Routledge, 2007.

Mertin, Evelyn. *Sowjetisch-deutsche Sportbeziehungen im 'Kalten Krieg'*. Sankt Augustin: Akademia Verlag, 2009.

Milza, Pierre. Sport et relations internationales. *Relations internationales* 38 (1984): 155–174.

Mittag, Jürgen. Europa und der Fußball. Die europäische Dimension des Vereinsfußballs vom Mitropa-Cup bis hin zur Champions League. In *Das Spiel mit dem Fußball. Interessen, Projektionen und Vereinnahmungen*, Jürgen Mittag and Jörg-Uwe Nieland (eds.), 155–176. Essen: Klartext Verlag, 2007.

Mittag, Jürgen and Benjamin Legrand. Towards a Europeanization of Football? Historical Phases in the Evolution of the UEFA Football Championship. *Soccer & Society* 11 (2010): 709–22.

Mittag, Jürgen and Jörg-Uwe Nieland. Auf der Suche nach Gesamteuropa: UEFA und EBU als Impulsgeber der Europäisierung des Sports. In *Freunde oder Feinde? Sportberichterstattung in Ost und West während des Kalten Kriegs*, Christoph Bertling and Evelyn Mertin (eds.), 208–229. Gütersloh: Medienfabrik Gütersloh, 2013.

Mittag, Jürgen. Negotiating the Cold War? Perspectives in Memory Research on the UEFA, the Early European Football Competitions and the European Nations Cups. In *European Football and Collective Memory*, Wolfram Pyta, Nils Havemann (eds.), 40–63. Palgrave Macmillan: Basingstoke, 2015.

Mittag, Jürgen and Philippe Vonnard. The role of societal actors in shaping a pan-European consciousness. UEFA and the overcoming of Cold War tensions, 1954–1959. *Sport in history* 37 (2017): 332–352

Monin, Eric and Christophe Maillard. Pour une typologie du boycottage aux Jeux olympiques. *Relations internationales* 162 (2015): 173–198.

Montez De Oca, Jeffrey. *Discipline and Indulgence: College Football, Media, and the American Way of Life during the Cold War*. New Brunswick, New Jersey and London: Rutgers University Press, 2013.

Murray, Stuart. The Two Halves of Sports-Diplomacy. *Diplomacy & Starecraft* 23 (2012): 575–592.

Naha, Souvik. 'Over the Border and the Gates?' Global and Transnational Sport. *Sport in Society* 20 (2016): 1347–1353.

Niggli, Nicholas. Diplomatie sportive et Relations internationales: Helsinki 1952, les 'Jeux olympique de la Guerre froide'. *Relations internationales* 112 (2002): 467–485.

O'Mahony, Mike. *Sport in the USSR: Physical Culture – Visual Culture*. London: Reaktion Books, 2006.

Ottogali-Mazzacavallo, Cécile, Terret, Thierry and Gérard Six. *L'histoire de l'escrime : 1913–2013, un siècle de Fédération internationale d'escrime*, Biarritz : Atlantica, 2013.

Parks, Jenifer. *Red Sport, Red Tape: the Olympic Games, the Soviet Sports Bureaucracy, and the Cold War, 1952–1980*. PhD, University of North Carolina en 2009.

Parks, Jenifer. 'Nothing but Trouble': The Soviet Union's Push to "Democratise" International Sports during the Cold War, 1959–1962. *The International Journal of the History of Sport* 30 (2013): 1554–1567.

Parks, Jenifer. Welcoming the 'Third World': Soviet Sport Diplomacy, Developing Nations, and the Olympic Games. In *Diplomatic Games: Sport, Statecraft, and International Relations Since 1945*, Heather Dichter and Andrew Johns (eds.), 85–114. Lexington: The University Press of Kentucky, 2014.

Peppard, Victor and James Riordan. *Playing politics: Soviet sport diplomacy to 1992*. Greenwich: JAI Press Inc., 1993.

Pernas López, Juli. *Barcelona 1955: els Jocs Mediterranis*. Barcelona: CG Anmar, 2012.

Pigman, Geoffray Alan. International Sport and Diplomacy's Public Dimension: Governments, Sporting Federations and the Global Audience. *Diplomacy & Starecraft* 25 (2014): 94–114.

Polley, Martin. *Moving the Goalposts: a history of sport and society since 1945*. London & New York: Routledge, 1998.

Prozumenŝlkov, Mihajl. Sport as a Mirror of Eastern Europe Crises. *Russian Studies in History* 49 (2010): 5–93.

Quin, Grégory. La Coupe de l'Europe Centrale (1927–1938), une compétition internationale oubliée? *Stadion. Revue Internationale d'Histoire du Sport* 37 (2013): 285–304.

Quin, Grégory. La reconstruction de la Fédération Internationale de Football Association (FIFA) après la Seconde Guerre mondiale (1944–1950). Jalons pour une histoire des relations sportives internationales. *STAPS* 106 (2014): 21–35.

Quin, Grégory. De la cure d'air à l'or blanc, une *Interassociation Suisse pour le Ski* face aux enjeux de l'essor du ski en Suisse (années 1920–années 1960). *Histoire des Alpes* 22 (2017): 135–155.

Quin, Grégory and Philippe Vonnard (eds.). Special Issue: International sports organisations. *Sport in history* 37 (2017).

Ramos, Ramón. *¡Que vienen los rusos!: España renuncia a la Eurocopa de 1960 por decisión de Franco*. Granada: Comares, 2012.

Rider, Toby. Eastern Europe's Unwanted: Exiled Athletes and the Olympic Games, 1948–1964. *Journal of Sport History* 40 (2013): 435–453.

Rider, Toby. *Cold war games: propaganda, the Olympics, and US foreign policy*. Urbana: University of Illinois Press, 2016.

Riordan, James. La politique sportive étrangère soviétique pendant l'entre-deux guerres. In *Sport et relations internationales (1900–1941): Les démocraties face au fascisme et au nazisme*, Pierre Arnaud and James Riordan (eds.), 127–142, Paris: L'Harmattan, 1998.

Riordan, James. *Sport, politics and communism*. Manchester: Manchester University Press, 1991.

Roche, Maurice. *Mega-events and modernity: olympics and expos in the growth of global culture*. London & New York: Routledge, 2000.

Roche, Maurice. Cultural Europeanization and the 'Cosmopolitan Condition': EU Regulation and European Sport. In *Cosmopolitanism and Europe*, Chris Rumford (ed.), 126–141. London: Liverpool University Press, 2007.

Rofe, Simon and Heather Dichter (eds.). Special Issue: Diplomacy and Sport. *Diplomacy & Starecraft* 27 (2016).

Roger, Anne and Thierry Terret. *European Athletics. Une histoire continentale de l'athlétisme*, Stuttgart : Neuer Sportverlag, 2012.

Santacana, Carles. Espejo de un régimen. Transformación de las estructuras deportivas y su uso político y propagandístico. In *Atletas y ciudadanos: historia social del deporte en España (1870–2010)*, Xavier Pujadas i Martí (ed.), 125–167. Madrid: Alianza Editorial, 2011.

Sarantakes, Nicholas Evans. *Dropping the Torch: Jimmy Carter, the Olympic Boycott, and the Cold War*. Cambridge: Cambridge University press, 2010.

Sbetti, Nicola. *Giochi diplomatici. Sport e politica estera nell'Italia del secondo dopoguerra (1943–53)*. PhD, University of Bologne, 2015.

Sbetti, Nicola, Umberto Tulli. La fine di una reciproca negazione: riflessioni sullo sport nella storia delle relazioni internazionali, *Ricerche di storia politica* 2 (2016): 193–202.

Sbetti, Nicola. La 'diplomazia sportiva' italiana nel secondo dopoguerra: attori e istituzioni (1943–1955). *Diritto dello Sport* 1 (2016): 27–44.

Sbetti, Nicola. Neutrally anti-Communists. International Sports Institutions and the Case of Trieste (1945–1954). *Sport in History* 37 (2017):273–289

Sbetti, Nicola. *Giochi diplomatici. Sport e politica estera nell'Italia del second dopoguerra (1943–1953)*. Treviso: Ludica (in press).

Schotté, Manuel. La structuration du football professionnel européen. Les fondements sociaux de la prévalence de la 'spécificité sportive'. *Revue française de Socio-Economie* 13 (2014): 85–106.

Schulze-Marmeling, Dietrich and Hubert Dahlkamp. *Die Geschichte der Fussball Europameisterschaft*, Göttingen: Verlag die Verkstatt, 2008.

Shaw, Duncan. *Fútbol y franquismo*. Madrid: Alianza, 1987.

Simon, Juan Antonio. La diplomacia del Balón. Deporte y relaciones internacionales durante el franquismo. *História e Cultura* 4 (2012): 165–189.

Simon, Juan Antonio. Fútbol y cine en el franquismo: la utilización política del héroe deportivo en la España de Franco. *Historia y communicación social* 17 (2012): 69–84.

Simón, Juan Antonio. Jugando contra el enemigo: Raimundo Saporta y el primer viaje del equipo de baloncesto del Real Madrid CF a la Unión Soviética. *RICYDE Revista Internacional de Ciencias del Deporte* 28/8 (2013):109–126.

Simón, Juan Antonio. Madrid-72: relaciones diplomáticas y Juegos Olímpicos durante el Franquismo. *Revista Movimento* 19/1 (2013): 221–240.

Simón, Juan Antonio. L'homme de l'ombre Raimundo Saporta et le basket espagnol et européen. In *Le continent basket: L'Europe et le basket-ball au XX siècle*, Fabien Archambault, Loïc Artiaga and Gérard Bosc (eds.), 215–231, Belgique: Peter Lang, 2015.

Singaravélou, Pierre and Julien Sorez (eds.). *L'Empire des sports. Une histoire de la mondialisation culturelle*. Paris: Belin, 2010.

Soares, Joan. Our Way of Life against Theirs. In *Diplomatic Games. Sport starecraft and international relations since 1945*, Heather Dichter and Andrew John (eds.), 251–296, Lexington Kentucky: University Press of Kentucky.

Svensson, Daniel. How Much Sport is There in Sport Physiology? Practice and Ideas in the Stockholm School of Physiology at GCI, 1941–1969. *The International Journal of the History of Sport* 30 (2013): 892–913.

Svensson, Daniel. Scientizing Performance in Endurance Sports: The Emergence of 'Rational Training' in Cross-country Skiing, 1930–1980. PhD, Kungliga Tekniska Högskolan, Stockholm, 2016.

Svensson, Daniel. Technologies of Sportification – Practice, Theory and Co-Production of Training Knowledge in Cross-country Skiing Since the 1950s. *European Studies in Sports History* 9 (2016): 1–29.

Tallec Marston, Kevin. A Lost Legacy of Fraternity? The Case of European Youth Football. In *The Routledge Handbook of Sport and Legacy: Meeting the Challenge of Major Sport Events*, Richard Holt and Dino Ruta (eds.), 176–188. London: Routledge, 2015.

Tallec Marston, Kevin. 'Sincere Camaraderie': Professionalization, Politics and the Pursuit of the European Idea at the International Youth Tournament, 1948–57. In *Building Europe with the Ball. Turning Points in the Europeanization of Football, 1905–1999*, Philippe Vonnard, Grégory Quin and Nicolas Bancel (eds.), 137–161. Oxford: Peter Lang, 2016.

Teichler, Hans-Joachim. *Internationale Sportpolitik im Dritten Reich*. Schorndorf: K. Hofmann, 1991.

Terret, Thierry (ed.). Special Issue: Sport in Eastern Europe during the Cold War. *The international journal of the history of sport* 26 (2009).

Thomas, Damion L. *Globetrotting: African American Athletes and Cold War Politics*. Chicago: University of Illinois Press, 2012.

Tomilina Natalia (ed.). *Belye igry pod grifom 'sekretno', sovetskij soûz i zimnie olimpiady, 1956–1988* [The white games under the clutches of secrecy, the Soviet Union and the winter games, 1956–1988]. Moscou: MFD, 2013.

Tomlinson, Alan and Christopher Young. Sport in Modern European History: Trajectories, Constellations, Conjunctures. *Journal of Historical Sociology* 24 (2011): 409–427.

Tulli, Umberto. Boicottate le Olimpiadi del Gulag! I diritti umani e la campagna contro le Olimpiadi di Mosca, *Ricerche di Storia Politica*, 1 (2013): 3–24.

Verschuuren, Pim. Les multiples visages du 'sport power'. *Revue internationale et stratégique* 89 (2013): 131–136.

Veth, Manuel. La Sbornaya, de l'URSS à la Russie de Poutine. In *Le football des nations. Des terrains de jeu aux communautés imaginées*. Fabien Archambault, Stéphane Beaud and William Gasparini (eds.), 121–131. Paris: Publications de la Sorbonne, 2016.

Vonnard, Philippe. *La genèse de la Coupe des clubs champions. Une histoire du football européen (1920–1960)*. Neuchâtel: CIES, 2012.

Vonnard, Philippe. A Competition that Shook European Football: The Origins of the European Champion Clubs'Cup, 1954–1955. *Sport in History* 34 (2014): 595–619.

Vonnard, Philippe, Grégory Quin and Nicolas Bancel (eds.). *Building Europe with the Ball: Turning Points in the Europeanization of Football, 1905–1995*. Oxford: Peter Lang, 2016.

Vonnard, Philippe. How did UEFA Govern the European Turning Point in Football? UEFA, the European Champion Clubs' Cup and the Inter-Cities Fairs Cup Projects (1954–1959). In *Building Europe with the Ball. Turning Points in the Europeanization of Football (1914–1989)*, Philippe Vonnard, Grégory Quin, Nicolas Bancel (eds.), 165–185. Oxford: Peter Lang, 2016.

Vonnard, Philippe. Genèse du football européen. De la FIFA à l'UEFA (1930–1960). PhD., University of Lausanne, December 2016.

Vonnard, Philippe and Grégory Quin. Did South America Foster European Football? Transnational Influences on the Continentalization of FIFA and the Creation of UEFA, 1926–1959, *Sport in Society* 20 (2017): 1424–1439.

Wagg, Steven and David L. Andrews (eds.). *East Plays West: Sport and Cold War*. London & New York: Routledge, 2007.

Wiese, René. *Kaderschmieden des 'Sportwunderlande' die Kinder- und Jugendsportschulen der DDR*. Hildesheim: Arete-Verl., 2012.

Wilson, J.J. 27 remarkable days: the 1972 summit series of ice hockey between Canada and the Soviet Union. *Totalitarian Movements and Political Religions* 5 (2004): 271–280.

Witherspoon, Kevin. 'Fuzz Kids' and 'Musclemen'. In *Diplomatic Games. Sport starecraft and international relations since 1945*, Heather Dichter and Andrew John (eds.), 297–326, Lexington Kentucky: University Press of Kentucky.

Young, Christopher, Tomlinson, Alan and Richard Holt (eds.). *Sport and the transformation of modern Europe: states, media and markets*, 1950–2010. London: Routledge, 2011.

Contributors (by alphabetical order)

Biographies

Anna Åberg has a PhD in History of Science, Technology and Environment (KTH – Royal Institute of Technology, Stockholm, Sweden). She is Assistant Professor in the History of Science and Technology at Chalmers University of Technology in Gothenburg, Sweden where she is working on energy- and resource history, often in relation to the Soviet Union. Currently she is involved in projects on Soviet fusion research, Swedish uranium import, and sea- and space mining, and her recent publications includes the chapter "Rising Seas: Facts, Fictions and Aquaria" (with Susanna Lidström), in *Curating the Future: Museums Communities and Climate Change* (Routledge, Environmental Humanities Series, 2017).

François Doppler-Speranza holds a PhD in American studies from the University of Strasbourg. A former student of the University of Missouri in St. Louis and instructor at Indiana University, he currently teaches languages and culture at the University of Strasbourg, as well as transatlantic history at Syracuse University (Strasbourg campus). He is also a member of SEARCH (Savoirs dans l'Espace Anglophone–Représentations, Culture, Histoire) and E3S (Sport and Social Sciences) research labs. His research focuses on the various forms of diplomacy – especially cultural and sports diplomacy – conducted by the United States in Europe after the Second World War. His doctoral research on the cultural aspects of the US military presence in France received the support from the French Institute of Advanced Studies in National Defense (IHEDN).

Sylvain Dufraisse has a PhD in Contemporary History (University Paris 1 Panthéon-Sorbonne, France). His work focuses on the social and political history of sports in the Soviet Union from the 1930s to the 1980s. He is currently senior lecturer at the University of Nantes. He has already published several articles on sports, physical education, and sportsmen in the Soviet Union and in contemporary Russia.

Kevin Tallec Marston is a Research Fellow at CIES and a Visiting Researcher and Lecturer at the International Centre for Sports History and Culture at De Montfort University, Leicester where he completed his PhD in History. His work has focused on the history of youth football, the question of age, the place of childhood in society, the evolving role of training and education of youth in and around sport, and the biography of sporting administrators as well as other themes such as legacy, diffusion, fraternity, and transnationalism. He also has a particular interest in the questions of governance in sport, specifically the historical, political and economic aspects of both European football and its main governing body UEFA as well as the global game and FIFA.

Claire Nicolas is currently a PhD student in Political Sciences (SciencePo Paris, France) and Sport Sciences (University of Lausanne, Switzerland), under the supervision of Professor Nicolas Bancel and Richard Banégas. She is doing a comparative study between Ghana and Côte d'Ivoire between the early 1950s to the late 1970s. Her work focuses on how sports, scouting, and physical education were used to perform nascent Nation-States in West Africa. In this respect, she gives special attention to life-course trajectories and individualisation process at work among youngsters.

Stefan Scholl holds a PhD in History (University of Bielefeld, Germany). He is currently working on a post-doc project about the transnational European cooperation in sport policies from the 1960s to the 1990s, focusing on institutions such as the Council of Europe, the European Sport Conference and the NGO-Club (later becoming the European Non-Governmental Sports Organisation). In this context, he has already published articles on the European Sport for All Charter and the mechanisms of sport policy cooperation within the Council of Europe in German language. He is currently editing a volume on the historical links between sport and biopolitics.

Souvik Naha holds a PhD in History (ETH Zurich, Switzerland). His thesis explored the network of cricket's mediated relationships, constituted by the mass media, readers, and spectators, and uncovered various strands of the public's mobilization as cricket consumers in Calcutta from 1934 to 1999. He has published research articles in journals such as the *International Journal of the History of Sport, Sport in Society, Soccer & Society, Sport in History,* and *Economic and Political Weekly,* and edited two special issues of *Sport in Society* on the FIFA World Cup and global sport respectively. He is currently a guest lecturer in History at West Bengal State University and the book review editor of *Soccer & Society.*

Martin Polley is the Director of the International Centre for Sports History and Culture, and a Professor of History, at De Montfort University, Leicester, UK. He previously taught at the University of Winchester and the University of Southampton. He gained his PhD on the history of British Foreign Office involvement in sport from the University of Wales in 1991. He is the author of *Moving the Goalposts: a history of sport and society since 1945* (1998), *Sports History: a practical guide* (2007), and *The British Olympics: Britain's Olympic heritage 1612–2012* (2011), as well as numerous articles and book chapters on such themes from sports history as diplomacy, professionalism, national identity, and gender. He is an editor of *Sport in History,* and edits the book series Palgrave Studies in Politics and Sport. Polley has contributed to news and documentary programmes on sports history on TV and radio in the UK, Canada, Japan, and Australia, and has given keynote papers and invited seminars at events in Sweden, France, Japan, and Switzerland.

Grégory Quin holds a PhD in Sport Science (University of Lausanne, Switzerland) and Pedagogy (University of Paris Descartes, France). He is senior lecturer at the University of Lausanne, where he is trying to promote sport history, through courses, research, and some public projects. After a PhD focused on the medical roots of physical education, he is currently working on Swiss and international sport history, especially trying to disclose some new archives while travelling all over Europe. He has recently edited a special issue for *Sport in History* (with Philippe Vonnard) on the history of international sports federation. Among others, he published, in 2016, *Building Europe with the Ball* (with Philippe Vonnard and Nicolas Bancel) and, in 2015, *Les liaisons dangereuses de la médecine et du sport* (with Anaïs Bohuon).

Nicola Sbetti holds a PhD in Politics, Institution and History (University of Bologna, Italy), working on the relations between sport and foreign policy in Italy from 1943 until 1953. His work focuses on the political history of sport in Italy and on the links between sport and international relation. He has already published several articles on these topics and *Giochi di Potere. Olimpiadi e politica da Atene a Londra (1896–2012)*, (Firenze. Le Monnier, 2012). He is currently contract lecturer of Contemporary History for the University of Bologna (branch of Forlì).

Juan Antonio Simón holds a PhD in Humanities (Carlos III University of Madrid, Spain). He is currently Head of Department of Sport Science and Lecturer in Sport History and Sociology of Sport at the European University of Madrid. His work focuses principally on the history of sport in Spain, the links between football and international relations, and on the history of mega sports event like the FIFA World Cup or the Olympic Games. Among others, he published *España-82: La historia de nuestro Mundial* (T&B Editores, 2012), *Construyendo una pasión el fútbol en España 1900–1936* (Unir, 2015) and, in 2016, the book chapter *De la furia espagnole au tiki-taka. Football et constructions identitaires en Espagne (1920–2015)* (Fabien Archambault, Stéphane Beaud and William Gasparini (dir.) Paris: Publications de la Sorbonne, 2016).

Daniel Svensson holds a PhD in History of Science, Technology and Environment (KTH Royal Institute of Technology, Sweden). He is currently researcher and lecturer at Chalmers University of Technology, Sweden. His research is mainly within the fields of sport history and environmental history. Svensson's dissertation (awarded with the ISHA Ullr Award 2017) focused on the scientization of training methods in cross-country skiing, and meetings between scientific and experiential knowledge in sport during the 20th century. He has also published books and articles about the history of Swedish women's football, and shifting ideas about landscape, sports heritage, and mobility during the 19th and 20th century.

Quentin Tonnerre is a PhD candidate in history of sport diplomacy (Sport Sciences, University of Lausanne, Switzerland). In his ongoing PhD thesis, he describes the involvement of both sport institutions and federal administration in the Swiss sport diplomacy from the 1920s until the 1980s. He has a Master degree in Social Sciences and Sport and wrote his Master thesis about "French Newspapers and 1936 Berlin Olympic Games. The Acceptance and Fascination Factors of the Nazi Propaganda". He is currently visiting PhD candidate at the Centre for British Studies (Humboldt-Universität Berlin).

Philippe Vonnard holds a PhD in Sport Sciences and Physical Education (University of Lausanne, Switzerland). His work focuses principally on the history of football in Europe (from the 1920s to the 1960s) and he has already published several articles on this topic and coordinated (with Grégory Quin and Nicolas Bancel) Building Europe with the Ball (Oxford, Peter Lang. 2016). He is currently doing a postdoc funded by the Swiss National Foundation for Sciences (SNSF) in Paris (at ISCC) where he is going on with researches about the Europeanization of football during the first period of the Cold War. In this matter, he has recently edited a special issue for Sport in History (with Grégory Quin) on the history of international sports organizations during the Cold War.

Index[1]

Alonso, Vega Camilo   61
Astavin, Sergei   187
Åstrand, Per-Olof   35, 38, 49

Baden-Powell, Robert   162–164
Bangstad, Ole J.   115, 121
Barassi, Ottorino   102
Bauwens, Joseph (Peco)   98
Bazennerye, René   123
Bengtson, Bo   114, 115
Ben-Gurion, David   170, 171
Bevilacqua, Antonio   30
Bombassei De Vettor, Giorgio   29
Briandt, Calle   39, 40, 51, 52
Blanco, Carrero   61
Boggs, Grace L.   173
Botvinnik, Mikhail   184, 185
Brady, Leslie S.   144, 154
Brenden, Hallgeir   48
Brezhnev, Leonid   186
Brundage, Avery   64
Brunt, Lo   96, 98, 100
Bulganin, Nikolaï A.   80

Carlson, Lief   146, 152
Castiella, Fernando María   59
Castro, Fidel   190
Cifuentes, Sergio   59
Cochet, Henri   74
Comăneci, Nadia   9
Cottur, Giordano   30–32
Crahay, José   91, 92, 96
Creel, George E.   138

De Gasperi, Alcide   26
Denker, Arnold   190
Delaunay, Henry   91–92, 101
Delaunay, Pierre   88, 101
Donskoi, Dmitrij D.   44, 48–49
Dunayevskaya, Raya   173

Edström, Sonja   48
Ekblom, Björn   35
Elola-Olaso, José Antonio   61
Euwe, Max   187
Ewald, Manfred   115, 122, 127–129

Fischer, Robert J. (Bobby)   12, 179–193
Franco, Francisco (General)   1, 55–67

Gafner, Raymond   207
Garrigues, Emilio   62
Gerö, Joseph   91
Gieseler, Karl-Heinz   115–116, 119, 122–127, 130
Gligoric, Svetozar   190
Gmelin, Hans   120
Graham, George   91
Gross, Hans Hansovič   44, 48

Haffner, Steffen   119, 123–124
Hartwig, H.C. (Colonel)   146, 151, 153

Jernberg Sixten   48

Kaganovič, Lazare M.   80
Kai-shek Chiang   199
Kamath, M. V.   189
Kamenskij, V.I.   47–50
Karpov, Anatoly   183
Kennan, George F.   17
Kharlamov, N. I.   45
Kincheloe, Jerry   146, 152
Kissinger, Henry   186
König, Walfried   109, 113
Krivcov, M. M.   42–45
Khrushchev, Nikita S.   78, 80
Kubala, László   9
Kulinkovic, Konstantin   122
Kuma, Bennard   170

---

1 This index gathers all the characters quoted in the chapters of this book.

Index

Lake, Michael 185–187
Larsen, Ben 192
Larsson, Lennart 40
López, Bravo 67
Lotsy, Johannes J. (Karel) 90, 96

Malenkov, Gueorgui M. 80
MacMillan, Harold 157
Moeller, Kurt 115, 120
Mikoân, Anastas I. 80
Mitri, Tiberio 32
Molotov, Viatcheslav M. 80
Mowbray, Elliott 163, 165, 175
Mussolini, Benito 19, 55

Nasser, Gamal Abdel 172, 174
Nixon, Richard 107, 182, 186, 195
Naumov, Vladimir N. 45–47, 49
Nehru, Jawaharlal 172
Nkrumah, Kwame 158–161, 165–167, 170–176

Okoh, Salome 167
Olander, Gösta 38–41, 50–52
Orwell, George 198, 214–215
Osborn, Frederik H. 141

Padmore, George 165, 172–173
Pawlow, Sergej 115, 121–123, 128–129
Pelletier, Louis 96
Perrott, Roy 186
Pervuhin, Mikhail 80
Pico, Benito 96

Redman, Earl 146, 152
Roosevelt, Franklin D. 140–141
Rous, Stanley 88, 96, 98–100, 102
Rowland, Robert R. 149–152

Saburov, Maksim 80
Salizzoni, Angelo 27

Saltin, Bengt 35
Saporta, Raimundo 64
Schaller, Marcel 205
Shardow, Zachary 167, 170, 175
Schwartz, Ebbe 85, 91, 96, 102, 104
Sebes, Gustav 91
Sedó, Ramón 65
Sisk, Robert E. 146, 151–154
Solís, José 61, 63
Spassky, Boris 12, 179–193
Stalin, Joseph (Iossif Djougachvili) 18, 21, 28, 31–32, 75
Stone, Donald 187
Streibert, Theodore C. 144
Sukarno Koesno Sosrodihardjo 172
Syme, Ajimburu 159, 170

Taimanov, Mark 185, 191, 192
Tal, Mikhail 192
Tetteh, Matthew N. 159, 174–176
Timms, Charles R. 145
Tito, Broz Josip (Marshall) 1, 18–21, 24, 28, 31–32, 172
Thommen, Ernst 90, 102

Vlot, Nicolaas 115, 122–123
Vogl, Joseph 96, 99
Vorošilov, Kliment 73, 80

Weyer, Willie 115, 119, 121–124, 126–127, 129
Wickhorst, Frank H. 141
Wilson, Woodrow 138
Wolf, Kaspar 205
Wotherspoon, William W. 135

Zaccagnini, Benigno 27
Zador, Ervin 216
Zátopek, Emile 9
Zedong, Mao 169
Zimmermann, Karl 96

www.ingramcontent.com/pod-product-compliance
Lightning Source LLC
Chambersburg PA
CBHW030620230426
43661CB00053B/2080